SCREWBALL COMEDY

Cary Grant and Katharine Hepburn in *Bringing Up Baby* (1938). This scene is the all-important finale. Hepburn has just collapsed Professor Grant's brontosaurus skeleton, which also symbolizes nicely what she has done to the last vestiges of his academic rigidity. No single scene better metaphorically captures the freeing spirit of the genre. (Photograph courtesy of the Museum of Modern Art/Film Stills Archive.)

SCREWBALL COMEDY
A Genre of Madcap Romance

Wes D. Gehring

Contributions to the Study of Popular Culture, Number 13

Greenwood Press
New York • Westport, Connecticut • London

aaq 6886

Library of Congress Cataloging-in-Publication Data

Gehring, Wes D.
  Screwball comedy.

  (Contributions to the study of popular culture,
ISSN 0198-9871 ; no. 13)
  Bibliography: p.
  Filmography: p.
  Includes index.
  1. Comedy films—United States—History and
criticism. I. Title. II. Series.
PN1995.9.C55G45 1986   791.43'09'0917   85-12703
ISBN 0-313-24650-5 (lib. bdg. : alk. paper)

Library of Congress Catalog Card Number: 85-12703
ISBN: 0-313-24650-5
ISSN: 0198-9871

First published in 1986

Greenwood Press, Inc.
88 Post Road West, Westport, Connecticut 06881

Printed in the United States of America

∞

The paper used in this book complies with the
Permanent Paper Standard issued by the National
Information Standards Organization (Z39.48-1984).

10 9 8 7 6 5 4 3 2 1

Copyright Acknowledgment

The author's poem, ''Now Showing: Screwball Comedy,''
originally appeared in *Literature/Film Quarterly,*
Volume 10, Number 4, 1982.

To Eileen, Sarah, and Emily; my Family;
and Professor John Raeburn

NOW SHOWING:
SCREWBALL COMEDY
by
Wes D. Gehring

Screwball comedy is essentially about
The crazy rich girl next door
And the comic antihero boy
Who doesn't love her . . . at first.

And though there are several
Recipes available to create
This fruitcake of a genre,
All require lots of mixed nuts.

For best results, add one
Zany heiress to the world
Of some mild-mannered male,
Unaware of his own unhappiness.

Then sprinkle lightly with comic
Character actors, childlike pets,
And oodles of decadent playtime
In the most la-de-da of settings.

Stand back as the ingredients start
To bubble, noting how the male's goose
Is cooked as the screwball heroine
Wears him out with her wackiness.

Properly prepared, this comedy dish
Has served audiences endlessly since
The 1930s, Hollywood's version of the loaves
And the fishes, in 35 mm. topsyturvydom.

CONTENTS

ILLUSTRATIONS

PREFACE

The goal of this work is to present an in-depth look at the illusive film genre called screwball comedy, keying on its relationship with the evolution of the comic antihero in American humor. With this in mind, the book is divided into eight chapters. Chapter 1 is an overview of the genre and its ties with the comic antihero.

Chapter 2 is a background look at the American origins of the comic antihero. Five schools of comedy are examined: fictional humor of New England, fictional humor of the Old Southwest, newspaper comic strips, slapstick farce, and vaudeville comedy. The chapter also includes a general overview of the beginnings of American humor and the Yankee, and the *New Yorker* comic antihero of the 1920s.

Chapter 3 is a detailed look at the genre according to the basic comic antiheroic characteristics: abundant leisure time, childlike naïveté, life in the city, apolitical nature, and frustration. In addition, the reasons why the post-*It Happened One Night* (1934) career of Frank Capra should best be seen as populist rather than screwball are thoroughly reviewed.

Chapter 4 analyzes the lives and careers of screwball comedy's four key directors (in order of importance): Howard Hawks, Leo McCarey, Preston Sturges, and Gregory La Cava. Also included are Hawks-personified approaches to comedy and film production which frequently reappear in the work patterns of these directors. Thus, the chapter also addresses such characteristics as a propensity for physical comedy; a tendency to improvise, with a relaxed, frequently fun atmosphere to the production; Hollywood in-house humor; and a greater degree of production control than was the norm during the studio era.

Chapter 5 discusses eight significant screwball comedy players: Cary Grant, Carole Lombard, Irene Dunne, Claudette Colbert, Katharine

Hepburn, Jean Arthur, Melvyn Douglas, and Fred MacMurray. Because of their unique status, Grant, Lombard, and Dunne rate special consideration.

Chapter 6 surveys the genre in terms of comedy theory—fixing on the theory of superiority as most applicable to screwball comedy. Despite the genre's frequent madcap activities, it is found to be inherently conservative, generally with the goal of capturing a male and breaking him—or saving him—from any real antisocial rigidity.

Chapter 7 is a bibliographical essay which organizes in chronological order those key reference materials which both address screwball comedy directly and are most helpful in studying the genre. There is always a temptation to note every source of related interest, but this can open such a floodgate of material that pivotal works are shortchanged. Consequently, this section maintains the most disciplined of configurations. The reader/researcher who must have other related sources is invited to study the scores of notes which close the other chapters. The bibliographical essay closes with a section on accessibility of sources, focusing on important archives.

Chapter 8 is a bibliographical checklist of all sources recommended in Chapter 7. The Appendix is composed of a chronological filmography of the genre.

Few books are solely the result of one person, and special thank yous are in order for a number of individuals: Cooper C. Graham, film reference librarian, Motion Picture Division of the Library of Congress; Dorothy L. Swerdlove, curator, the Billy Rose Theatre Collection (New York City); Mary Corliss, who heads the stills division of the Museum of Modern Art, New York City, and her assistant Terry Geesken.

Interviews with a number of filmmakers, many of which took place years prior to the planning of this book, have been of great value. I would especially like to acknowledge talks with the late William Wellman, Pandro S. Berman, the late George Seaton, and Eddie Bracken.

In May 1983 I presented the paper "'Screwball Comedy and the Comic Antihero" (a blueprint for Chapter 3 of the present work) at the Society for Cinema Studies Conference at the University of Pittsburgh. The comments of film comedy historians Gerald Mast (who chaired my panel) and Donald McCaffrey were most helpful.

The encouragement of my interest in 1930s film comedy by friend, former teacher, and Capra scholar John Raeburn, professor and chairperson, Department of English, University of Iowa, has been greatly appreciated. Most important was John's support that Capra is better understood when examined outside the screwball camp.

Closer to home, additional thank yous are in order for my department chairperson, John Kurtz, for lightening my teaching load while this work was being finished; Janet Warrner, my typist and general troubleshooter; and Veva McCoskey, interlibrary loan librarian at Ball State University's Bracken Library.

Further acknowledgments are in order for the support and suggestions of friends, colleagues, and students (especially members of my recent American film comedy seminar) for their contributions to this volume. I would particularly like to recognize the ongoing support my past writing on comedy has received from Professor Larry Mintz, editor of *American Humor* (University of Maryland); and Professor Timothy J. Lyons, chairperson, Department of Cinema and Photography, Southern Illinois University at Carbondale.

Finally, my family deserves a wheelbarrowful of thanks for their patience and understanding through all the mini-dramas that constitute writing a book.

SCREWBALL COMEDY

1.

INTRODUCTION

"Chivalry is not only dead, it's decomposing." John D. Hackensacker III (Rudy Vallee) to Gerry Jeffers (Claudette Colbert) in *The Palm Beach Story* (1942).

In the mid-1930s a new genre arose in American cinema based upon the old "boy-meets-girl" formula turned topsy-turvy.[1] It generally presented the eccentric, female-dominated courtship of the American rich, with the male target seldom being informed that open season had arrived. The genre was called "screwball comedy."

The birth and initial success of the genre were tied to a period of transition in American humor which had gained great momentum by the late 1920s. The dominant comedy character had been the capable cracker-barrel type of a Will Rogers; it now became an antihero, best exemplified by the writing of Robert Benchley and James Thurber or by the film short subjects of Leo McCarey's Laurel & Hardy. The new genre dressed up the surroundings and added beautiful people, but this was more a reflection of the need to mass-market feature films than a substantive difference. The outcome was essentially the same: an eccentrically comic battle of the sexes, with the male generally losing.

There is no easy way of explaining why the transition from capable to incompetent comic hero took place. Yet, if an explanation were attempted, it would probably focus on the issue of relevance. In a world that seems more irrational every day, the antihero is fated to be forever frustrated. His frustration is the result of his attempt to create order—as did his nineteenth-century comedy counterparts—but now in a world where order is impossible. The commonsense platitudes of any updated crackerbarrel philosopher are inadequate in today's crises. The antihero is "incapable of inventing homespun maxims about hundred-megaton bombs, or of feeling any native self-confidence in the face of uncontrollable fallout."[2] He eventually deals with this frightening outside world by not dealing with it at all. Instead, he focuses "microscopically upon the individual unit . . . that interior reality—or hysteria. . . . In consequence, modern humor deals significantly with frustrating trivia."[3]

The term "screwball" first appeared in the mid-1930s and referred to an eccentric person.[4] The word probably has ties with such late nineteenth-century colloquial expressions as having a "screw loose" (being crazy) and becoming "screwy" (drunk).[5] Since the mid-1930s "screwball" has also been used in baseball to describe both an eccentric player and "any pitched ball that moves in an unusual or unexpected way."[6] All these characteristics describe performers in screwball comedy films: the crazy Carole Lombard, the often drunken William Powell, and the unusual or unexpected movement of Katharine Hepburn.

The use of the term in baseball may have been stimulated by the 1934 world champion St. Louis Cardinals, a team noted for its nutty behavior and nicknamed the "Gas House Gang." The team's success was largely the result of pitching brothers "Dizzy" and "Daffy" Dean, with Dizzy being the principal source of Cardinal eccentricity. The zany antics of Dizzy were not, moreover, limited to the sports page. On April 15, 1935, he made the cover of *Time* magazine, with the accompanying article noting:

> it was clear that with Shirley Temple, Father Coughlin, the Dionne Quintuplets and Mrs. Roosevelt, Jerone Herman Dean was definitely one of that small company of super-celebrities whose names, faces and occupations are familiar to every literate U.S. citizen and whose antics, gracious or absurd, become the legend of their time.[7]

While there was hardly a preponderance of baseball references in screwball comedy literature, they occasionally occurred. For example, *Variety*'s review of *My Man Godfrey* (1936) observed:

> Lombard has played screwball dames before, but none so screwy as this one. From start to finish, with no letdowns or lapses into quiet sanity, she needs only a rosin bag to be a female Rube Waddell [a Dizzy Dean-type, turn-of-the-century pitcher][8].

Study of screwball comedy should begin with the realization that the genre satirizes the traditional love story. The more eccentric partner, invariably the woman, usually manages a victory over the less assertive,

1. The beautiful as well as zany Carole Lombard in *My Man Godfrey* (1936). (Photograph courtesy of the Museum of Modern Art/Film Stills Archive.)

easily frustrated male. The heroine is often assisted by the fact that only she knows that a "courtship" is going on. By the time the male becomes aware of the courtship, the final buzzer has sounded, signaling an end to his comfortably rigid bachelor life-style. Film theorists/historians Thomas Sobchack and Vivian C. Sobchack have appropriately defined "the predatory female who stalks the protagonist" as a basic genre convention.[9] The inevitability of the woman's victory is nicely summarized by Barbra Streisand at the close of *What's Up, Doc?* (1972, a film largely derived from the Katharine Hepburn-dominating screwball classic *Bringing Up Baby*, 1938). Streisand accepts Ryan O'Neal's romantic surrender at film's close with the apt observation, "You can't fight a tidal wave."

Screwball comedy is not part of the traditional ("determinate space") genres in which action must occur at a specific time and place, as with the western, the war film, and the gangster picture.[10] The screwball comedy is less obvious and more ambiguous. It is not limited to one period and place, although it is often set in the present in the milieu of the rich. The genre actually is defined by the eccentric courtship of the screwball couple and by the often tenuous plot, which revolves around their slapstick romantic encounters. Thus, the performers become unusually significant; the recurrent appearance of a Cary Grant or a Carole Lombard might be the only immediately discernible unifying element.

Little has been written about the development of screwball film as a genre of comedy. Much about it remains unclear and even controversial. Sociological film historians Lewis Jacobs and Andrew Bergman regard the genre as an outgrowth of 1930s depression America; film critics Molly Haskell and Andrew Sarris suggest that the suppression of sexuality in the films of the 1930s, a consequence of the imposition of the Motion Picture Production Code in 1934, stimulated development of screwball comedy.[11].

Whatever the origins of the genre, most analysts suggest that 1934 should be considered as its beginning because of the appearance of three films. Frank Capra's *It Happened One Night* was a prototype, although this tale of a runaway heiress (Claudette Colbert) had a stronger male lead (Clark Gable) than would become the genre norm. While *It Happened One Night* was a bigger commercial hit, Howard Hawks's *Twentieth Century* (from the Ben Hecht and Charles MacArthur play) had more of what would typically be considered screwball in years to come, including the escaped meandering of one certified crazy (who bankrolls John Barrymore's play with nonexistent money) and an ongoing comic battle royal between Barrymore and Lombard.

Pivotal 1934 also produced W. S. Van Dyke's adaptation of Dashiell Hammett's comedy mystery *The Thin Man*. In *The Thin Man,* the central character, Nick Charles, is more capable than the usual screwball comedy male, but he does represent a transition toward the type. He is not of the Sherlock Holmes mold, a hero who can deduce six dozen things about a suspect merely from his footprints. Charles can be frustrated. He is more vulnerable, more human, and decidedly funnier than the classical detective, attributes that make him a first cousin to the screwball male. Moreover, Hammett biographer William F. Nolan has described Charles as

> a self-indulgent fellow who just wanted to be left alone with [wife] Nora and her dollars, and who came out of retirement to solve the case of the missing thin man only because his wife nagged him into it.[12]

Accordingly he seems all the closer to the screwball male.

In 1934 the antihero, screwball-like male even appeared in the comedy gangster film *The Whole Town's Talking* (not released until early 1935), in which mild-mannered accountant Mr. Jones (Edward G. Robinson) is a dead ringer for Public Enemy Number One, "Killer" Bannion (also played by Robinson). Although the film does not display the high-society trappings that characterize most screwball comedies, it does include many of the genre's other essentials, most notably in the nature of Robinson's relationship with costar Jean Arthur. In fact, Arthur's impersonation of a gun moll during one of the film's many mistaken-identity scenes may have served as Katharine Hepburn's model for her own gun moll scene in screwball comedy's celebrated *Bringing Up Baby*.

The script for *The Whole Town's Talking* (1935) was adapted from a story by W. R. Burnett, probably best known for his novel *Little Caesar*, from which the classic gangster film of the same name was adapted (1930). Interestingly, however, Thurber's story, "The Remarkable Case of Mr. Bruhl" (anthologized in *The Middle-Aged Man on the Flying Trapeze*, 1935) also deals with a mousey little man and a lookalike gangster. There seemed to be an antiheroic Zeitgeist in the air.

What is forgotten today is the period significance of *My Man Godfrey* (1936). Though seldom left off anyone's list of classic screwball comedies, during the 1930s it also rated near pioneer status. More than any of its predecessors, including the zany *Twentieth Century, My Man Godfrey* offered a whole houseful of screwballs. Thus, for many, *My Man Godfrey* represented a more obvious starting point for the genre. The great 1930s film critic Otis Ferguson suggested just this when he credited it with having been the first film to rate the label screwball: "With *My Man Godfrey* in the middle of 1936, the discovery of the word screwball by those who had to have some words to say helped build the thesis of an absolutely new style in comedy."[13]

This 1936 coming of age also helps explain why 1937 seems to have been such a watershed year for the genre. Five screwball classics appeared: *Easy Living, Topper, The Awful Truth, Nothing Sacred,* and *True Confession.* Leo McCarey would win an Academy Award for his direction of the film frequently labeled the definitive screwball comedy: *The Awful Truth.* And while the heavens dropped riches on *Easy Living*'s Jean Arthur in the form of a mink coat, *Topper* examined how two "ectoplasmic screwballs" could work their way to heaven.[14]

Topper gave the genre a whole new excuse for eccentricity—visitation by the most free-*spirited* of couples (Cary Grant and Constance Bennett). As *New York Times* film critic Frank S. Nugent so nicely put it, "their car crashed and turned them into double-exposures."[15] Thus, their good deed to guarantee their safe entry into heaven was to be the loosening up of the most rigid of milquetoast males—Roland Young as Topper. The vanquishing of rigidity, which is the goal of all good screwball comedies, would naturally succeed, but not before Young comically gyrated himself through this film and two sequels, *Topper Takes a Trip* (1938) and *Topper Returns* (1941). Receiving an Academy Award nomination for Best Supporting Actor (1937), Young's Topper performances quite possibly inspired Steve Martin's more recent screwball gyrations in the splendid *All of Me* (1984). In the latter case, however, Martin's body becomes partially inhabited by a spirit (Lily Tomlin), something with which not even Young had to contend.

The successive late 1937 releases of *Nothing Sacred* and *True Confession* (both starring Carole Lombard) also inspired film critic Nugent to write a special *New York Times* salute to the actress. Nugent, never one to avoid complementing a film comedy review with additional comedy, as already exemplified with his "double-exposures" observation, appropriately labeled his article "A Christmas Carole."[16] Coming upon the previous year's *My Man Godfrey*, Lombard was given a screwball comedy notoriety which is still associated with her name.

Cary Grant also starred in two of those 1937 screwball classics—*Topper* and *The Awful Truth*. And with his next two films (*Bringing Up Baby* and *Holiday*, both 1938), Cary Grant was fast approaching an eclipse of even Lombard. As film critic Andrew Sarris would later observe, Grant was "the only actor indispensable to the genre."[17] Grant was able to mix comic frustration (frequently in the most slapstick manner) with traditional leading-man handsomeness. In fact, film critic Ferguson might have been describing Grant when he said of the genre:

> The funny character with or without the funny pants, the funny incidents, the gag and the breakaway and the washtub full of cake-dough, were assimilated into the progression of a main effect—namely the whole story and the whole show.[18]

The early forties films of writer/director Preston Sturges, particularly *The Lady Eve* (1941) and *Palm Beach Story* (1942), are also of major importance to the genre. As the initial thrust of the movement faded, Sturges's work was a comic culmination of the genre's mixture of slapstick and sophistication.

2. Roland Young experiences comic trouble in *Topper Returns* (1941). (Photograph courtesy of the Museum of Modern Art/Film Stills Archive.)

9

Screwball comedies continue to be made, as evidenced by Blake Edwards's *10* (1979) and Steven Gordon's *Arthur* (1981), both of which star today's economy-sized Cary Grant—Dudley Moore. But they appear with neither the fanfare nor the frequency of the 1930s and early 1940s films. There are no easy explanations for this decline, but it is undoubtedly true that both screwball comedy's antiheroics and its "new image of courtship and marriage . . . with man and wife no longer expecting ecstatic bliss, but treating . . . living as a crazy adventure sufficient to itself" are now the norm in American humor.[19]

Despite screwball comedy's significance in both film and comedy history, its nature remains something of a mystery. Film critic Brian Henderson, whose "Romantic Comedy Today: Semi-Tough or Impossible? is one of the more ambitious essays on the subject, observes, " 'screwball comedy' [is] a term one finds in critical contexts of all sorts. Beneath the common term, however, there is no agreement, neither from critic to critic nor within the work of a single critic."[20]

To understand the genre fully, it is necessary to examine the relationship between the screwball comedy characters of the 1930s and the full blossoming of the comic antihero in American humor during the preceding decade. The emergence of the antihero marked a pivotal period in American humor. He supplanted the crackerbarrel philosopher, marketing the full transition from a rural figure full of wisdom learned through experience to a frustrated urban misfit, more childlike than manly.

The comic antihero is characterized by five key elements: his abundant leisure time, his childlike naïveté, his life in the city, his apolitical nature, and his frustration—all of which are in marked contrast to the traits of the crackerbarrel figure. The screwball comedy character follows the antihero pattern, except that the feature films tend to glamorize the surroundings with beautiful people in luxurious settings and soften the battle of the sexes.

The evolution of the comic antihero also paralleled the adaptation of film to another new phenomenon—the "talkie." Appropriately, only the picture-plus-sound could adequately showcase the marriage of slapstick to witty dialogue, which was screwball comedy's method of portraying of the antihero. The popular birth date given the genre (1934) coincides with the time it took sound technology to catch up to the visual technology. Sound also defused the comic centralness of the silent clowns. Thus, the lesser nature (the in-film frustrations) of the antiheroic screwball comedy male was reinforced by a sound system more geared to a decentralized focus, such as the comic battle of the sexes.

Examining the screwball comedy within the framework of American humor also sheds light on a key misunderstanding of the genre: the tendency to include the films of director Frank Capra. After *It Happened One Night*, this director's career took a fascinating, but decidedly non-screwball, turn. The Capra heroes who follow, like the classic trio of Mr. Deeds, Mr. Smith, and John Doe, are from the American humor tradition of the political crackerbarrel, hardly that of screwball comedy. In fact, the genre has, on occasion, even parodied Capra's work. For example, the opening of *Nothing Sacred* (1937) is a comic send-up of the positive small-town beginning of *Mr. Deeds Goes to Town* (1936). And Ralph Bellamy's failed attempt to read his romantic poetry to Irene Dunne in *The Awful Truth* (1937)—as well as sing it to her in *Lady in a Jam* (1942)—parodies Gary Cooper's poetry recitation to Jean Arthur in *Mr. Deeds*.

Capra has given the world a unique film comedy heritage, but it is a cultural endowment better understood from a crackerbarrel than an antiheroic point of view. His post-*It Happened One Night* career is best studied along populist rather than screwball lines.

This is not to say that populist tendencies can never appear in the genre. They surface on occasion in *My Man Godfrey*, for example. However, the difference between a Capra film from his celebrated trilogy and a true screwball comedy is that whereas Capra's work invariably makes populist politics the central focus (as well as a Christ-like central hero), screwball comedy simply keys on madcap romance.

Screwball comedy characters were instrumental in making the antihero a significant comedy type in American humor today. Drawing from a rich antiheroic tradition that existed in 1920s America, the screwball comedy feature film was able to broaden the audience for this comic misfit. It is time the genre's ties with this evolution in American humor were recognized.

NOTES

1. A key element of Henri Bergson's theory of comedy, as applied to character development, addresses situations of "inversions" or "topsyturvydom," where one takes "certain characters in a certain situation" and pulls a switch:

> Thus, we laugh at the prisoner at the bar lecturing the magistrate; at a child presuming to teach its parents; in a word, at everything that comes under the heading of "topsyturvydom."

"Topsyturvydom" seems an especially appropriate term for a genre born in the depression, especially one in which the stereotyped sexual role models of the American courtship system are reversed. See also Henri Bergson, "Laughter," in *Comedy*, ed. Wylie Sypher (Garden City, New York: Doubleday Anchor Books, 1956), p. 121.

2. Hamlin Hill, "Modern American Humor: The Janus Laugh," *College English* (December 1963), p. 174.

3. Hill, "Modern American Humor: The Janus Laugh," p. 174.

4. Joseph Weingarten, *American Dictionary of Slang and Colloquial Use* (New York: Joseph Weingarten, 1954), s.v. "screwball"; William Freeman, *A Concise Dictionary of English Slang* (1955; rpt. London: English Universities Press Ltd, 1958), s.v. "screwball"; Harold Wentworth and Stuart Flexner, eds., *The Pocket Dictionary of American Slang* (1960; rpt. New York: Pocket Books, 1967), s.v. "screwball."

5. Eric Partridge, *Dictionary of Slang and Unconventional English* (1937; rpt. New York: Macmillan Company, 1970), s.v. "screw loose" and "screwy."

6. Wentworth and Flexner, *The Pocket Dictionary of American Slang,* p. 287.

7. "Me 'n Paul" (cover story), *Time,* April 15, 1935, p. 52.

8. *My Man Godfrey* review, *Variety,* September 23, 1936, p. 16.

9. Thomas Sobchack and Vivian C. Sobchack, "Genre Films," in *An Introduction to Film* (Boston: Little, Brown and Company, 1980), p. 208.

10. Thomas Schatz deals with determinate and indeterminate space throughout his "Hollywood Film Genre As Ritual: A Theoretical and Methodological Inquiry" (Ph.D. dissertation, University of Iowa, 1976, which served as the foundation for his recent *Hollywood Genres: Formulas, Filmmaking, and the Studio System* [New York: Random House, 1981]). The determinate space category refers to genres in which action occurs at a specific time and place, while indeterminate genres are defined more in terms of character interaction. The latter category includes the melodrama and musical genres, as well as screwball comedy.

11. Lewis Jacobs, "Significant Contemporary Film Content," in *The Rise of the American Film* (1939; rpt. New York: Columbia University Teachers College Press, 1971), pp. 535-36; Andrew Bergman, "Frank Capra and Screwball Comedy, 1931-1941," in *We're in the Money: Depression America and Its Films* (1971; rpt. New York: Harper & Row, 1972), pp. 132-34; Molly Haskell, "The Thirties," in *From Reverence to Rape: The Treatment of Women in the Movies* (Baltimore: Penguin Books, 1974), p. 124; Andrew Sarris, "The Sex Comedy Without Sex," *American Film,* March 1978, pp. 8-15.

With reference to the Haskell-Sarris hypothesis, it should be noted that screwball comedies still appeared after the code was eliminated in the 1960s. In fact, the beginning of the end for the code occurred with the 1953 release of the screwball comedy *The Moon Is Blue.* The film was both a commercial and critical success, despite being the first film by a major American studio (since the inception of the code) to be released without the code's "Seal of Approval."

12. William F. Nolan, *Hammett: A Life at the Edge* (New York: Congdon & Weed, 1983), p. 129.

13. Otis Ferguson, "While We Were Laughing" (1940), in *The Film Criticism of Otis Ferguson,* ed. Robert Wilson (Philadelphia: Temple University Press, 1971), p. 24.

14. *Topper* review, *New York Times,* August 21, 1937, p. 21.

15. Frank S. Nugent, *Topper Takes a Trip* review, *New York Times,* December 31, 1938, p. 11.

16. Frank S. Nugent, "A Christmas Carole," *New York Times,* December 19, 1937, p. 7 (section 10).

17. Sarris, "The Sex Comedy Without Sex," p. 15.

18. Ferguson, "While We Were Laughing," p. 24.

19. Raymond Durgnat, "Lightly and Politely," in *The Crazy Mirror: Hollywood Comedy and the American Image* (1970; rpt New York: Dell Publishing Co., 1972), p. 122.

20. Brian Henderson, "Romantic Comedy Today: Semi-Tough or Impossible?" *Film Quarterly,* Summer 1978, p. 12.

2.

BACKGROUND OF THE COMIC ANTIHERO

"Marriages are made in heaven, an' very few o' them ever git back t' the factory."

Kin Hubbard's *Abe Martin* (1926).[1]

A GENERAL LOOK AT THE BEGINNING OF
AMERICAN HUMOR AND THE YANKEE

Native American humor can be dated from approximately 1830, taking Seba Smith's Jack Downing as a starting point.[2] A fictional character, Jack was a tall, long-legged New Englander from Downingville, Maine. He was bright and ambitious and had a great interest in politics. Today we would recognize Downing under a different title: Uncle Sam. "But a hundred years ago or so, before Uncle Sam had become . . . [a national] symbol, the cartoonist would have used a figure better known at the time—the pawky, impudent Yankee, Jack Downing."[3] Yet even in 1830, the Yankee was not new to America.

During the Revolutionary War the British had composed the tune "Yankee Doodle" to deride the colonists.[4] Instead, the rebels took up the ditty and it became an unofficial theme song. With a birth that parallels that of the nation, it is appropriate that the Yankee's first debut should occur in 1787, the year the United States Constitution was framed. The setting was Royal Tyler's comedy play *The Contrast*, and the Yankee was named Jonathan—"the first full portrait of the New-Englandman. The earliest attempt at characterizing the real American, he became the progenitor of a long line of stage Yankees."[5]

Tyler's play proved very influential and "by 1797 . . . the Yankee was an established small part [often as a servant], though by no means a conspicuous figure on the stage."[6] But even more influential were the farmer's almanacs of the time, for instance,

> R. B. Thomas (1766-1846), whose *Old Farmer's Almanac,* started in 1793 . . . was perhaps the most popular publication of its kind in the early years of the century. Thomas . . . hit upon the idea of putting advice to rural readers . . . into the form of salty [comic] speeches presumably made by an actual farmer.[7]

In and of itself this was nothing new. John Gerber placed the Yankee in the tradition of *The Book of Proverbs, Aesop's Fables*, the essays of Bacon, and even America's Benjamin Franklin.[8] But what was unique for America and the character of the Yankee was that under the guise of Smith's Jack Downing, "the Yankee emerged in a new role, as oracle."[9] Previously the figure of the Yankee had been thinly drawn, more often the butt of the joke than its originator.

With Downing, the "lowly Yankee first took an important place in American political and social satire."[10] The Yankee was capable; he could take care of himself. Walter Blair called this capability "horse sense," even entitling a book *Horse Sense in American Humor*. The character had "learned everything from experience. When he gets into a new situation, he whittles his problem down to its essentials, sees how it compares with situations in his past and how it differs from them, and then he thinks out what he should do—figures out the right answer."[11] He does not need any "book learnin'." It was a rational universe and life could be planned in a rational manner. Comedy resulted from characters who had trouble planning their existence. But the Yankee established a positive, rational plan and/or advised others of the correct procedure open to them.

The New England Yankee, of course, was not the only comedy type to exist in nineteenth-century American humor. There were, for example, the Local Colorists, the Literary Comedians, who, despite an interest in political satire, drew much of their humor from word sight gags on the printed page (misspellings, slang, clichés), and the Southwesterner humorists, who focused on having fun, often through sneaky practical jokes (putting a lizard in someone's nightshirt). These, and most other forms of American nineteenth-century humor, do have one thing in common, however. They are based on the premise that their protagonists exist in a rational world, where comic misfortune is a product of human error or meanness (pranks) instead of a total system gone awry—an irrational world.

The Yankee dominated American humor until well into the twentieth century. Will Rogers's death in 1935 is usually considered the end of this character as a dominant national figure of American humor. "From the day of Downing's appearance to 1935 . . . America was at no time without at least one homespun philosopher.''[12] The rustic wiseman of American fiction was hard pressed to maintain a national audience after the 1920s. The nation's ever-increasing urbanization and sophistication made the country philosopher's down-home wisdom (usually delivered in dialect or ungrammatical English) seem old fashioned and irrelevant. More importantly, America's view of itself was undergoing a change.

The breakthrough of the comic antihero in American humor took place in the middle- to late 1920s. The antihero, who tries to create order in a world where order is impossible, is actually not new to American comedy. He even surfaces on occasion in the nineteenth-century world of the New England Yankee, as well as in the wild and woolly frontier humor of the Southwest. In fact, few comedy types are ever entirely new. But what is different about the American antihero of the twentieth-century is his advancement to center stage. Previously he had been a character often on the fringe of American humor, an irrational figure in a world still considered rational. Or, if some antihero did manage center stage, he was atypical, far from the then contemporary status quo in comedy. As these antiheroic roots are examined in pre-*New Yorker* schools of comedy, it should also be mentioned that filmmaker Leo McCarey's teaming and molding of Laurel & Hardy also constituted an important part of the antihero's coming of age in the 1920s.[13] Because of the ongoing popular culture significance of the team, and their many parallels with the antiheroic frustrations of the *New Yorker* group, it also frequently provides the new student of the comic antihero a more mainstream example with which he might have greater familiarity.

AMERICAN ROOTS OF THE COMIC ANTIHERO

This section examines the American background of the comic antihero in five different areas prior to its full blossoming in the 1920s: fictional humor of New England, fictional humor of the old Southwest, newspaper comic strips, slapstick farce, and vaudeville comedy.

These five areas are not meant to represent every example in American culture of the comic antihero's roots. It is merely an attempt to give a general impression of the rich American tradition, already in place, even in the 1920s. By the late 1920s the American comic antihero had evolved into a mirror opposite of the crackerbarrel figure. The antihero is characterized by his abundant leisure time, childlike nature, urban life, apolitical outlook, and basic frustration (especially in relationships with women). Earlier precedents, however, will not need to match each of the criteria but rather be in the general spirit of the antihero; an example might be a life-style grounded in general frustration.

Humor of New England

The humor of New England is most famous for the wisdom of its Yankee figure, the antithesis of the antihero. The Yankee's world is bound up in employment, political involvement, success, fatherly image, and rural residency (all antihero opposites)—though he can handle the city. Yet it is wrong to assume that there were no antihero types in Yankee humor. There were actually a goodly number, but often they did not receive the attention afforded the capable Yankee. Sometimes that attention became the focus of a moral, as for example, in "My Neighbor Freeport," a very early archetype of the antihero, from Robert Thomas's *The Farmer's Almanac* (1813).

Freeport is the town entertainer. He has "a knack at telling a story, cracking a joke and singing a song."[14] Whatever the social event, Freeport is sure to be the center of attention. Soon his neighbors start to reward him for his efforts with a glass of grog and the tavern becomes more of a home than his farm.

The neglected farm means a neglected family, and Freeport has failed in his duties as a father; "the poor children were shoeless and coatless."[15] Eventually the farm is lost to debts, the children go on public support, and Freeport "died drunk in the highway!"[16] He had paid appropriately for his neglect of the Yankee virtues. Freeport is antiheroic in that he is only concerned with fun and he knows frustration.

This is not to imply that the antihero in the Yankee tale must be made to suffer or that the Yankee himself is devoid of antiheroic characteristics. Even Seba Smith's Yankee Jack Downing, considered the first full articulation of a native comic figure, is not without antiheroic characteristics. Downing's walking journey from Downingville (Maine) to Washington and President Jackson's search for a suitable job for him display frustration.

Moreover, descriptions of eccentric, comically physical acts, with even an accompanying cartoon, were not foreign to Yankee humor. For example, in "Letter LIX: in which Major Downing shakes hands for the President at Philadelphia, while on the grand tour down East," Downing is literally pictured and described as helping the president when Jackson became tired greeting well-wishers—"Then I kind of stood behind him and reached my arm around his, and shook for him for about an hour as tight as I could spring."[17]

More often than not antihero characterics are present in a supporting player in the Yankee cast. Thus, in Thomas Chandler Haliburton's Sam Slick tale "Taming a Shrew," Slick stops at the home of a friend who is having wife problems. The friend, John Porter, is as henpecked as any antihero, a state of affairs Slick plans on changing. That night, under cover of darkness, Slick calls upon one of his many talents (ventriloquism) and gains access to the house as Porter. He then proceeds to gain some womanly respect for Porter by whipping the wife. The story closes with "A woman, a dog, and a walnut tree, The more you lick 'em the better they be.''[18] These are words the antihero would hardly venture to think, let alone vocalize.

Probably the most effective use of the antiheroic character in the Yankee tale is, however, in terms of a more direct, sustained comparison with the capable Yankee. Just such a sustained articulation is to be found in *The Biglow Papers* of James Russell Lowell. These letters juxtapose Yankee Hosea Biglow against antiheroic Birdofredum Sawin.

The complete stupidity of Birdofredum underlines the capabilities of the Yankee Hosea Biglow. Moreover, by their placement on opposite ends of a political issue, the position of Biglow is reinforced all the more. For example, Biglow opposes the 1848 war with Mexico, while Sawin is an often wounded soldier still parroting rhetoric to the glory of war:

> I've lost one eye, but thet's a loss its easy to supply
> Out o' the glory thet I've gut, for thet is all my eye;
> An' one is enough, I guess, by diligently usin' it.[19]

Sawin eventually loses an arm, the fingers of his other hand, and a leg, all in the name of glory. He becomes something of a comic Ahab, forever destined to surrender new limbs to a great white whale called war. The humor arises from the grizzly repetition of his frustration.

Yankee humor, therefore, despite its general reliance on homely verbal advice, is not without antiheroic elements. Because of an interest in politics and national issues there is a certain seriousness to even the most comic of Yankee advice. Because of this, the generally nonpolitical antihero is less likely to stand out in Yankee humor. But there is no doubt that he has some New England roots, especially as a device to build up the image of the Yankee.

It should be noted, however, that despite the presence of antiheroes, the Yankee world is still the product of eighteen-century rational thinking. That is, the antihero found himself in a comic dilemma more or less due to his own incompetency. Since the world was assumed to be rational, the character could right himself by making his own life well ordered. After all, he had the example of the Yankee. And Yankee success was based merely on common sense (nonintellectual) practices in a rational world. But in the later world of Laurel & Hardy, the whole system was out of order.

Humor of the Old Southwest

Southwestern humor contemporaneous with that of the Yankee school (1830-67) is different from its proper eastern neighbor.[20] This humor, born of the American frontier, has been defined by John Gerber through a contrast with the Yankee: The Southwesterner is amoral where the Yankee is moral, impractical where the Yankee is practical, shrewd as opposed to

Yankee common sense, interested in upsetting the status quo versus Yankee contentment, and suspicious of authority where the Yankee is trustful.[21] Obviously this rough and tumble character sounds little like the antihero, as if you were to match Daniel Boone against Laurel & Hardy. And in truth, they are probably more different than alike, yet Southwestern humor foreshadows the antihero in two essential ways: humor through the frustration of physical discomfort and the pursuit of leisure time activities. These traits may be found in the work of George Washington Harris, Johnson J. Hooper, and Mark Twain, as well as T. B. Thorpe's "Big Bear of Arkansas" and William Tappan Thompson's "A Coon Hunt in a Fency Country."[22]

First, Walter Blair notes that the humor of the Southwest is largely "derived from physical discomfort."[23] The primer of primers on this topic is Harris's Sut Lovingood. F. O. Matthiessen notes that Lovingood "delights to put lizards in a parson's pants, or to turn loose a hornet's nest at a prayer meeting; and he strews unconscious bodies around the scene of a fight with as much gusto as Fielding."[24]

Johnson's Simon Suggs is just as likely as Lovingood to inflict physical frustration. For example, early in *Simon Suggs's Adventures* (Johnson's only published book) a young Suggs rides away from home for the final time, content that he had "stolen into his mother's room, and nicely loaded the old lady's pipe with a thimble full of gunpowder; neatly covering the 'villainous saltpetre' with tobacco."[25]

Twain goes well beyond this early variation on the exploding cigar when he makes Tom Sawyer a master of frustration at the close of *Huckleberry Finn*. He and Huck must rescue Jim from his woodshed jail. But what should have amounted to a ten-minute mission stretched on for days as Jim was submitted to a bevy of pains to make this an authentic rescue, in the best traditions of the eighteenth-century romance. Thus, Jim's pleasant "cell" had to become a hovel, thanks to Tom's acquisition of rats, spiders, and snakes:

> But we got them laid in . . . and you never see a cabin as blithesome as Jim's was when they'd all swarm out for music and go for him . . . spiders . . . lay for him, and make it mighty warm for him. And he said that between the rats and the snakes . . . there weren't no room in bed for him . . . and when there was, a body couldn't sleep, it was so lively . . . always lively . . . because they never all slept at one time, but took turn about, so when the snakes was asleep the rats was on deck.[26]

The Southwestern figure does not just cause frustration; he can also be the victim. Twain's "The Notorious Jumping Frog of Calaveras County" is the tale of Jim Farley's luck at betting, until someone fills his prize jumping frog Dan'l Webster full of quail shot up to his chin. Thorpe's "Big Bear of Arkansas" is about another hoodwinking, this time by a bear. And Thompson's "A Coon Hunt in Fency Country" is about the realization that the demon in a bottle of rum can make a man climb the same fence time and again, even on a simple hunting expedition.

Southwestern humor, however, more often has a focus figure more likely to instigate frustration than to suffer it. As Gerber's definition implies, the Southwestern figure is nothing if not sneaky. In fact, the sneakiest of the sneaks, Simon Suggs, practically opens his *Adventures* with his favorite aphorism: "IT IS GOOD TO BE SHIFTY IN A NEW COUNTRY" (his emphasis).[27] Thus, Southwestern figures of frustration are often of secondary importance.

Even when the main Southwestern figure is frustrated, it is different in one essential way from the antiheroic world. That is, Southwestern humor still functions in the world of eighteenth-century rationality, as does Yankee humor. Thus, frustrations occur as the result of human deceit (Dan'l Webster full of quail shot) or human foolishness (coon hunting with rum), instead of the collapse of the system itself—which is the case in the world of the antihero.

The second manner in which the humor of the Southwest foreshadows the antihero is in its persistent focus on leisure time activities, on having fun. For example, Harris's Sut Lovingood relates that:

> Men wer made a-purpus jis' tu eat, drink, an' fur stayin awake
> in the yearly part ove the nites: an' wimen wer made tu cook the
> vittils, mix the sperits, an' help the men du the stayin awake.[28]

Jeannette Tandy notes that:

> When Hooper's character Simon was a boy of sixteen, his
> father, an old "hardshell' Baptist" preacher, caught
> Simon . . . playing seven-up . . . he tells his father that it is no
> use to whip him. He intends to play cards as long as he lives, and
> some day to make his living by it.[29]

The story eventually finds Simon playing (and cheating) his preacher father for a pony; thus begins the recorded history of the free spirit Simon Suggs.

Tom Sawyer represents a boyhood guide to classic American examples in leisure: Tom selling opportunities to whitewash Aunt Polly's fence (his workload for that Saturday), Tom and friends playing hooky from homework and escaping to their own private island, Huck never even going to school (except for his short stay with the widow), Huck and Jim floating down the Mississippi on a raft and "borrowing" their food when necessary, and so on and so on.[30]

There is, however, an essential difference between the backgrounds to the leisure-time activities of the Southwesterner and the antihero, despite the fact that both groups like to party. To maintain his leisure time, the Southwestern figure must be on a constant hustle. Thus, Suggs can play the part of a reborn Christian and take up a collection for himself at a revival ("Simon Suggs Attends a Camp Meeting"), while Tom Sawyer can sell chances on whitewashing Aunt Polly's fence. The antihero has neither the need nor the ability to hustle. And whereas the Southwesterner often combines business and fun for a profitable leisure time, the antihero adds to his collection of frustrations.

Newspaper Comic Strips

After the rather mature content of Southwestern humor, Arthur Asa Berger terms the first years of the American comic strip (1900-20) the "innocents," from Henry May's book *The Age of American Innocence*.[31] Among the comic strips that appear during this period are four that seem especially to foreshadow the later antihero: Rudolph Dirks's "Katzenjammer Kids" (1897), Bud Fisher's "Mutt & Jeff" (1907), George Herriman's "Krazy Kat" (1913), and George McManus's "Bringing Up Father" (1913).[32] These strips anticipate antihero characteristics in three significant ways: large degree of leisure, presence of frustration, and a nonpolitical nature.

First, these comic strip characters tend to take their leisure more for granted than do the Southwestern figures. This is best exemplified in McManus's "Bringing Up Father" by Jiggs, the male member of a nouveau riche couple, not pressured about making an income. Jiggs can on occasion be seen in the office, but it is much more likely that he will be lounging at home or heading for friend "Dinty's" Saloon (a New York vaudeville hangout) for poker or pool.

If Jiggs represents the closest facsimile to later leisure-laden antiheroes, Dirks's "Katzenjammer Kids" represents the most exotic of archetypes. The strip is located somewhere in the jungles of East Africa, "perhaps the former German East Africa colony, if not Polynesia.' "[33] Its principal characters—the Kids—know only the pursuit of pleasure, particularly the culinary delights of Mama.

The second manner in which the strips anticipate the antiheroic is through depiction of a great deal of frustration, often displayed in the most physical manner. In fact, certain violent acts are repeated so often that they literally can be considered trademarks of each strip, for example, Mama beating the Kids or the Captain with her ever-ready rolling pin or frying pan, Mutt giving Jeff one more black eye, Ignatz Mouse braining Krazy Kat with still another brick, and Jiggs finding himself the permanent target of Maggie's vases or rolling pins.

Close attention should be paid to the source of these frustrations. As in most antiheroic situations, the female makes the rules and administers the punishment (though Mutt and Ignatz are both males, each strip plays upon the concept of a feuding "couple"). Thus, Jiggs's constant goal seems to be to slip out of the house for a night of poker with the boys, while Maggie represents a determined and a sizable roadblock (one is reminded of the huge wives McCarey sometimes gave Laurel & Hardy). Jigg's pride, daughter Nora, is actually a junior wife, also keeping tabs on her father. Between Maggie and Nora, Jiggs's world is often reduced to a female force-field, where women not only control conversation but often anticipate male adventures, just as the McCarey Laurel & Hardy wife does.

Frustration in these strips, however, can go beyond a single focus and foreshadow the irrational world of the antihero. This is particularly true of Herriman's "Krazy Kat." Even the title—"Krazy"—underlines this fact. The strip features a docile cat who loves a brick-toting mouse (Ignatz) who is often arrested by a cat-loving police dog (Offissa Pupp). This bizarre situation, however, goes one step further, as Gilbert Selden explains:

> back to the days of Cleopatra . . . a mouse fell in love with Krazy, the beautiful daughter of Kleopatra Kat . . . advised . . . to write his love, he carved a declaration on a brick and, tossing the "missive" . . . he had nearly killed the Kat . . . "it has become the Romeonian custom to crease his lady's beam with a brick laden with tender sentiments."[34]

Thus, each time Krazy gets beaned, he sees hearts and arrows, while Ignatz feels confident that he has knocked that cat silly still one more time. Neither animal, then, really knows what is going on. Such is the stuff of the antiheroic world.

The antiheroic is anticipated in a third manner—its nonpolitical nature. But unlike later antihero examples, it is not due to a childlike quality. Despite the fact that these strips concern themselves with the "Kids" or a situation called "Bringing Up Father," the characters are more in the capable, sneaky tradition of a Southwestern Simon Suggs. Thus, the "Kids" are capable of tunneling into the kitchen, stealing a roast, and placing the blame on the Captain, while even Jiggs manages to beat the radar systems of Maggie and Nora occasionally. That is, they are essentially capable types too busy for politics because of the constant battles with their partners. In contrast, antiheroes like Laurel & Hardy are incapable children who need the help of a wife-mother because time and again they prove their own inadequacy.

Slapstick Farce

At the same time that the comics were being born, slapstick farce was popular in American theatres. Playwright Charles H. Hoyt had begun the

American version of this genre in the late nineteenth century.[35] In the
twentieth century years before World War I, George Ade and George M.
Cohan followed the path of Hoyt.[36] Together their work foreshadows the
plight of the comic antihero in an essential way—frustration that borders on
the irrational.

Two examples from Hoyt and Ade nicely describe these frustrations. In
Hoyt's *A Tin Soldier* (1886), the practical plumber Vilas Canby dryly
informs the play's central character,

> I might go over and see it and shut off the water and bring away
> the faucets and connections and meter—that will hold the job
> for us till we are ready to attend to it.[37]

Ade's *The Sultan of Sulu* (1902) deals with the Americanization of a
Philippine potentate and his harem. Americanization means womanization,
even in 1902. Thus, this new "royal" American begins his education on the
sticky situation of divorce proceedings by all his wives—with each entitled
to one-half his income.[38]

Frustration in these plays often turns on a situation Hoyt introduced to
American theatres:

> a man takes over a business that he knows nothing about and
> attempts to run it, an endeavor which forces him to deal with
> unfamiliar circumstances mirth provoking in their
> consequences.[39]

This is nicely demonstrated in Cohan's *Broadway Jones* (1912), about a
New York spendthrift who falls heir to the Jones Chewing Gum Company
in Jonesville, Connecticut. Knowing nothing about chewing gum, he must
rely on the company's executive secretary for advice.

As should be expected of a school of comedy called slapstick farce,
frustration is displayed in a physical manner. Theatre historian Margaret G.
Mayorga has even moved to associate the slapstick process with the mental
workings of Ade's and Cohan's work, while Montrose Moses compares
Ade's work to the cartoon.[40]

Ironically enough, the full frustration potential for *Broadway Jones* and
similar works by Hoyt and Ade are seldom realized. Instead of going the
final mile to the totally irrational environment of "Krazy Kat," these plays
bounce back into celebrations of Americana and revamped Horatio Alger
values, particularly that of experience over education. In the case of Jones,
he decides to fight the gum trust. With dialogue suddenly echoing the
"bullies" of former trust-busting President Theodore Roosevelt (he was in
the news again in 1912 as the presidential candidate of his own Bull Moose
party), Jones beats the trust, learns the gum-chewing business, and marries
the secretary.

All three playwrights end up riding success themes. Mayorga has made the further observation that both Ade and Cohan tend to present these themes in the "spirit of a game."[41] Cohan, of course, is the ultimate symbol of all-American drive, but he has nothing on the energetic character of Spangle Ade's *Sulu Revisited* (1904):

> He . . . builds pickle and "butterine" factories, promotes a national interest in Goo-Goo Chewing Gum, unionizes the workers, . . . turns the royal palace into a department store, converts the temple of Sho-Gum into a bowling alley . . . and considers plans for opening seven additional corporations the next day.[42]

The real story of these works, then, is that their protagonists start out in the irrational world of the antihero and surface as successful Yankees. Thus, it is hardly a coincidence that Cohan is most famous for his American associations: his patriotism, the "Yankee Doodle" theme song, a joint birthday with Uncle Sam (July 4). It also should be noted that Ade is probably best known for his "Fables in Slang," which first appeared in Chicago papers in the late nineteenth century. These fables, though in the tradition of the literary comedians (much of the humor derived from the words themselves—slang, misspellings, clichés) do deal with worldy wisdom.[43]

Vaudeville Comedy

As with the foreshadowing of the antiheroic in slapstick farce, vaudeville comedy at the turn of the century had its own contribution to make. In *Vaudeville as Ritual* Albert F. McLean, Jr., notes that again and again after 1900 critics implied that a "new humor" had developed in this country. And though he mentions other media, he gives the biggest nod to vaudeville, because it "was both the major market and the leading innovator in this revolution in popular taste."[44]

The primary manner in which this new vaudeville comedy seemed to anticipate the antiheroic comedy was in its focus on the urban area. Big industry had come to the cities, and behind it, tens of thousands of immigrants anxious for success. Yet as shown in Upton Sinclair's *Jungle* (written in the first years of the century), few of these immigrants succeeded. Thus, McLean suggests that urban-based frustrations created a demand for a "new humor":

> The task of relieving social tensions had been taken from the . . . deadpan. Yankee wits, and a whole new generation of comics, for the most part city-bred, competitive hustlers, had

sensed the utility of humor in oiling the psychic wheels of an industrial democracy.[45]

According to McLean, "The new humor was the antidote for larger doses of the Myth of Success."[46] Moreover, it is important to note that these vaudeville "new humor" comics are, in McLean's terms, "city-bred," a fact John E. Dimeglio corroborates in *Vaudeville U.S.A.*[47] It is logical that they should deal with urban frustrations, just as it is logical that most of the playwrights of slapstick farce, who were from rural, small-town areas—the traditional harborer of the American dream—naturally often pushed the success story.

If the McLean hypothesis is correct, these antiheroic elements appeared much earlier in vaudeville. For example, Douglas Gilbert has noted the popularity of Irish and Dutch comedy acts in vaudeville of the 1880s as "indicative of the huge immigration of those nationals in the days when Liberty beckoned them up the bay in boatloads."[48]

Initially, then, the urban-based humor of vaudeville relied on dialect and "such stylized figures as the blackfaced coon, the Jew, the Irishman, the Wop, or the Urban Dandy . . . but, on the whole, the audience seemed to accept these figures . . . as symbolic . . . of loneliness and alienation as opposed to racist figures."[49]

In vaudeville's pre-turn-of-the-century days, an examination of period literature (primary sources, such as the archives of the Billy Rose Theatre Collection, New York Public Library at Lincoln Center), would seem to indicate that the ethnic order of popularity among performers was Irish acts first, followed by blackface, and then Dutch/German dialects.

For the contemporary viewer, the early vaudeville days of the Marx Brothers (see the Billy Rose Collection) represent a perfect case study of the evolving nature of ethnic humor in vaudeville. The Marx Brothers's early vaudeville days, beginning just after the turn of the century, reflect the continued pervasiveness of dialect humor in American entertainment. Groucho would, for a time, use a German dialect, while Harpo would briefly essay an Irish accent. Chico also developed his Italian accent during this period, continuing it, of course, through the Brothers' later film career.

In time, when these stylized figures were more apt to be misused or misunderstood (through the increased sensitivity of minority groups and acquiring Germany as a World War I enemy), the vaudeville comic "drew upon a strong American tradition in humor . . . the monologue."[50] Gilbert notes in his chapter on "Great Comics of the 1900's" that Ed Wynn's act was sidewalk conversation.[51] Yet even a sidewalk conversation could underline urban affronts to personal dignity; a popular turn-of-the-century monologue chronicles the crowded unpleasantness of travel by public conveyance, a product of the high population density of many cities:

He was endeavoring to expectorate on the ceiling, not having the necessary five hundred for doing it on the floor, the unexpected expectoration of the expectorator, in the opening of the man's map hit the conductor a wallop in the eye. I beg your pardon, says he. My fault says the conductor, I had no right getting in front of a hose.[52]

There is no better primary source on this combination of comedy and urban frustration than the copyrighted sketches of W. C. Fields, which are only available at the Library of Congress (see the "W. C. Fields Papers," Manuscript Division—Madison Building). Fields, who was already a headliner by the turn of the century, copyrighted much of his stage material during the 1910s and 1920s. These sketches frequently showcase a frustrated urbanite. In fact, the most entertaining of the sketches parallels the aforementioned comic dilemma of the traveler on a public conveyance. The Fields sketch in question, "Off to the Country" (of which he copyrighted three variations), finds Fields trying to get his family onto a busy subway train for a trip to the peace of a rural setting.

The family is composed of Babby Sammy, "Sap"; daughter Ray, "Tut"; a nagging wife, Mrs. Fliverton; and Emmeline Fliverton, apparently Mr. Fliverton's (Fields's mother). Besides the difficulty Fields's character has in directing this crew, they are weighed down by a massive collection of vacation items, including a mandolin in a case, a tennis racket, a parrot cage, a suitcase, balloons, an all-day sucker, a can of worms, folding fishing rods, a gun, various bundles, a big doll, a teddy bear, an umbrella, a ukelele in a case, a small phonograph, a baseball mask, a bat, and a hatbox.[53]

"Off to the Country" is full of missed trains, troublesome children, a bothersome wife, a surly ticket taker, a sneaky revenue officer ("Pussyfoot Anderson"), and loads of slapstick—largely due to that warehouse of props. The Flivertons never do get their trip; instead, Papa is arrested for violation of the Volstead Act—he is found to have a bottle of brandy, although it was used only "for medicinal purposes."[54] And the family follows in tears as Mr. Fliverton is dragged off to jail.

As these new comics were slowly weaning themselves from the more obvious gimmicks, such as blackface and dialects, a rather apropos characteristic was descending upon them—apropos, that is, for comics dealing in urban frustration. Gilbert defines it as:

a combination of outrageous distortion, noisy satire, and mad humor, adding up to an insanely imaginative entertainment— "nut" acts, in the argot of the profession.[55]

Again, one is reminded of the Marx Brothers *after* their initial old-style focus on dialect.

These "nut" acts seem to join "Krazy Kat" in foreshadowing the irrational world of the comic antihero. Another well-known example of these "nut" performers, through later appearances on radio and television, is Ed Wynn. Long before the radio birth of his zany "fire chief" character (complete with helmet), he was "The Perfect Fool" of vaudeville.

But at the time, the "Biggest of the nut headliners was Joe Cook," whose comedy props were of special interest—"Joe depended largely upon ridiculous mechanical contrivances."[56]. One such device was a huge machine with a sleeping man beside it. Cook defined it as a device to get the hired man to supper, and gave a mini-lecture on the parts of the machine. Finally, he would activate the machine,

> [setting] . . . in motion a number of crazy-looking gears, and pistons, eventually liberating a slapstick which smacked the sleeping man who woke up and struck a gong with a mallet. This called the hired man to dinner.[57]

Unlike McCarey's nonmechanical Laurel & Hardy, Cook does successfully operate the machine. But it obviously goes a long way toward explaining both the frustration and fear (through mechanical replacement in urban industry) under which the typical American suffered, even at the turn of the century.

The copyrighted stage material of W. C. Fields again provides a pivotal primary source example. That is, the surname Fliverton appears frequently in the copyrighted sketches, including the previously noted "Off to the Country." The name underlines how often the modern comic frustrations of the twentieth-century man are tied to the mechanical. Fliverton is unquestionably a thinly veiled reference to the most antiheroic of machines, the Model-T Ford, then frequently called the flivver. (One of the sketches in which the Flivertons appear is called "The Family Ford." Fields copyrighted three versions of it.) The Model-T Ford was so associated with comic frustrations that countless jokes circulated on the subject. For example: "The guy who owns a secondhand flivver may not have a quarrelsome disposition, but he's always trying to start something."[58] Several later comedy careers are closely identified with this car, including that of Laurel & Hardy. Thus, to name a comedy family (actually, several of them) Fliverton is strongly to suggest modern comedy antiheroic tendencies. A reading of the sketches bears this out.

Unfortunately, the antiheroic nature of the comedian's career has often been neglected.[59] While some of Fields's routines were committed to film in the silent era, it took the advent of sound for him to arrive fully as a film comedian. Yet, even today, his con-man characteristics generate more attention than the antiheroic ones. Still, McLean's *Vaudeville as Ritual* has observations on "new humor" which would seem to point to Fields. (See chapter 4 for material on Gregory LaCava and J. P. McEvoy, with whom Fields worked in the 1920s.)

The Comic Antihero in the 1920s: *The New Yorker*

The 1920s represented a significant decade for the comic antihero. He was hardly a new figure in American humor, as the preceding examination has shown. Yet this period saw him take on an increased visibility, particulary because of *The New Yorker* magazine. In fact, credit for this antiheroic blossoming of the 1920s as *the* American Humor historian Walter Blair observes in his watershed *Native American Humor*, is usually given to it—"The magazine which was more responsible than any other medium for the rise of a new type of humor."[60] More specifically, this responsibility fell to four writers: Clarence Day, Robert Benchley, James Thurber, and S. D. Perelman. Walter Blair also noted:

> though they did not entirely break with the past—no humorist is
> likely to do this—they wrote humor based upon assumptions
> quite different from those of older humorists and employed
> techniques contrasting with older techniques.[61]

This is not to suggest, however, that other period humor magazines, in an era particularly rich with such publications, did not showcase similar comedy pieces, sometimes even both predating *The New Yorker* as well as drawing from what would be its pantheon four. Thus, one might note *Judge, Life* (the humor magazine, not the later pictorial), and *College Humor* (which drew largely from the then pervasive college humor journals) as other important 1920s comedy journals. *Judge-New Yorker* ties are possibly most interesting, because *The New Yorker*'s celebrated founder and first editor Harold Ross was a one-time assistant to *Judge* editor Norman Anthony. Moreover, S. J. Perelman first rose to prominence as a writer and cartoonist at *Judge.*

None of this, however, negates the significance of *The New Yorker*. In fact, this chapter thus far has examined antiheroic precedents in American humor which even surfaced in the most crackerbarrel of nineteenth-century sources. Besides, rare is the movement, literary or otherwise, where the discerning critic cannot uncover some earlier precedent. Such precedents should not be ignored, but neither should they be allowed to distract from genuinely pivotal events. With regard to the antihero, the birth of *The New Yorker* was one such genuinely pivotal event. Its birth was a *conscious* celebration of this new urban humor. Ross's prospectus for the magazine, which might be comically summarized by noting its most quoted line—"*The New Yorker* will be the magazine which is not edited for the old lady in Dubuque"—is dedicated to this change. Moreover, as humor historian Norris W. Yates has observed, *The New Yorker*:

> was to give the highly literate but nimble [antiheroic] humorists their most important outlet of publication and to carry respect for competence in general and for stylistic smartness without brashness in particular to an extreme that amounted almost to fetishism concerning the word and the precise phase.[62]

It also should be kept in mind that there were direct ties between these *New Yorker* writers and the film world itself. Both Benchley and Perelman were active in Hollywood early in their writing careers. In fact, Benchley logged time in Hollywood as early as 1926, a year before he joined the *New Yorker* staff. Moreover, he starred in his first film comedy short almost as early (*The Treasurer's Report*, 1928). Perelman did not officially join the magazine until 1931, the same year he did the story for the Marx Brothers' film *Monkey Business*. Thus, if there was any antihero influence from either coast, there is a good chance Hollywood would receive the nod as more influential.

A less direct but no less important influence of the New Yorker writers on the antiheroic screwball comedy film movement was their leisure-time party antics off the job. Perfectly consistent with the antihero's leisure focus, the writers' early 1930 party circuit served as the inspiration of Hammett's good-time backdrop in *The Thin Man*. The real-life good-time backdrop was something with which Hammett and his companion the author Lillian Hellman (the models for *The Thin Man*'s Nick and Nora Charles) were well acquainted. In fact, the novel itself was written at the hotel of Hammett's friend Nathanael West, an author and the brother-in-law of Hammett's buddy S. J. Perelman.

Of the four *New Yorker* writers, particular attention will be given to the work of Benchley and Thurber because it best exemplifies the comic American hero and the two were most productive during the 1920s and 1930s. Through the character of his father, Day represents something of a transition from Yankee to antihero; Perelman anticipates comedy pushed to the extremes of absurdity in the post-World War II period.

The comic antihero of these *New Yorker* writers always has time on his hands. The Benchley character is a wealthy bachelor (on occasion he implies a wife, but she is nowhere to be seen), usually observed in his tuxedo or his robe, depending on when the party was over. His at-home free time is spent figuring out ways to kill time: "How to Eat," "The Care of Fish," "How to Break 90 in Croquet." In the last lesson one is told:

Let us take the first shot which you will be called upon to make—through No. 1 wicket. As No. 1 wicket and No. 2 wicket are very close together, you ought to be able to go through them both at once, unless you have been drinking. (I naturally do not mean that you actually try to go through the wickets yourself—unless you have been drinking.)

For this first shot, I usually use the mallet called the "massie," because it has a blue band around it. Taking an easy grip on the handle with both hands something in the manner of a flute player, only more virile, you bend over the ball, with the feet about two feet apart and both pointing in the same direction.[63]

As the aforementioned titles suggest, the Benchley essay could be presented as a comic lecture, the ramblings of an absent-minded professor. Interestingly enough, Benchley soon became something of an absent-minded professor screen personality through his appearances in a number of film short subjects. His *How to Sleep* (1935) even won an Oscar for Best Short Subject. (See chapters 3 and 6 for more on the absent-minded professor.)

The Thurber figure tends to be middle-aged, married, and most probably dressed in a rumpled brown suit that could double as an army blanket at a Shriner's picnic. But like the Benchley character, he has nothing but free time. On occasion he too will fall into the comic lecture "how to" posture—"How to See a Bad Play" or "How to Listen to a Play"[64]—but he is more likely to drop into the memories of his eccentric childhood. This is best chronicled in *My Life and Hard Times*, with tales of "The Dog That Bit People," "The Night the Bed Fell," and "University Days"—complete with antiheroic professors and students. Probably Thurber's most popular use of this leisure time, however, as well as the one most commonly associated with the antihero (thanks to "The Secret Life of Walter Mitty") is in his fantasy daydreams of bravery and high adventure. It is the fate of the antihero to be a hero only in dreams:

Captain Mitty stood up and strapped on his huge Webley-Vickers automatic. "It's forty kilometers through hell, sir," said the sergeant. Mitty finished one last brandy. "After all," he said softly, "what isn't?" The pounding of the cannon increased; there was the rat-tat-tatting of machine guns. . . .

Something struck his shoulder. "I've been looking all over this hotel for you," said Mrs. Mitty. "Why do you have to hide in this old chair?"[65]

The *New Yorker* antihero virtually never seems to have the opportunity or the inclination to foster an interest in politics. His is a nonpolitical but frustrating domestic life, occasionally punctured by an equally frustrating sortie to the store or small social gathering. These minor domestic chores must take first priority for him to maintain some hold on reality. This hold, slipshod at best, would be put to a precarious imbalance by world events and political figures.

One might still wonder if, just on occasion, the comic antihero were allowed to escape his self-enforced domestic security blanket, would he then not take at least a passing fancy to world and political events? But even then he would probably miss, most likely because of an ailment one might call "derby disease." Benchley, in a well-documented study of news photographs taken on "cataclysmic events" found that:

> If you want to get a good perspective on history in the making, just skim through a collection of news-photographs which have been snapped at those very moments when cataclysmic events were taking place throughout the world. In almost every picture you can discover one guy in a derby hat who is looking in exactly the opposite direction from the excitement, totally oblivious to the fact that the world is shaking beneath his feet. That would be me, or at any rate, my agent in that particular part of the world in which the event is taking place.[66]

Thurber biographer Charles S. Holmes insightfully notes that the antiheroic author has also made a humorously major nonpolitical comment in titling his comic autobiography *My Life and Hard Times.* "*Hard Times* would remind all readers that the book was written in the middle of a great economic depression and had absolutely nothing to say about it."[67]

The antihero's lack of political interest may be explained by the fact that he does not interact well with people. Whereas the Yankee enjoys people coming to him for advice and often works at a profession dependent upon these contacts, the antihero enjoys none of this. Either because of his leisure time or through a conscious effort to so use it, outside parties play a very insignificant part in his comedy.

The ultimate move for the Yankee is to enter politics for the common good. For the easily intimidated antihero, the ultimate move is to hide. His primary goal is just to survive; this leaves very little opportunity for saving the masses through politics.

The antihero finds the world a generally unordered place. Any attempt to lead a rational life is destined to end in constant frustration. Where the Yankee could fall back on a history of past personal experiences that represented the logical pattern of a rational world, the antihero finds that nothing works. It is an irrational world for him and any attempt to bring order to it results in total frustration.

For *The New Yorker* writers, there is one key danger to the antihero male: women represent a severe frustration spot. The secret to this female power can be found in Thurber's "Destructive Forces in Life."[68] Near the story's beginning he pens a drawing of an unhappy man and smiling wife, entitling it "A Mentally Disciplined Husband with Mentally Undisciplined Wife." This domestic mugshot leads to the sad story of one more frustrated male. But the key at this point is the conclusion of that tale:

> the undisciplined mind [that of the woman] runs far less chance of having its purpose thwarted, its plans distorted, its whole scheme and system wrenched out of line. The undisciplined mind, in short, is far better adapted to the confused world in which we live today than the streamlined mind [the undisciplined mind of the man]. That is, I am afraid, no place for the streamlined mind.[69]

It should be kept in mind, moreover, that the frustrations of the antihero, be they precipitated by females or other irritants, are often largely based in physical terms, just as with earlier American schools of comedy.

Appropriately enough, we associate the humor of the *New Yorker* group with cartoons, from the celebrated drawings of Thurber to the delightful caricatures by Gluyas Williams that grace the Benchley books. Thus, favorite antihero stories are quite likely not only to bring to mind our own mental cartoons but also the actual cartoons that accompanied the stories, such as the two-page drawing of "Two thousand people . . . in full flight" from Thurber's "The Day the Dam Broke" or Williams's comic fascimile of a rather irate Benchley pitching a roll of mints onto the sidewalk in "Rapping the Wrapper!"

The comic antihero represents a child figure. This is most effectively shown in the eight stories comprising "Part One: Mr. and Mrs. Monroe" of Thurber's *The Owl in the Attic*, especially in "Mr. Monroe and the Moving Men." In this story once the wife leaves, the husband is helpless. This helplessness occurs despite the fact that before she had left "little Mrs. Monroe had led her husband from room to room, pointing out what was to go into storage and what was to be sent to the summer place."[70]. But now "little Mrs. Monroe was away, unavoidably away, terrifyingly away,"[71] and he could not remember where things went and what she had said. And he certainly has no ready answers for the moving men's questions. Their names for him progressively fall in respect from "chief" and "mister" to "buddy" and "pardner" to the child's nickname "sonny." By the story's end he is reduced to tears.

The comic antihero represents the big city. *The New Yorker* was literally founded on an attack against the old value system, as a "magazine which is not edited for the old lady in Dubuque . . . a magazine avowedly published for a metropolitan audience." *The New Yorker* focuses on the city, yet what is written about metropolitan living hardly constitutes a love letter.

The city represents a severe trial for Benchley. He has a poor sense of direction and the complex modern city only compounds this. In "Spying on the Vehicular Tunnel" he becomes lost on a walking tour of the Holland Tunnel.[72] When he attemps to leave the driving to someone else (especially on formal dress occasions) by taking a taxicab, he invariably enters a musty vehicle that more closely resembles "the old sleigh which used to stand up in the attic at Grandpa's barn in Millbury" than an automobile.[73] Moreover, there are so many people squeezed into the city that he must stand in long lines for everything. For Benchley this is best exemplified by the post office: "It has been estimated that six-tenths of the population of the United States spend their entire lives standing in line in a post office."[74]

Thurber finds the city just as frustrating as Benchley. "The Monroes Find a Terminal" chronicles the difficulty of urban navigation; a more logical title might be "The Monroes Find Everything but a Terminal"[75] Not surprisingly, Thurber's real-life feelings on New York closely resemble the old rural adage, "It's a nice place to visit but . . .":

> One more or less holds on there. It is an achievement to have lived there, not a pleasure to do so. It has to be seen now and again, visited . . . but I swear that all the laws of nature and of the constitution of man make it imperative not to live there.[76]

The antihero, then, actually agrees with the Yankee's anti-city position through his constant urban-based victimization. But difficulty with women and mechanical objects are frustrations the Yankee does not even know. Thus, it should be kept in mind that the Yankee is usually seen as a superior visitor to an inferior world (a city), whereas the antihero is usually seen as a victim of that world. In either situation, the country usually comes out like the proverbial rose, while the city resembles a bit of crabgrass. That is, the country represents the ideal state that produced the Yankee and is the protected haven he will return to after solving urban problems. On the other hand, the antihero is the frustrated child of a frustrated state, the city, with no open avenues of escape. Thus, antiheroes minimize the outside world and concentrate on getting through the little things—a battle which is still being fought today.

NOTES

1. Kin Hubbard, *Abe Martin: Horse Sense and Nonsense* (Indianapolis: Bobbs-Merrill Company, 1926), p. 31; Abe Martin was, in most respects, a typical

nineteenth-century crackerbarrel figure, yet he was increasingly at home in the twentieth-century world of the antihero. The book title from which this saying is taken suggests just that. See Wes D. Gehring, "Kin Hubbard's Abe Martin: A Figure of Transition in American Humor." *Indiana Magazine of History,* March 1982, pp. 26-37.

2. Walter Blair, *Native American Humor* (1937; rpt. San Francisco: Chandler Publishing Company, 1960), p. 39.

3. Walter Blair, *Horse Sense in American Humor* (Chicago: The University of Chicago Press, 1942), p. 51.

4. Blair, *Native American Humor*, p. 17.

5. Jennette Tandy, *Crackerbox Philosophers in American Humor and Satire* (New York: Columbia University Press, 1925), p. 2.

6. Ibid., p. 6.

7. Blair, *Native American Humor,* p. 19.

8. John Gerber, "Lecture on New England and Crackerbarrel Philosophy," in the class "American Humor and Satire" (Iowa City: University of Iowa, 1975).

9. Constance Rourke, *American Humor: A Study of the National Character* (1931; rpt. New York: Harcourt Brace Jovanovich, 1959), p. 23.

10. Tandy, *Crackerbox Philosophers,* p. 2.

11. Blair, *Horse Sense in American Humor*, p. vii.

12. Blair, *Native American Humor*, p. 39.

13. See Wes D. Gehring, *Leo McCarey and the Comic Anti-Hero in American Film* (New York: Arno Press, 1980).

14. "My Neighbor Freeport," in *Native American Humor*, ed. Walter Blair (1937; rpt. San Francisco: Chandler Publishing Company, 1960), p. 199.

15. Ibid., p. 200.

16. Ibid.

17. Seba Smith, *The Life and Writings of Major Jack Downing* (1833; rpt. New York: AMS Press, 1973), p. 200.

18. Thomas Chandler Haliburton, "Taming a Shrew," in *The Sam Slick Anthology*, ed. Walter S. Aris (Toronto: Clark, Irwin & Company, 1969), p. 49.

19. James Russell Lowell, *The Biglow Papers* (1848; rpt. Philadelphia: Altemus, 1910), p. 150.

20. Blair, *Native American Humor*, p. 62.

21. John Gerber, "Lecture on Southwestern Humor," in the class "American Humor and Satire" (Iowa City: University of Iowa, 1975).

22. Mark Twain is America's greatest humorist and thus, to a certain degree, rises above any one particular school of comedy. Yet, he certainly owes the vast majority of his comedy skills to the Southwestern. Another reason, in fact, for including the very representative Southwestern writers of Harris and Hooper is that they seemed to have influenced Twain considerably. Bernard DeVoto, *Mark Twain's America* (Boston: Little, Brown and Company, 1932), p. 257.

23. Blair, *Native American Humor*, p. 75.

24. F. O. Matthiessen, *American Renaissance: Art and Expression in the Age of Emerson and Whitman* (1941; rpt. New York: Oxford University Press, 1954), p. 642.

25. Johnson J. Hooper, *Simon Suggs' Adventures* (1867; rpt. Americus, Georgia: Americus Book Company, 1928), p. 26.

26. Mark Twain, *Huckleberry Finn* (1885; rpt. New York: Scholastic Book Services, 1967), p. 339.

27. Hooper, *Simon Suggs' Adventures*, p. 12.

28. George Washington Harris, "Sicily Burn's Wedding," in *Native American Humor*, ed. Blair, p. 375.

29. Tandy, *Crackerbox Philosophers,* p. 84.

30. Appropriately, John Gerber links the amoral Sut Lovingood with Tom Sawyer, in that both (and no doubt most Southwestern characterizations) derived a great deal of their mischief-making popularity as a reaction against sappy juvenile fiction of the time. Tandy goes on to call Sut "the first well-developed example of the bad boy." (Tandy, *Crackerbox Philosophers*, p. 93).

31. Arthur Asa Berger, *The Comic-Stripped American* (Baltimore: Penguin Books, 1973), p. 19.

32. Rudolph Dirks later moved from the *New York Journal* to the *New York World*, continuing the strip under the name of "The Captain and the Kids," while H. H. Knerr maintained the "Katzenjammer Kids" at the *Journal*. "Bringing Up Father" is often referred to as "Jiggs & Maggie."

33. Berger, *The Comic-Stripped American*, p. 36.

34. Gilbert Seldes, *The Seven Lively Arts* (New York: Harper & Brothers, 1924), p. 237.

35. Margaret G. Mayorga, *A Short History of the American Drama* (New York: Dodd, Mead & Company, 1934), p. 193.

36. Ibid., p. 244.

37. Arthur Hobson Quinn, *A History of the American Drama* (New York: Harper & Brothers, 1927), p. 98.

38. Lee Coyle, *George Ade* (New York: Twayne Publishers, 1964), p. 58.

39. Mayorga, *A Short History of the American Drama*, p. 195.

40. Ibid., p. 241.

41. Ibid., p. 245.

42. Coyle, *George Ade,* p. 85.

43. It should also be noted that one of Ade's most popular, though atypical, plays is *The Country Chairman* (1903), which deals with a nineteenth-century small-town Yankee politician. Appropriately enough, it later became a screen adaptation for Yankee Will Rogers (1935).

44. Albert F. McLean, Jr., *American Vaudeville as Ritual* (Lexington: University of Kentucky Press, 1965), p. 106.

45. Ibid.

46. Ibid., p. 109.

47. John E. DiMeglio, *Vaudeville U.S.A.* (Bowling Green, Ohio: Bowling Green University Press, 1973).

48. Douglas Gilbert, *American Vaudeville: Its Life and Times* (New York: McGraw-Hill Book Company, 1940), p. 70.

49. McLean, *American Vaudeville as Ritual*, p. 120.

50. Ibid., p. 122.

51. Gilbert, *American Vaudeville: Its Life and Times*, p. 253.

52. McLean, *American Vaudeville as Ritual*, pp. 122-23.

53. W. C. Fields, "Off to the Country" (W. C. Fields Papers, Library of

Congress, Manuscript Division—Madison building. Copyrighted May 25, 1921, first of three versions), p. 1.

54. Ibid., p. 6.

55. Gilbert, *American Vaudeville: Its Life and Times*, p. 251.

56. Ibid., pp. 255, 256.

57. Ibid., p. 256.

58. Floyd Clymer, *Those Wonderful Old Machines* (New York: Bonanza Books, 1953), p. 151.

59. Wes D. Gehring, *W. C. Fields: A Bio-Biography* (Westport, Connecticut: Greenwood Press, 1984).

60. Blair, *Native American Humor*, p. 168.

61. Ibid., p. 169.

62. Norris W. Yates, *The American Humorists: Conscience of the Twentieth Century* (Ames: Iowa State University Press, 1964), p. 228.

63. Benchley, "How to Break 90 in Croquet," pp. 27-28.

64. James Thurber, *The Middle-Aged Man on the Flying Trapeze* (New York: Harper & Brothers, 1935).

65. James Thurber, "The Secret Life of Walter Mitty," in *The Thurber Carnival* (New York: Harper & Brothers, 1945), p. 51.

66. Robert Benchley, "Johnny-on-the-Spot," in *From Bed to Worse: Or Comforting Thoughts About the Bison* (New York: Harper & Brothers, 1934), p. 255.

67. Charles S. Holmes, *The Clocks of Columbus: The Literary Career of James Thurber* (New York: Atheneum, 1978), p. 156.

68. James Thurber, "Destructive Forces in Life," in *Let Your Mind Alone! and Other More or Less Inspirational Pieces* (1937; rpt. New York: The Universal Library, 1973), p. 12.

69. Ibid., p. 18.

70. Thurber, "Mr. Monroe and the Moving Men," in *The Owl in the Attic* (1931; rpt. New York: Harper & Row, 1965), pp. 25-26.

71. Ibid., p. 125.

72. Benchley, "Spying on the Vehicular Tunnel," in *The Early Worm* (New York: Henry Holt and Company, 1927), pp. 241-45.

73. Robert Benchley, "Here You Are—Taxi!" in *No Poems: Or Around the World Backwards and Sideways* (New York: Harper & Brothers, 1932), p. 121.

74. Benchley, "Back in Line," in *No Poems: Or Around the World Backwards and Sideways*, p. 158.

75. Thurber, "The Monroes Find a Terminal," in *The Owl in the Attic: And Other Perplexities,* pp. 32-38.

76. Burton Bernstein, *Thurber: A Biography* (1975; rpt. New York: Ballantine Books, 1976), p. 410.

3.

SCREWBALL COMEDY WITHIN AMERICAN HUMOR: DEFINING A GENRE

"Men don't get smarter as they grow older, they just lose their hair."

> Gerry Jeffers (Claudette Colbert) to Tom Jeffers (Joel McCrea) in *The Palm Beach Story* (1942).

The most obvious base from which to examine the screwball comedy genre, the structural change of American humor in the 1920s and 1930s, has been completely neglected. This failure has led to the continued misunderstanding of the genre. To clarify the nature and role of screwball comedy, the films of the genre can be examined for five key characteristics of the comic antihero: abundant leisure time, childlike nature, urban life, apolitical outlook, and basic frustration (especially in relationships with women).

Screwball comedy focuses on the leisure life, often in "high-society" style. A review of the fantasy screwball comedy *I Married a Witch* (1942) nicely describes the condition with the phrase "caviar comedy."[1] The titles of two other celebrated examples of the genre express the films' ambience quite nicely: Mitchell Leisen's *Easy Living* (1937) and George Cukor's *Holiday* (1938). Other classic examples of this mode of living occur in *Twentieth Century* (1934), *The Gilded Lily* (1935), *My Man Godfrey* (1936), *Theodora Goes Wild* (1936), *The Awful Truth* (1937), *Topper* (1937), *Bringing Up Baby* (1938), *Midnight* (1939), *My Favorite Wife* (1940), *The Lady Eve* (1941), and *The Palm Beach Story* (1942).

A 1938 *New York Times* article, "Laughter at So Much Per Tickle," even examined how the high society screwball comedy eventually led to higher production costs:

> The current vogue of goofy [screwball] comedies necessitates more elaborate sets than those used for the ancient laugh-makers. The old-fashioned gag comedies could be played in front of any kind of scenery, but the characters in the modern mad cycle are invariably millionaires, and their antics must be chronicled in settings befitting their wealth.[2]

From wealth to high society decadence, the beautiful people of *My Man Godfrey* can find no more meaningful activity than a scavenger hunt at the city dump; the whole focus of the characters in *Topper* is to learn how to spend leisure time with the correct amount of frivolity. Melvyn Douglas's character in *Theodora Goes Wild* is said to be a painter, but there is little proof; he is too busy being a New York playboy. Director Leo McCarey does not even attempt to establish an occupational cover for Cary Grant in *The Awful Truth*, a situation basically repeated in *My Favorite Wife*, which McCarey also produced. That this was a conscious effort by McCarey is best illustrated by his response to the difficulty Grant has in playing a scene in *The Awful Truth*, when Grant's character offers to assist his estranged wife monetarily:

> When Cary came to that scene he stopped and laughed. "Where am I supposed to have gotten any money?" he asked. "I never work . . . you never show me doing any sort of a job." My reply was that the audience would not be interested in how he got the money, but merely in the efforts of the two young people to straighten out their married life.[3]

If a character does flirt with a profession in a screwball comedy, it is usually in a field middle America does not view as serious or "real" employment. Instead, the genre showcases the actors in *Twentieth Century* or "painter" Douglas of *Theodora Goes Wild*. In fact Douglas's martinet film father puts pressure on him at one point, saying, "You owe at least that much to me, especially after your choice of a profession."

Probably the most celebrated example of a character in a profession seemingly nebulous to many Americans is the absent-minded professor, a type fully realized by Cary Grant in Hawks's *Bringing Up Baby*. Grant plays a professor-scientist who, when not socializing with rich patrons of the arts to obtain contributions to his museum, is busy assembling the giant skeleton of a brontosaurus. The tools of his socializing "trade" include nine irons and cocktail attire. Hawks had a penchant for the absent-minded professor; he created many such characters in the screwball milieu. After

Bringing Up Baby, there were the seven little professors of *Ball of Fire* (1941), headed by Professor Gary Cooper; the film was actually a parody of Disney's *Snow White and the Seven Dwarfs* (1938). Hawks's 1951 comedy *Monkey Business* gave us Professor Barnaby Fulton, once again played by Grant, who thinks he has discovered a youth serum. In 1964 Hawks cast Rock Hudson as a professorial author in *Man's Favorite Sport?*

Screwball comedies focusing on professors were not, however, limited to the work of Hawks. Opening nearly simultaneously in 1938 with *Bringing Up Baby* was George Stevens's neglected *Vivacious Lady*, which features James Stewart as another milquetoast academic. Between that year and the entry of the United States into World War II, more than a few films in the genre would follow this lead. Examples include Alexander Hall's *Good Girls Go to Paris* (1939, with "Professor" Melvyn Douglas) and *The Doctor Takes a Wife* (1940, with "Professor" Ray Milland), Preston Sturges's *The Lady Eve* (Henry Fonda is a professor-like ophiologist), and W. S. Van Dyke's *The Feminine Touch* (1941, with "Professor" Don Ameche). The end of 1941 represents a full circle return to Hawks, because the director's *Ball of Fire* was a major critical and commercial success at year's end.

Billy Wilders's 1942 *The Major and the Minor* was an excellent but rare reworking of the theme during the war years, with Ray Milland as a military school instructor revitalized by Ginger Rogers—masquerading as a twelve-year-old schoolboy. Though it was Wilder's American directing debut, he was hardly a stranger to the genre; he had co-scripted (with Charles Brackett) screwball *Midnight* and the densely professor-populated *Ball of Fire*.

Even when a basic working-class job is allowed in the screwball genre, it can rarely be trusted to be what it seems. In *Easy Living*, Jean Arthur's eventual beau (Ray Milland) works as a busboy in a food automat; in reality he is the rebellious son of a millionaire father. The scavenger hunt bum (William Powell), whom Carole Lombard recycles into first a butler and then a husband, also turns out to be a rebellious wealthy son. It is generally difficult to escape wealth and easy living in the genre. In fact, many screwball comedies have to cope with what a 1938 *Time* magazine article called the "chief problem" facing the hero and heroine of *Holiday*: "The prospect of having too much money."[4] What better "dilemma" could a genre called screwball have?

The only major occupational intrusion into the normally leisure-oriented screwball comedy is that of occasional newspaper reporter. But even here the focus seems almost entirely on the leisure life, exemplified by the journey of ex-reporter Clark Gable and heiress Claudette Colbert up the East Coast in *It Happened One Night* (1934). Even with reporters, the focus not only often continues to be on leisure but also encompasses high society, from the newspaper spy (William Powell) who enters the world of the Four

Hundred in *Libeled Lady* (1936) to the frustrations of editor-reporter Henry Fonda in *Mad Miss Marton* (1938) whenever he encounters the upper-class eccentric Miss Marton (Barbara Stanwyck).

The best example of how this leisure orientation enters and completely dominates the newspaper world depicted in screwball comedy occurs in *Nothing Sacred* (1937). A small-town girl (Carole Lombard) is wined and dined in New York City for two weeks, all at the expense of the *Morning Star*. This great benevolence on the part of the newspaper is purely commercial: Lombard supposedly has only a short time to live and has always wanted to visit New York. The *Star* hopes to increase circulation by covering the unfortunate girl's last days as she fulfills her dream visit. Of course, there has been a mistake; nothing is wrong with Lombard, although neither she nor her doctor tells anyone, and they proceed to cash in on this cynical "nothing sacred" offer from the *Star*. The film follows the high-living Lombard from one leisure activity to another as she goes on a long joy ride at the expense of the paper and the city.

Naturally, reporter Fredric March, whose brainstorm is turned into a freebie by Lombard, falls for her. Lombard reciprocates and together they survive the melodramatic story within this comically dark film—a story which should end with her death. (New York is "let down" easily by another manufactured story—that Lombard committed suicide.) Regardless, chances are good that antiheroic March will not be continuing in the newspaper world, since his previous "exclusive" story (prior to Lombard's con) had him believing in a philanthropic oriental potentate who turned out to be a Harlem shoeshiner on the lam from a wife and four children.

The second commonality between the antihero and the screwball comedy male is that both are childlike. Traditionally, one associates the childlike with comedy, but the association has a special focus here. Whereas the capable crackerbarrel figures were caretakers for a nation, the screwball comedy male is often in a situation where he quite literally is being taken care of, from the fiftyish Egbert (Charles Ruggles) getting a haircut under the supervision of his wife in *Ruggles of Red Gap* (1935) to the middle-aged Douglas of *Theodora Goes Wild* taking orders from his father.

The childlike males, in the apparent antiheroic tradition of James Thurber, often have a dog—an obvious corollary of childhood. Thurber wrote about the dog because he felt it was the one animal that had been domesticated so long that it had taken on most human frustrations. A dual focus of frustration, male and canine, plays an important part in several screwball comedies, including such pivotal examples as *The Awful Truth, Theodora Goes Wild*, and *Bringing Up Baby*, a film that also incidentally adds a leopard. In Neil Simon's recent script for *Seems Like Old Times* (1980), the frustrations of the husband are mirrored repeatedly in his wife's (Goldie Hawn) pack of dogs. This final example is especially important because *Seems Like Old Times* is a conscious celebration of the screwball genre, from story-line parallels such as the use of dogs to the inclusion of stills from earlier screwball films in its own theater release posters. This male-canine dual focus is best illustrated by McCarey's *The Awful Truth*, where Grant and the dog Mr. Smith (the same dog that appears as Asta in the screwball-related *Thin Man* series) show a great propensity for similar slapstick frustration. For example, each (at different times) performs a monumental pratfall from a precariously balanced chair—all while investigating the activities of Irene Dunne.

The dog sometimes represents a surrogate child for a screwball comedy couple who "play house" when one partner, usually the male, is not adult enough for a real marriage. A custody fight over Mr. Smith at the divorce proceedings in *The Awful Truth* allows McCarey to extend his parody of divorce without the real pathos a human child would have given the scene. Since a dog is used, any sexuality between the couple is not undermined by a "family" situation. (In *Bringing Up Baby* having a pet represent a surrogate child is addressed much more baldly, for "Baby" in the title is actually a tame leopard.)

In *Theodora Goes Wild* Douglas tries to use the image of child and dog as a defense against real housekeeping, the responsibility of marriage. Near the end of the film, when the unmarried Dunne returns to her small town as an infamous sex novelist, she is holding a friend's baby. Given the X-rated reputation of her work, everyone assumes the child to be hers. Douglas, there finally to declare his love, is taken aback at the sight of the baby. In every ensuing scene Douglas cradles his dog Jake, just as Dunne does the baby, the contrast in bundles underscoring the "I'm just a boy playing at being a husband" nature of the male's role.

In addition, the dog can represent a metaphor for the pet-like existence to which the screwball comedy child/man is frequently reduced by the genre's female. This is best examplified by Preston Sturges's *The Palm Beach Story,* in which Princess's (Mary Astor) latest male satellite is named Toto (Sig Arno). No doubt playing upon the celebrated dog Toto from *The Wizard of Oz* (the film version starring Judy Garland just having appeared in 1939), Sig Arno could not have played a more obedient pooch to Mary Astor's Princess. Moreover, since Arno's Toto could not speak English (no one knew or tried to decipher his comically obscure tongue), he was in the same situation as any barking-at-the-heels neglected pooch.

The male also reveals his childishness in several other ways. Traditionally the screwball characteristic is associated with the female in the genre, but the male, too, may have a screwball tendency. While the heroine is either pleasantly potty to begin with or merely assumes that comic role to better control the situation, the male is just as likely to become a screwball as a result of female shenanigans. Examples can be found in Grant's classic breakdown in *Bringing Up Baby* and the Stanwyck-engineered breakdown of Fonda in *The Lady Eve*. Such incidents have a close affinity to the frustrations and resultant temper tantrums of childhood. (In *Bluebeard's Eighth Wife,* Claudette Colbert's antics actually result in the institutionalization of her victim/husband Gary Cooper.)

The settings for these films often accent the childlike quality in the male. In *Holiday*, Grant, Hepburn, and her brother (Lew Ayres) spend much of their time in the Seton family mansion's only comfortable setting—the childhood playroom. The playroom is full of toys: a stuffed giraffe named Leopold, a Punch-and-Judy show, a sailboat, dolls, a globe, drums, and miniature furniture. The "adult" trio actually play there, with Ayres banging away at his old drum set and Hepburn and Grant doing acrobatics. The playroom setting further exemplifies the childlike quality of the characters because it is the one place where all positive members of the film can interact in the natural, uninhabited manner of children. A term McCarey often used seems applicable here: spontaneity. Screwball players are nothing if not spontaneous. In *Holiday* this natural trait of childhood is underlined by the fact that the only two Setons worth saving (Hepburn and Ayres) generally are spontaneous only in this playroom, their actions no doubt triggered by an association with the freedom of childhood.

This toyshop mise-en-scène occurs throughout the genre, from the previous examples to Robert Benchley's playroom "office" in *Take a Letter, Darling* (1942). More recently, Dudley Moore's toy-strewn bedroom in *Arthur* (1981) also exemplifies the condition, as well as the playthings with which Moore gifts his servant/friend John Gielgud. (The periodic use of the tune "Santa Claus Is Coming to Town" further reinforces Arthur's toyshop mise-en-scène.) But the best example occurs at the close of *My Favorite Wife*. The frustrated Cary Grant is still faced with a which-wife-should-I-choose problem. (The film had opened with Grant marrying Gail Patrick shortly before the surprise return of first wife Irene Dunne—missing for the past seven years in the South Pacific.) Grant finds himself in a child's bed stored in the attic, surrounded by toys. He is obviously on the verge of making his decision in Dunne's favor but he is too frazzled by this point to know how to express it. Moreover, at bedtime Dunne does not hurt her cause any by attractively and yet forcefully assigning separate rooms—she to the *master* bedroom, he relegated to the attic.

The effect of Grant's trek upstairs is that of a small boy sent to his room without supper. It is heightened by the nursery surroundings of the attic and the little bed in which he must sleep. The setting is a scaled-down version of the children's bedroom in McCarey's celebrated Laurel & Hardy short subject *Brats* (1930), in which the duo play doubled roles as fathers and little boys.

Grant gets ready for bed with toys literally hanging from the low ceiling. As he crawls into the squeaky bed, knocking things down, the viewer's eyes focus on two specific toys—a doll beside the bed and a toy cannon just underneath. (Without being overly metaphorical, this reduction of male to toy cannon, subservient to the female on high, nicely describes *My Favorite Wife* and numerous other screwball comedies.) As if to accent the childlike focus while revealing Grant's thoughts, the doll falls and says "mama." With this suggestion, he does, in fact, get up and go to "mama's" room.

After Grant has made the long trek down to Dunne's room, she reinforces the earlier suggestion of the supperless child by asking in the most motherly of ways, "Are you hungry?" Needless to say, the true answer is something of a yes and a no, but Grant replies in the most appropriate of little boy styles that he cannot sleep. There are no "nice mattresses" in the attic as there are here—referring to the spare bed in Dunne's room. She coyly says that, then, he can sleep on the unoccupied one. After his face has sufficiently lit up, like a little boy's at Christmas, she tells him he would be most welcome to take the mattress upstairs.

The crestfallen child then takes the mattress out of the room, but McCarey's camera remains with Dunne. Grant returns in seconds complaining that the mattress does not fit, adding quietly in befuddlement, "I'm stuck. This could go till doomsday. I'm stuck but I don't care what people think." After this pointed regression, we once again see the two in their separate beds.

Grant must somehow express to Dunne that she truly is "my favorite wife." But because of his long puzzlement over the decision and this complete childhood regression, which itself could be seen as the actualization of a childish male ego that refuses to admit a mistake, Grant seems to be literally struck dumb—unable even to communicate with normal speech patterns.

When you note this verbal incapacity of Grant's, you also remember that "'Do it visually'" was McCarey's byword.[5] Grant therefore can be expected to perform some very comically symbolic act to resurrect the marriage. Moreover, whatever symbol is chosen to represent the uniqueness of this day should be commensurate with a red-letter day in childhood. Grant is obviously operating with the mind of a child, and it is only natural that he should communicate as such. (A key point to keep in mind, however, is the earlier suggestion by Grant that he take an ocean cruise alone to help him choose his favorite wife—a cruise which would last until Christmas.)

After individual shots of Grant and Dunne in their separate beds, the camera remains on Dunne. The viewer then hears Grant's attic bed collapse, another crash, the squeal of the attic door, and finally jingle bells. Grant then bursts in dressed as Santa Claus and cries "Merry Christmas!" Since Christmas is probably the most anxiously awaited moment of childhood, Grant's happiness over this apparent reconciliation proves to be a most effective communication, as well as suggesting the aforementioned possible reconciliation date. Moreover, just as in childhood, Grant plays his game by dressing up as someone else and imagining it to be a different time. And, despite the fact that "good-night" is then written across the screen, ending the film with Grant's Santa Claus entry maintains the asexual nature of the child (and the comic antihero).

The concept of the child-husband and mother-wife are essential factors in the husband-wife reconciliation at the close of several McCarey films. Throughout these films, the males have assumed somewhat asexual roles, As with McCarey's Laurel & Hardy films, extramarital activities in screwball films are not condoned, though their rejection does not match the physical degree of rejection of feminine advances shown by Laurel in *We Faw Dawn* (1928) in which a flirt gets too familiar with his Adam's apple. The antihero of McCarey's features is more apt to be in a state of intense confusion and frustration.

This husband-wife reconciliation thus takes on rather significant consequences in several McCarey films. In *The Awful Truth, My Favorite Wife,* and to a certain extent, *Six of a Kind*, the child-husband attempts to have himself tucked in by the mother-wife, or be enabled to slip into bed with "mother." It occurs at the film's close, and is symbolic of the new world—the new marriage—that traditionally ends comedy, for at this point the McCarey male-child is finally allowed the suggestion of sexual manhood. But for the viewer, he remains forever the child.[6]

In *Too Many Husbands* (1940), Jean Arthur finds she must decide between two husbands, after husband number one returns from having been lost in the Atlantic, thus reversing the sudden romantic comedy triangle of *My Favorite Wife*. Here the male species of the screwball genre displays still another example of his childlike nature. The two husbands in question (Fred MacMurray and Melvyn Douglas) compete, schoolboy style, in "events" like chair jumping, spelling, and playing sick for the interest of their joint wife. Jean Arthur will later admonish that "You two men act like children!" but she really enjoys the interest. Frequently she slips into the role of mother, checking for brushed teeth and tucking the two into bed.

Sometimes, however, a central male in screwball comedy suffers from "comic rigidity"; his "character is so tightly jammed into the rigid frame of his functions that he had no room to move or to be moved like other men"—the complete opposite of the child.[7] It thereby becomes the goal of the genre to bring the joy of childhood's spontaneity to an adult grown brittle. The focus of *Ruggles of Red Gap* is bringing a stuffy British butler back to life, with an amusement park playing a major part; in *Topper* it is a stuffy banker who must be saved, with a playground-like nightclub assisting in the transformation. Hepburn performs much the same task in *Bringing Up Baby* when she rescues Professor Grant from his studies and a stuffy fiancée; this is beautifully summarized in the film's close, when Hepburn collapses the last remaining vestige of his academic rigidity—the brontosaurus skeleton. Celebrated film critic Robin Wood insightfully observed that this skeleton and the film's leopard (the dog might also be substituted) are a perfect metaphor for the contrasting life-styles of rigid professor Grant and free spirit Hepburn—"living and dead."[8]

Fantasy author Thorne Smith, whose work was so often adapted for the genre, articulates perfectly this sense of screwball rebirth in his novel *Topper*. Marion Kirby, one of the two ghosts resparking the staid banker Cosmo Topper, says after the transformation: "It's almost like leaving a son—my own creation."[9]

The screwball comedy male can also experience another combination of rigidity and childlike nature. This occurs when the male begins the story with a youthful, fun-loving nature but a proposed romantic union threatens to trap him in a cobweb of rigidity until a free-spirited heroine arrives. This is best demonstrated in Cukor's *Holiday,* where the rich and haughty Doris Nolan cages her once-happy fiancé Cary Grant, but Nolan's "sister" Hepburn comes to the rescue as "the spirit of foolishness and freedom."[10] The cage, in this case, would have been the big business world of Nolan and Hepburn's father. Hepburn's liberation of Grant is especially important because he represents an idealized alternative to rigidity—he possesses both youthfully limber mental *and physical* states (his expression of joy is executing cartwheels).

More recently, a similar threat of rigidity faces Dudley Moore in *Arthur*. His childlike character role (enhanced by the actor's youthfully small size; he is known in the press as "Cuddly Dudley") is the ultimate fun-loving little boy. But all this is to change after Moore's marriage, arranged by his wealthy family, to a proper daughter of high society. Like Grant in *Holiday,* he is to become fossilized in his future father-in-law's big business. Moore's screwball comedy deliverance is made possible by the arrival of the most free thinking of heroines: Liza Minnelli.

Hawks's late screwball comedy, *Monkey Business* (1952), provides another comment on the childlike nature of the male within the genre. Where other screwball males have a pronounced tendency toward regression to childhood, even though they may be unaware of it, the goal of Professor Barnaby Fulton (Cary Grant) is to invent a youth serum. Ironically, a real serum is created as a result of a laboratory monkey's play among the chemicals, but people are unaware that they are drinking it; the monkey mixture has accidentally been dumped into the water cooler. Initially these people are also oblivious to the regression to youth taking place. The film ultimately represents a salute to childhood and "monkey business."

Another parallel between the worlds of the antihero and the screwball comedy male is that both focus on an urban setting. (The elegance of the urban playgrounds of the idle rich—the art deco nightclubs, restaurants, town houses, and Hollywood-style fantasy settings—helps to explain the popularity of screwball comedy with a depression-era audience.) Unlike the capable crackerbarrel hero, who had a close rapport with his setting—rural America—the screwball comedy male does not fully identify with his milieu: For him the city is symbolic of the irrationality of modern life. He remains frustrated no matter where he is; the city gives him at once a luxurious setting for his frustration and another cause for it besides the female. Indeed, for him the urban environment may even represent victimization: like Egbert in *Ruggles of Red Gap*, who both literally and figuratively gets his hair cut, the genre's city-based male is forever in danger of losing his masculinity.

Nothing Sacred (a perfect title for a film of a genre that displays little respect for anything), directed by William Wellman and written by Ben Hecht, is impartial in its deployment of jabs at both city and country, with New York described in an opening title as a place "where the slinkers and know-it-alls peddle gold bricks to each other and where truth, crushed to earth, rises again more phony than a glass eye." But the country is the ultimate winner in this film, for the small-town girl (Carole Lombard), through her faked illness and free dream vacation, puts one over on the biggest city of them all.

Wilder's *The Major and the Minor* also opens with a titled attack on *the* big city: "The Dutch bought New York from the Indians in 1626 and by May 1941 there wasn't an Indian left who regretted it." Unlike *Nothing Sacred*'s Lombard, however, small-town girl Ginger Rogers begins the film in New York and is very anxious to return to her Iowa home. Appropriately, the final straw which sends her back is a comically fumbled pass from pivotal antiheroic author/actor Robert Benchley. His dialogue even manages to include: "Why don't you get out of that wet coat and into a dry martini," a slight variation on the famous line by Benchley's *New Yorker* colleague Dorothy Parker.

In Sturges's *The Palm Beach Story* (1942), inventor Joel McCrea loses his wife (Claudette Colbert) because he is an urban outcast, unable to peddle his futuristic municipal airport system. McCrea wins her back only after he finds himself on a country estate, where a buyer for his invention eliminates his urban jinx. In *My Man Godfrey* men are either assigned to the city dump (the depression's "forgotten men") or to living as some sort of gigolo protégés. Even the often capable Godfrey (Powell) initially assumes the negative "city dump" position. The urban Grant in *My Favorite Wife* is contrasted both in physique and forcefulness with "muscle man of the wilderness" Randolph Scott, who is shipwrecked with Grant's wife for seven years.

Too Many Husbands also showcases a comparison between a man of nature (the formerly shipwrecked MacMurray) and a more docile urbanite (Douglas). Though the contrast is not as striking as in *My Favorite Wife,* Douglas suggests that MacMurray is the "missing link between ape and man," frequently cowering before the comic anger of his formerly lost rival. In the earlier *Theodora Goes Wild*, Douglas had seemingly already relinquished part of his masculinity and freedom for the leisure-life temptations of a playground city. He is also bested by Theodora (Dunne) in all their nature excursions.

Romantic screwball comedy interludes, frequently at the film's close, are likely to occur in the country, as if that is the only place where the male can regain a semblance of sexuality. Even there, however, he is generally frustrated in every other way. In both *The Awful Truth* and *My Favorite Wife* problem relationships are patched up only after the characters leave the city and go to cabins in the country. In *Theodora Goes Wild* it is in an atmosphere of fishing and berry picking that Dunne and Douglas build a positive relationship, after an initially negative first encounter in the city. It is the country-oriented close of *Take a Letter, Darling,* centered on a camper, that suggests the permanency of the Rosalind Russell-Fred MacMurray relationship after problems first encountered in the city. In Alfred Hitchcock's excursion into screwball comedy, *Mr. and Mrs. Smith* (1941), Carole Lombard and Robert Montgomery work out a reconciliation at a Lake Placid winter resort. *Bringing Up Baby* is largely a country film, with Grant and Hepburn hunting leopards in the "forests" of Connecticut.

This country vein is rather ironic, since screwball comedy characters often exhibit antirural and anti-small-town values, a trait illustrated by Cary Grant's baiting of Albany insurance salesman Ralph Bellamy in *His Girl Friday,* or the viciously comic small-town victimization of reporter Fredric March in *Nothing Sacred* (1937). But although screwball comedy characters occasionally attack the country hayseed, they seldom attack the country setting itself, no doubt because Western culture has long considered the pastoral backdrop a classic location for the awakening of romance, even screwball style.

This love-hate relationship with the rural setting is also sometimes present in the work of Regionalist painters of the 1930s, particularly the canvases of Grant Wood. Wood, though best known for his satirizations of small-town rural pretentiousness, such as the pitchfork-toting couple of *American Gothic* and the senile *Daughters of Revolution*, was at the same time painting love letters to the Iowa countryside (*Young Corn, Fall Plowing, Near Sundown, Trees and Hills,* and *Spring Turning*). E. H. Gombrich's description of *Spring Turning* even seems worded with the childlike antihero male of the screwball comedy in mind, with its "charm of a toy landscape."[11] Such idealized country settings are a perfect embodiment of the romantic rural backdrop sometimes used in the screwball comedy.

Other Regionalist painters who paralleled Wood's celebration of the land would also include Thomas Hart Benton and John Stewart Curry. What effect these painters had on the romantic rural mise-en-scène of the screwball comedy would be difficult to measure, though it is interesting that the movement achieved national recognition in 1934, the same year often given as a starting point for the screwball genre.[12] Hollywood was not unaware of the movement; for example, in the American Film Institute's Oral History of George Cukor, director of *Holiday* and other screwball comedies, Cukor speaks very highly of his impressions of Grant Wood in the 1930s.[13]

Stanley Cavell posits a provocative hypothesis on the relationship between screwball comedy and the country in *Pursuits of Happiness: The Hollywood Comedy of Remarriage.* Cavell observed that a number of screwball comedies spend some time in Connecticut country settings, particularly *Bringing Up Baby*, which becomes a pivotal example for him.[14] Attempting to place these films in the "tradition of romance," he draws upon what theorist Northrop Frye calls "the green world," best exemplified by the country settings in several Shakespearean comedies—the most important for Cavell being the forest of *A Midsummer Night's Dream.*[15]

Using the phrase "the green world" in the most metaphorically universal manner—as a place of restful renewal—one might very generally link it to the use of the country in screwball comedy. Cavell seems to suggest this when he defines Frye's green world as "a place in which perspective and renewal are to be achieved."[16] However, drawing such an analogy, particularly between the forest background of *A Midsummer Night's Dream* and the country settings of screwball comedy, appears to have three strong drawbacks.

First, as Cavell notes, the forest of *A Midsummer Night's Dream* is enchanted, as is often the case in Shakespeare's comedies. More specifically, a delightfully mischievous sprite named Puck, through magic and mistake, creates a romantic comedy uproar in the forest. But it is Puck's magic which causes the musical chair romances of the play, and it is Puck's magic which corrects things. The couples remain innocent victims. In contrast, the romantic comedy friction of screwball comedy (an Irene Dunne suddenly deciding to be the sister of her nearly ex-husband in *My Favorite Wife,* or Barbara "Eve" Stanwyck toying with the most antiheroic of Adams in *The Lady Eve*) is caused by one of the lovers—usually the woman. To these romantic comedy manipulators, innocence is an unknown commodity. Thus, while screwball heroines are frequently enchanted, the forests are not.

In addition, Cavell later draws a parallel between the dream-credited forest activities of *A Midsummer Night's Dream* and the slapstick forest events of *Bringing Up Baby*. He quotes Frye on Shakespearean romantic comedy conclusions to the effect that the extremes of forgiving and forgetting almost demand the explanation that the previous activities took place in a dream or a comic nightmare.[17] This is a fascinating analogy, but it does not address the fact that while screwball comedy can end in a state of time-worn acceptance (forgiveness seems too strong), the players never awaken to another personality—they do not suddenly become less eccentric, as in *A Midsummer Night's Dream. Bringing Up Baby* closes with Hepburn as comically dominate as ever, right down to orchestrating a proposal out of Grant's inarticulateness, following the accidental destruction of his dinosaur skeleton. Dunne reduces Grant to a puppet on a string at the close of both *The Awful Truth* and *My Favorite Wife*, while she makes Melvyn Douglas literally run scared at the conclusion of *Theodora Goes Wild*.

Second, the green world placement in the structure of the Shakespearean comedy plot generally differs from its location in screwball comedy. Drawing directly from Frye, "the action of the [Shakespearean] comedy begins in a world represented as a normal world, moves into the green world, goes into a metamorphosis there in which the comic resolution is achieved, and returns to the normal world."[18] In contrast, when a true pastoral setting appears in a screwball comedy, it frequently represents merely a brief respite—a temporary promise of romantic escape—at the close of the film. This is McCarey's approach to the mountain cabin closings of *The Awful Truth* and *My Favorite Wife*, just as it is applied to *True Confessions* (Wesley Ruggles, 1938), *Four's a Crowd* (Michael Curtiz, 1938), *Mr. and Mrs. Smith* (Alfred Hitchcock, 1941), and *Take a Letter, Darling* (Mitchell Leisen, 1942). More recently the excellent Neil Simon-scripted homage to screwball comedy *Seems Like Old Times* included a short country finale to strongly suggest stars Goldie Hawn and Chevy Chase will again become romantically involved.

Unlike the pastoral resolution Frye discusses, the screwball comedy country conclusion is merely a lull in the story. The audience leaves content with a happy ending but knowing nothing has really changed: the Grants and the Lombards will be just as distracted next time out. After all, this constant is the attraction of any genre. Lombard's zany Helen Bartlett suggests just this when she gets that spacey cast to her eyes and rolls her tongue into her cheek at the lakeside conclusion of *True Confession*—an action which always telegraphs the message that she has just come up with the most screwball of lies. It is as if to say—"Well, here we go again!" There is no resolution here, nor is there any in all but a few screwball comedies.

Third, while Cavell's comparison of forest scenes in *Bringing Up Baby* and *A Midsummer Night's Dream* is insightful, the frantic country activities of this screwball comedy are not typical of the rural sojourns in most films of the genre which include a rural sidetrip. Generally such an outing provides both audience and actors with a film-closing breather, full of more resignation (the real screwball of the film's focus couple is just not going to change) than resolution. Even those screwball comedies which commit more time to their country excursions, commensurate lengthwise with that in *Bringing Up Baby*, rarely showcase the comic nightmare intensity of this film. For example, in *Theodora Goes Wild*, there is a leisurely pace to the fishing and berry picking of Dunne and Douglas. In fact, the segment's biggest laugh depends upon it. The two are returning from an early morning fishing trip on foot and unhurried, content in each other's company. They are so blissfully oblivious that neither realizes their slow steps have positioned them (in the most casual of fishing attire) right in front of *the* church in town just as the Sunday service is letting out. The result is an obvious comedy scandal, particularly since Dunne's conservative aunts and the even more conservative members of the town's women's society (particularly the wonderful busybody Spring Byington) all seem to be in attendance. As in most screwball comedies, the real zaniness in *Theodora Goes Wild* takes place in the city. In this case, that is quite literally where Theodora goes wild.

There are even occasions in the genre when this slowed country pace (after all, this is still the rural stereotype) strays from thoughts of romance to such uncomedic subjects as death and dying. This was often the case when fantasy infiltrated screwball comedy in the late 1930s. The pivotal incident in the film which gave new vitality to the genre even represents a metaphorical statement on this city-country dichotomy. The film is *Topper*, and the scene is the car crash which kills George and Marion Kerby (Cary Grant and Constance Bennett), though a contemporary (1937) reviewer's description of them "as a pair of ectoplasmic screwballs" is to be preferred.[19] The city-country metaphor of the scene, with an additional pun, is that these fast-paced, party-happy urbanites (appropriately speeding along in a "futuristic automobile"[20]) are stopped dead in the country by a tree. These two spirits then proceed to contemplate their now-past lives in the most rural of settings, save for a wrecked car. It is there that they concoct the good-deed plan to convert their milquetoast banker Topper (who though still alive is more dead than the Kerbys) to the fun life.

Regardless of how one interprets the use of the country in screwball comedy, it is important to note that the genre is still about urban-based misfits—antiheroes—and spends proportionately more time in urban settings. And while the country has never been without eccentrics, the wider circle of contacts with which a city is equated provides the genre with a limitless supply of zany types. Screwball comedy takes America's fundamental Jeffersonian democracy-based fear of cities, the unnatural mixing of too many people, and turns it into fun. The genre is full of "crazies," such as the lunatic asylum escapee who thinks he is rich and "bankrolls" John Barrymore's play and also puts up "repent" stickers everywhere in *Twentieth Century*, or the "weiner king" with a real bankroll who pays Claudette Colbert's bills and gives her culinary advice in Sturges's *Palm Beach Story*. Barrymore, while not without his wacky moments in *Twentieth Century*, had graduated to full daftness in *True Confession*, where he plays the comically demented Charley. Lombard, who also starred in both *Twentieth Century* and *True Confession*, had made an equally qualitative jump in dementedness by the latter film. But the real source for her out-to-lunch comedy persona was her role in *My Man Godfrey*, which seems to have inspired both the first link of the term "screwball" to the genre, as well as encouraging a marked increase of zanies in post-*Godfrey* productions. The *New York Times* described her most famous character in the pivotal *Godfrey* as "a one-track mind with grass growing over its rails."[21] *Variety* added that "she has no exclusive on eccentricity, for her whole family, with the exception of the old man, seem to have been dropped on their respective heads when young."[22] A further loony list would seem pointless as well as redundant for a film genre already labeled screwball.

Urban crazies symbolize both a warning and an answer in the genre. The warning implies that the fast-paced, emasculating urban life-style—modern living itself—could eventually put all of us in mental jeopardy if something is not done. Just as medical science derives vaccines from the bacteria that cause diseases, screwball comedy recommends a small dose of the irrational. As a practical defense the male needs to assume a certain eccentricity as the female of the genre and American humor in general have done, such as the half-baked females on Thurber's family tree in *My Life and Hard Times*. In an irrational world, it is safest and most productive to behave irrationally.

Unfortunately, the urban male of the genre has difficulty breaking with the tradition of rationality; he does not see why things cannot be pursued logically. This trait is best examplified in Hawks's absent-minded professors, comfortable in academia but lost in the real world. Yet the dilemma goes beyond some cloistered naïveté of the professional scholar. It is a comic problem afflicting most males within the genre. When these males begin to act strangely, their behavior is seldom the (sometimes assumed) eccentric pose of the female, but rather a full-fledged breakdown.

A fourth characteristic shared by the antihero and the screwball comedy protagonist is the absence of political interest. Unfortunately, by mistakenly including in the screwball genre Capra's political films (those produced after *It Happened One Night*, though even here there are strong crackerbarrel qualities in Gable's role), as Andrew Bergman has done, some writers have discussed politics as characteristic of the genre.[23] To do this is to misunderstand basic trends in American humor. The Capra protagonists of *Mr. Deeds Goes to Town* (1936), *Mr. Smith Goes to Washington* (1939), and *Meet John Doe* (1941), the key trilogy of the director's career, are in the tradition of American humor's capable crackerbarrel Yankee. These Capra films helped fill the void created by the untimely death in 1935 of crackerbarrel figure Will Rogers, who dominated American movie box offices in the first half of the decade.[24]

Capra was not being opportunistic when he filled the crackerbarrel void left by Rogers's death. At the very beginning of Capra's career (when Capra worked a short time for Hal Roach), Rogers, also on contract, had taken the young man under his wing. Capra writes warmly of this period in his autobiography.[25] He no doubt was influenced by Rogers, especially when parallel political subjects can be drawn between an early Rogers work like *Going to Congress* (1924) and Capra's later *Mr. Smith Goes to Washington* or *Meet John Doe*. But Capra would also seem to have drawn from early American prototypes of the crackerbarrel figure.

The crackerbarrel tradition focuses on politics, often with the small-town Yankee going to Washington to straighten things out: Seba Smith's pivotal crackerbarrel character Jack Downing assisted President Jackson in the 1830s and Capra's Jefferson Smith purified the Senate in the 1930s. The long-legged backwoods Downing anticipates several Capra figures besides the long-legged backwoods Smith. There are close parallels with the down-home wisdom, political stance, and small-town, country background of Capra's *Mr. Deeds Goes to Town* and *Meet John Doe* (both played by Gary Cooper) as well as Doe's best friend, the "Colonel" (Walter Brennan). Capra underscores this link to crackerbarrel humor when he has Jefferson Smith "worship" at the Lincoln Memorial, the monument to America's greatest real-life crackerbarrel figure. This is just one of several references to historic Yankee heroes in the Capra trilogy.[26]

Thus, it should be underlined that while Capra's 1930s and '40s films after *It Happened One Night* invariably centered on populist politics, screwball comedy keyed on madcap romance. Indeed, as film critic Jim Leach has observed, Capra's post-*It Happened One Night* films "would much better be described as populist comedies."[27] Leach expands upon this by adding:

> Capra's vision is not really screwball at all . . . whereas the only positive strategy in screwball comedy is to accept the all-pervasive craziness, the populist comedy argues that what society regards as crazy (Mr. Deeds' attempt to give away his fortune) is really a manifestation of the normal human values with which society has lost touch.[28]

Moreover, while Deeds must face a sanity hearing, a true screwball comedy would not progress at all if eccentric behavior (the genre norm) were subject to the courtroom. The inherent naturalness of kookiness to the genre is best articulated by the matter-of-fact fashion in which Rudy Vallee tells his *Palm Beach Story* sister (Mary Astor): "You know Maude, someone meeting you for the first time, not knowing you were cracked, might get the wrong impression."

None of this negates the unique film comedy heritage Capra has given the world, but it is a cultural endowment better understood from a cracker-barrel than an antiheroic point of view. As noted film comedy historian and critic Raymond Durgnat's writing on populist film would suggest, Capra's post-*It Happened One Night* career is best studied not as a screwball auteur but rather as a populist one.[29] In 1978 this author did an article differentiating the 1930s comedy characterizations of Capra and Leo McCarey.[30] While not addressing the screwball genre by name, the essay juxtaposed the crackerbarrel nature of Capra's work with the antiheroic case of McCarey's. In later correspondence with Capra concerning another essay, the director expressed in an aside his enjoyment of the Capra-McCarey piece.[31] This article later became a major impetus to the author's 1983 monograph *Screwball Comedy: Defining a Film Genre.*[32]

The only post-*It Happened One Night* Capra films to approach screwball comedy are projects adapted from already successful works: the George S. Kaufman-Moss Hart Pulitzer Prize-winning play *You Can't Take It with You* and Joseph Kesselring's play *Arsenic and Old Lace.* In both of these the screwball characteristics were well developed before Capra acquired the film rights. Moreover, the dominant character in *You Can't Take It with You,* Grandpa Vanderhof (Lionel Barrymore), is still formed in the crackerbarrel mold. And Capra added the political conflict found in his version of *You Can't Take It with You*—making the father (Edward Arnold) of the suitor (James Stewart) of Grandpa's granddaughter (Jean Arthur) a munitions magnate needful of the Vanderhof property for a factory.

In contrast to the problem-solving crackerbarrel figure, the screwball comedy character is constantly buffeted about by the day-to-day frustrations of a seemingly irrational world. He is hardly capable of planning his leisure time, let alone entering politics. Crucial issues that arise in the genre are how to dunk a donut (*It Happened One Night*); who gets custody of the dog in divorce proceedings (*The Awful Truth*); how not to stay on a toboggan (*I Met Him in Paris*, 1937); whether a dog hid Cary Grant's missing dinosaur bone, and, if so, where (*Bringing Up Baby*); how to cheat when racing toy trains (*Four's a Crowd*, 1938); whether one can buy a pajama top or bottom and break up the set (*Bluebeard's Eighth Wife*, 1938); combining courtship and chair jumping (*Too Many Husbands*); how one keeps Henry Fonda from spilling things (*The Lady Eve*); the proper method to flatten and unflatten a top hat (*Take a Letter, Darling*); why hunting should be discouraged in passenger trains (*The Palm Beach Story*); and more recently, the need for martinis while bathing (*Arthur*). Political material just does not fit the genre. On the rare occasions when a central character deals seriously with politics, such as William Powell's speech near the close of *My Man Godfrey*, it entirely destroys the comedic pace of the film.

This does not exclude the occasional appearance in a minor role of a one-dimensional parody politician obviously not meant to be taken seriously, such as the crooked mayor (Clarence Kolb) in Hawks's *His Girl Friday* (1940). To best demonstrate, however, the *reductio ad absurdum* position a politican occupies on that rare appearance in the antiheroic world, one has only to return to that classic Robert Benchley volume *The Early Worm*, and his "interview" with Mussolini:

Mussolini seemed to be a good man to interview; so I got an interview with him. "Mr. Mussolini," I said, "as I understand your theory of government, while it is not without its Greek foundations, it dates even further back, in essence to the Assyrian system."

"What?" asked Mussolini.

"I said, as I understand your theory of government, while it is not without its Greek foundations, it dates even further back to the ancient Assyrian system. Am I right?

"Assyrian here seen Kelly? K-E-double-L-Y. That was a good song, too," said Il Duce.

"A good song is right," I replied. "And now might I ask, how did you come by that beard?"

"That is not a beard," replied the Great Man. "That is my forehead. I am smooth-shaven, as a matter of fact."

"So you are, so you are," I apologized. "I was forgetting."

We both sat silent for a while, thinking of the old days in Syracuse High.[33]

While appearances such as Hawks's crooked mayor or Benchley's version of Mussolini are uncommonly rare, they are not unsettling. Conversely, politicians in the crackerbarrel world of a Capra are more than unsettling. They stop at nothing to achieve their ends, whether it is running Boy Rangers off the highway in *Mr. Smith Goes to Washington*, or nearly driving the hero to suicide in *Meet John Doe*.

Consequently, the crackerbarrel film by necessity has a message. Capra once observed, after noting *Mr. Deeds Goes to Town* was his first conscious attempt to make a social statement: "I use comedy to, in a sense, warm people to my subject. . . . I get them in the spirit of laughter and then, perhaps, they might be softened up to accept some kind of a moral precept."[34]

While Capra mixed message with merriment, screwball comedy was all madcap merriment. Two key directors in the genre, Leo McCarey and Howard Hawks, both concede this point. McCarey has said:

Let other people take care of sordidness and ugliness. I string along with Disney. I think the biggest message of all is Who's Afraid of the Big Bad Wolf. The way I look at it, it's larceny to remind people how lousy things are and call it entertainment.[35]

Hawks adds:

A very astute and wise man gave me a chance to direct, and I made a picture that I don't think anybody enjoyed except a few critics. And he said, "Look, you've shown you can make a picture, but for God's sake go out and make entertainment." . . . And from that time on, I've been following his advice about trying to make entertainment.[36]

Moreover, Preston Sturges, the last great screwball director in what might be considered the genre's golden age (1934-44), observed that his sometimes screwball comedy *Sullivan's Travels* (1941) was "the result of an urge, an urge to tell some of my fellow filmwrights that they were getting a little too deep-dish and to leave the preachings to the preachers."[37] Capra is obviously one, if not *the*, targeted filmmaker, especially with the Christ-like allegory *Meet John Doe* having opened early in 1941. (A later Sturges screwball comedy—*The Miracle of Morgan's Creek*—has, in fact, been called a "sophisticated parody" of *Mr. Smith Goes to Washington* and *Meet John Doe*.[38]

Ironically, considering that Sturges felt so strongly about this pro-entertainment statement, *Sullivan's Travels* does not qualify as a full-fledged screwball comedy. As Sturges biographer James Curtis observed, *Sullivan's Travels* becomes "a message picture whose message is that we don't need any more message pictures."[39] It is clear, however, that Sturges has the same entertainment philosophy as McCarey and Hawks. In fact, Sturges visually anticipates McCarey's "I string along with Disney" statement when the pivotal scene in *Sullivan's Travels* uses the joyful response of a troubled audience to a Mickey Mouse cartoon to accentuate the importance of merely entertaining.

A fifth commonality between the worlds of the antihero and the screwball comedy male is that both focus on frustration. The antihero is always frustrated by women, a situation also generally evident in the screwball comedy, from Cary Grant's domination by Irene Dunne in *The Awful Truth* to his pursuit by Katharine Hepburn in *Bringing Up Baby*. Preston Sturges articulated the tendency toward female ascendency in the genre in the title of *The Lady Eve*, which also features a cartoon serpent in the delightful opening and closing credits. Not surprisingly, the Lady Eve (Barbara Stanwyck) wraps the sweet boob of a man-child (Henry Fonda) around her little finger during two different courtships, after appropriately starting things off by hitting him with an apple. So great is her mastery of this simple male Stanwyck even convinces Fonda she is two different women. (Not quite a year later Greta Garbo will persuade Melvyn Douglas of the same thing in the aptly titled George Cukor film *Two-Faced Woman*, 1941. While the film revives nicely today, the 1940s audience was not ready for Garbo as a screwball heroine.)

The Adam and Eve story is sometimes suggested in the screwball film at a nearly subliminal level, as in *Theodora Goes Wild*. Theodora (Irene Dunne) is a small-town girl who has written a successful novel about a big city girl,

3. Preston Sturges (circa 1941). (Photograph courtesy of the Museum of Modern Art/Film Stills Archive.)

The Sinner, using the pen name of Caroline Adams. Her hometown is straight out of Lysistrata, with female domination underscored by a name that suggests a female garden: Lynnfield. Dunne, who will go on to prove herself the most daring and daffy of this female tribe, ends up courting and besting the man (Melvyn Douglas) in several Garden of Eden encounters, from picking berries to catching fish. Even when Douglas momentarily flees, his note explains he has gone "to tend other gardens." His eventual fall, however, has been foreshadowed by the painting he was working on when they first met: *Eve and the Serpent*.

Eve is also the name of Claudette Colbert's delightfully manipulating character in *Midnight*; Irene Dunne brought her own brand of comic manipulation to a character nicknamed Eve in *My Favorite Wife*. (Dunne's shipwrecked island companion, Randolph Scott, is, naturally, Adam.)

As the genre entered the 1940s, the image of the screwball heroine as a power broker Eve-type became progressively stronger—culminating in Sturges's *The Lady Eve* and *The Palm Beach Story*. Sturges, as if somehow aware of *The Palm Beach Story*'s historical placement at the close of the initial screwball movement, even provides this Eve character with a gold digger's summation or bill of grievances. Joel McCrea has just discovered that a stranger called the "weiner king" has given wife Claudette Colbert enough money to pay all their numerous bills. When he asks whether sex entered into it, she replies:

> Oh, but of course it did, darling. I don't think he would have given it to me if I had . . . little short legs like an alligator. Sex always has something to do with it, dear. From the time you're about so big and wondering why your girlfriends' fathers are starting to get so arch all of a sudden. Nothing wrong. Just an overture to the opera that's coming . . . but from then on you get it [the sexual come-on look] from cops, taxi dancers, bell-boys, delicatessen dealers . . . the "how about this evening, babe?"

Put more succinctly, Colbert later observed, "You have no idea what a long-legged girl can do without doing anything."

While *It Happened One Night* did not showcase Colbert as an Eve type, most of her best pictures in the genre would take this route. Moreover, when Columbia unofficially remade *It Happened One Night* as a 1945 "B" film, someone even seemed anxious to correct this Eve omission by renaming the movie, *Eve Knew Her Apples*.[40]

In Hawks's much later screwball comedy, *Man's Favorite Sport?*, a modern-day visit to Eden is all the more obvious. Film critic Molly Haskell notes, the director "gives us Rock Hudson and Paula Prentiss as primordial man and woman, Adam and Eve in the lush, hazardous Eden of a hunting and fishing resort.''[41] Haskell also wisely notes that it is ''an Adam and Eve saddled with a bitter, comical heritage of sexual distrust, bravado, and fear, archetypes that are infinitely closer to the American experience.''[42] This observation could be applied to most antiheroic/screwball comedy—the why behind the significance of the Adam and Eve metaphor to the genre.

Haskell goes on to note the ''sexual allegory'' of the film—how Hudson has written the book on fishing but has never actually sunk hook into water—he is a ''how to'' sexual author who is really a cowardly virgin.[43] Other genre examples include the *Bringing Up Baby* Cary Grant bone which ''belongs in the tail'' and his later missing ''intercostal clavicle'' (a la ''Adam's rib'')—the latter of which Cavell also refers to as ''sexual allegory.''[44] Peter Bogdanovich's *What's Up, Doc?*, which borrows heavily from *Bringing Up Baby*, is much more bald about its sexual allegory—''Professor'' Ryan O'Neal, who mixes musicology and early stone study, is constantly endangering or losing ''his rocks.''

The best sexual allegory in the genre, however, which also plays nicely upon the interrelatedness of antiheroic and screwball comedy, occurs in *The Lady Eve* when the question is posed: ''Are snakes really necessary?'' which immediately brings to mind the title and text of the 1929 antihero classic by James Thurber and E. B. White—*Is Sex Necessary? Or, Why You Feel the Way You Do*.[45] The book anticipates the timid, virginal characteristics of many antiheroic/screwball males, particularly Henry Fonda's role in *Lady Eve*.

The domination by the female sometimes takes a more extreme course: reversal of sex roles. Such a switch occurs often in the genre, as in works by McCarey, Hawks, Sturges, George Stevens, and Mitchell Leisen. And with the increased 1940s visibility of women in society (due to the war), there was more opportunity for screwball comedies like Leisen's neglected *Take a Letter, Darling* (1942), which finds Rosalind Russell as a chief executive and Fred MacMurray as her private secretary.

Female domination is most prevalent in the works of Hawks; one of his films is even entitled *I Was a Male War Bride* (1949). The sex role-reversal tendency is showcased most entertainingly in his *Bringing Up Baby*, just after the masculine-willed Katharine Hepburn has kidnapped Cary Grant to her aunt's Connecticut home. Since his clothes are rather disheveled after a minor collision with a truck of crated chickens, he decides to shower. Hepburn, continuing to assert herself, takes his clothes, and he ends up donning her aunt's bathrobe and furry slippers. When confronted by another female, the bathrobe's owner, Grant has a complete comic breakdown, and whatever ''male'' resistance he had is completely dissipated.

The most extreme example of sex role reversal in the genre occurred under Hal Roach's direction in *Turnabout* (1940), from Thorne Smith's 1931 novel of the same name. A husband and wife, John Hubbard and

Carole Landis, exchange bodies, thanks to a genie-like oriental bust named Mr. Ram. Unlike onlookers in similar "exchanges" in the genre, the other characters in *Turnabout* are well aware that everything is not right with Hubbard and Landis. Although the exchange unfortunately lasts so long that its humor evaporates, the film remains *the* example of the screwball "turnabout."

Frustration continues for the dominated male as he attempts, like the comedy figures of the past, to follow a rational life-style, but it is an irrational world now, and he finds it nearly impossible. The female, just as irrational as this modern twentieth-century world, is somehow capable of getting through because she makes no rational demands. Appropriately enough, one of the first screwball comedies is called *Twentieth Century*, although in this film the male enjoys a surprising victory.

Accompanying this transition in American humor from competence to frustration is a further innovation. Women are given a major part, something American humor had previously largely neglected. The nineteenth-century crackerbarrel world had little place for women. The focus was too much on interests then labeled "male," from New England humor based in politics and business, as with Thomas Chandler Haliburton's Sam Slick character, to the emphasis in the comedy of the Old Southwest on raising hell, best exemplified by Johnson J. Hooper's world of Simon Suggs.

There had been earlier female comedy types, the vast majority seemingly products of New England humor, such as Frances M. Whitcher's Widow Bedott or B. P. Shillaber's Mrs. Partington, also a widow. These female characters tended to be rather screwball themselves. But since they existed in the world of the capable Yankee, their irrational characteristics, their malapropisms and long-winded chatter, were shown to be liabilities in what was seen as a rational world. They survived merely because their late husbands, presumably Yankees, had provided nicely for them.

Later, with the antihero *New Yorker* writers and with screwball comedy, a premium was set on female eccentricities, the logic no doubt being that the best defense against an illogical world is an illogical nature.

The key example of the female eccentric in the *New Yorker* group is found in Thurber's *My Life and Hard Times*, especially in the personality of his grandmother,

> who . . . lived the latter years of her life in the horrible suspicion that electricity was dripping invisibly all over the house. It leaked . . . out of empty sockets if the walls switch had been left on. She would go around screwing in bulbs, and if they lighted up she would hastily and fearfully turn off the wall switch . . . happy in the satisfaction that she had stopped not only a costly but dangerous leak.[46]

Yet, as eccentric as Grandma Thurber may be, she makes decisions and then gets on with living. The male attempts to make sense of situations, both with women and the world, and goes nearly crazy in the process. He cannot proceed without understanding, and there is no understanding.

Screwball film comedy adopted and developed the female eccentrics of antihero fiction and soon produced such celebrated mad hatters as Carole Lombard in *My Man Godfrey* (though she showcased her special craziness in numerous other outings) and Katharine Hepburn in *Bringing Up Baby*. In contrast, the genre's most underrated heroine, Irene Dunne, skillfully shifts into kookiness as the need arises, which is demonstrated by the title of her first screwball outing: *Theodora Goes Wild*. (Her favorite out-to-lunch persona is that of a wise fool Southern belle.) Among recent heroines, Barbra Streisand and Goldie Hawn have been the genre's most honored oddballs.

Because the illogical screwball heroine is better prepared than the male for an illogical world, she frequently meets new challenges in a radically different manner from her counterpart. For example, whereas Cary Grant is just this side of a nervous breakdown trying to decide which wife to choose in *My Favorite Wife*, Jean Arthur relishes a similar comic dilemma in *Too Many Husbands*. Arthur's near constant enjoyment of having two husbands competing for her is aptly captured in her evolving dialogue from three different points in the movie: "This is awful [having two husbands] but I love it." "Let's wait another day; I shouldn't be hasty about this [choosing just one]." "It [a doubled courtship] was wonderful while it lasted."

In the end it is the law, not Arthur, who decides upon husband Fred MacMurray. But it is more than obvious that Arthur will sustain indefinitely a degree of doubled romance by having her runner-up husband forever in the wings as insurance against MacMurray's travel habits (which originally led to his shipwreck). *Too Many Husbands* closes with Melvyn Douglas "accidentally" turning up at the same nightclub as Arthur and MacMurray. And as she dances back and forth between them, Arthur observes: "We'll have to do this often."

There can also be a darker side to this female dominance. This is best exemplified by Colbert's measured antics in *Bluebeard's Eighth Wife* (1938), antics which land husband Gary Cooper in a mental ward. In many ways—particularly female domination—screwball comedy of the 1930s and early 1940s anticipates the more sinister woman-as-predator film noir movies of the 1940s. One might even call screwball comedy an upbeat flipside of noir—in both cases it is a frequently irrational world with women hunting vulnerable men (though one merely desires a husband while the other desires his money). Screwball comedy regulars Fred MacMurray and Barbara Stanwyck even star in an early archetype of the genre—*Double Indemnity* (1944), with sometime screwball comedy writer/director Billy

Wilder co-scripting and directing. Moreover, while screwball heroines do not murder people (though zany Lombard claims she did in *True Confession*), murder is not alien to the genre. For example, madcap merriment joins murder in such genre works as *The Ex-Mrs. Bradford* (1936), *True Confessions* (1937), *Mad Miss Manton* (1938), and *Topper Returns* (1941). In fact, the quasi-screwball comedy *Thin Man* series (see Introduction) might be seen as a bridge between the two genres, especially with the original novel being penned by Dashiell Hammett, also author of *The Maltese Falcon*, which as closely adapted in 1941 became an early noir prototype.

The late 1930s influx of fantasy into screwball comedy also reinforced the frequent tendency toward female dominance in the genre. Pivotal films, such as *Topper* (1937, which triggered the movement), *Topper Takes a Trip* (1939), *Turnabout* (1940), *Topper Returns* (1941), and *I Married a Witch* (1942)—all of which are drawn from the work of novelist Thorne Smith—frequently favor the female lead via her supernatural powers. Even *Turnabout*, which is more about comic fantasy victims (the misadventures of a husband and wife who exchange bodies), ends with a decidedly pro-woman screwball twist. While female star Carole Landis howls with laughter, it is revealed that though genie-like Mr. Ram has returned the husband and wife to their correct bodies, the baby Landis has been carrying did not leave Papa's body. But this surprising final plot twist was anything but hidden in the film's print ad campagin, where *the stork* gives an overview of the plot, closing with "And who's to get Baby? Makes my face red!"[47] Thus, husband John Hubbard is soon to make medical history, and screwball comedy registers another "turnabout."

The best example, however, of the fantasy female carrying the day is Veronica Lake's eye-filling witch Jennifer in *I Married a Witch*. The actress, a contemporary reviewer was moved to note, "is turning out to be a first rate comedienne, in addition to being one of the sultriest ladies on the screen, and when you get a combination like that, in a figure like Miss Lake—brother, you've got a handful."[48] (Not surprisingly, the Thorne Smith novel upon which it is based—finished by Norman Matson after Smith's death—is entitled *The Passionate Witch*.)

It seems the most logical of developments that the generally bewitching screwball heroine should evolve into a real witch. *I Married a Witch* also offers an added bonus with a historical chronicle on the decline of a particular family of males named Wooley.

In 1690 Jennifer and her father Daniel (Cecil Kellaway) were burned for sorcery. Before their deaths, they put a curse upon denouncer Jonathan Wooley (Fredric March) that Wooley and his descendants should never be happily married. Comic montage reveals generation after generation of Wooleys marrying the wrong women.

All the while the spirits of father and daughter have been locked in the

4. Roland Young caught between "spirited" Joan Blondell and screwball wife Billie Burke in *Topper Returns* (1941). (Photograph courtesy of the Museum of Modern Art/Film Stills Archive.)

roots of an oak tree planted on the site of their execution. But a bolt of contemporary (1942) lightning splits the tree and frees Lake and Kellaway. Plans are made to continue the curse upon the most up-to-date Wooley, and the powers which this could release are nicely described in a dialogue between March and a now beautifully materialized Lake:

"Remember the Decline and Fall of the Roman Empire, that was our work."
"And the Fall of Pompeii, I suppose that was your work, too."
"Sure."

As in most screwball comedies, however, Lake becomes taken with the reluctant male (March is about to uphold the long Wooley tradition of marrying the wrong woman—Susan Hayward). Thus, Lake still causes havoc in his life, but now it is in the name of love. And as is the case in all romantic comedy, even of the madcap variety, love triumphs over all—even over Lake's revengefully comic father, who uses every available supernatural trick. (She eventually is able to keep him comfortably sealed up in his favorite hiding place—a rare bottle of Old Prairie Whiskey. What better place for an old "spirit"!)

The female's domination of the screwball male also exists upon a more self-conscious level. Stanley Cavell has written of his fascination with *The Lady Eve*'s "daring declaration" of its "awareness of itself, of its existence as a film."[49] The "daring declaration" he has in mind is what might be called the Barbara Stanwyck-directed scene of the handsome but awkward, naïve Henry Fonda first entering the ship's dining room/nightclub. The viewer watches the reflected image of Fonda in Stanwyck's makeup mirror as she narrates to the point of providing dialogue and direction for both the antihero and the many coquettes interested in the fortune from his family's brewery ("Pike's Pale, the Ale That Won for Yale").

Cavell's observation "that the woman [Stanwyck] is some kind of stand-in for the role of director fits our understanding that the man [Fonda], the sucker, is a stand-in for the role of the audience."[50] Cavell's realization of the Stanwyck-as-director, film-within-a-film nature of this scene is insightful. But while he relates this incident to the generally self-conscious nature of the genre, he misses the opportunity to add two other observations: here is another strong screwball comedy heroine (what he would call a Hollywood comedy of remarriage heroine), and such woman-as-director scenes occur in other films of the genre.

Excellent variations occur in both *My Favorite Wife* and *The Ex-Mrs. Bradford*. The funniest and most traditional example presents Irene Dunne's in-film manipulation of Cary Grant in *My Favorite Wife*, when she "directs" the reenactment of his marriage proposal to his second wife

(Gail Patrick). While Stanwyck's "direction" of Fonda might be labeled omnipotent narration because the antihero male is unaware of her, Dunne's assumption of the director's role follows more customary lines.

She discusses Grant's motivations and his lines, defining his physical movement in an imaginary set of her own design. She also portrays her version of the second wife, a delightful parody somewhere between the stereotype of the icy, self-centered socialite which Gail Patrick played so well (see also her Cornelia Bullock in *My Man Godfrey*) and the comically bored attitude of a Gabor sister discussing her collection of husbands. And as in *The Lady Eve*, the female "director" has the male jumping through hoops.

The heroine as director of a film-within-a-film scene goes beyond the merely metaphorical in *The Ex-Mrs. Bradford*. In this *Thin Man*-like film (though a more vulnerable William Powell is now teamed with Jean Arthur), Arthur orchestrates a movie-closing marriage to Powel using a minister who has already been filmed going through the ceremony (with more apparent direction from Arthur). Thus, Powell and Arthur face a truly "cinematic" minister on a screen within the movie, while the viewer becomes witness to probably the best example of screwball heroine as film director.

Despite this growth of the female role, there are occasionally screwball comedies in which the male apparently is in a more commanding position, like wheeler-dealer Cary Grant of *His Girl Friday* (1940) or suave and cerebral William Powell of *My Man Godfrey*. But this commanding position is only apparent; there are three qualifiers.

The most obvious qualifier is that if a screwball comedy allows one male more than average power, it creates one or more additional female-dominated males. The genre maintains a balance that never allows maleness much total power. The Grant figure of *His Girl Friday* is more than balanced by a host of frustrated milquetoast antiheroes, especially Rosalind Russell's comic "yes-man" financé Ralph Bellamy, an insurance man living with his mother (Bellamy being the period's favorite romantic also-ran), and such engaging characterizations as Billy Gilbert's Silas F. Pinkus, a much buffeted-about messenger. (Gilbert's other credits already included two-reeler frustrations at the hands of *the* antihero "couple," Laurel and Hardy, and as the voice of cartoon character Sneezy in Walt Disney's *Snow White and the Seven Dwarfs,* 1938.)

In *My Man Godfrey* the key milquetoast qualifiers to Powell are the female-dominated Bullock father (Eugene Pallette, who specialized in this type of role—see *The Lady Eve*) and his wife's art "protégé" (Mischa Auer, whose characterization of family pet Carlo and his ape imitations rated a nomination for Best Supporting Actor Oscar in 1936).

The second balance or qualifier to any depiction of male strength is that the focal male initially is shown in a lowly or weak situation. The wealthy

5. Maintaining male balance, Rosalind Russell is between Cary Grant and Ralph Bellamy during the production of *His Girl Friday* (1940). (Photograph courtesy of the Museum of Modern Art/Film Stills Archive.)

6. The delightful character actor Billy Gilbert is flanked by Rosalind Russell, Cary Grant, and Clarence Kolb in *His Girl Friday* (1940). (Photograph courtesy of the Museum of Modern Art/Film Stills Archive.)

7. Mischa Auer is in comic regression while Eugene Pallette, Carole Lombard (seated), and Alice Brady look on in *My Man Godfrey* (1936). (Photograph courtesy of the Museum of Modern Art/Film Stills Archive.)

Powell is first seen as a tramp, a "forgotten man," at the city dump, and later as the Bullock butler, which makes him Lombard's servant. Grant's newspaper editor character is overpowered by Russell, verbally and physically, at the opening of *His Girl Friday*. By initially leaving Grant, she defeats him in professional as well as private life, having formerly been both his wife and his reporter. Throughout the rest of the film he must play catchup. (Russell's delightfully overwhelming reporter in *His Girl Friday* draws heavily on a similar role she had in *Four's a Crowd,* a fact that has seemingly gone unnoticed.)

A final qualifier to any male strength is that on the rare occasion when the central male seems to win, the victory is Pyrrhic. For example, at the close of *My Man Godfrey* Lombard masterminds a marriage with Powell (more "direction" by the female), something he has been avoiding during the whole film, and one's last impression of the two records that inevitable transfer of power from male to female. The *New York Times* even put it more strongly, claiming Powell's Godfrey never had a chance against

> the forthright emotional processes of that bovine divinity (or vice versa) Irene [Lombard], who is somewhat surer than death or taxes. Godfrey, when we leave him, is being led to the slaughter and it's enough to bring tears to the eyes of an Eli.[51]

Lombard has, quite literally, made Powell "my man Godfrey."

Before closing this examination of frustration—the fifth commonality between the world of the antihero and the screwball comedy male—it should be highlighted that while females are frequently at the center of male problems, the male is capable of individual blundering. Witness Cary Grant's inability to watch a music recital without flipping over his chair in *The Awful Truth* or Henry Fonda's general homespun density in *The Lady Eve* (so nicely explained in terms of sexual naïveté by the recurring joke he has been up the Amazon a year). Even when the female is on the scene, she cannot always be blamed for male incompetency and frustration. For example, when Lombard contemplates ending it all in the East River during *Nothing Sacred,* March accidentally pushes her in while trying to prevent her jumping. And then, only after March goes to the rescue, does he remember he cannot swim; Lombard must save him!

The world of screwball comedy is antiheroic in nature. The genre should be seen as part of the general movement taking place in American humor during the late 1920s from the capable to the frustrated character, a movement that has come to be associated with the problems of coming to terms with an irrational modern world. The antiheroic nature of screwball comedy is also reflected in the relationship between the development of the genre and the times. From about 1934 to the early 1940s American humor felt the first full impact of the antihero. Later, while some screwball comedies such as *What's Up, Doc?* still appeared, antiheroic characteristics had become so pervasive in American humor that they were commonplace.

Because the distinctive edge of uniqueness was off screwball films, new comedy directions began to appear as early as the war years, including McCarey's populist films of faith, *Going My Way* (1944) and *The Bells of St. Mary's* (1945). World War II hurried along this transition. Some directors, like McCarey in *Once Upon a Honeymoon* (1942), produced flawed films by trying to combine war themes with screwball comedy. In *Honeymoon*, the whole film comes to a halt when Cary Grant and Ginger Rogers find themselves in a concentration camp, hardly a suitable subject for nonpolitical screwball comedy. Other directors like Hawks merely moved into more war-related adventure genres, from *Sergeant York* (1941) and *Air Force* (1943) to the 1944 restructuring of Hemingway's *To Have and Have Not*, to reflect the creeping evil of Nazism.

Lubitsch's *To Be or Not to Be* (1942) also addressed the war directly, following the misadventures of a troupe of Polish actors during the Nazi occupation of that country. Jack Benny is outstanding as the nearly cuckolded antiheroic husband who leads the group; Lombard provides excellent support as the romantically dizzy wife. But as with McCarey's *Once Upon a Honeymoon*, the film frequently is punctuated with concentration camp-type issues. And though Lubitsch's film is far superior, it is superior on a black comedy level; McCarey attempts to maintain a screwball comedy norm and fails. Thus, *To Be or Not To Be* succeeds as a black comedy, not as a screwball comedy.

The only real holdout of the war years in screwball comedy was latecomer Preston Sturges, who represented a summing up of the genre. His *The Lady Eve* (1941) and *The Palm Beach Story* (1942) are almost flawless examples of the antiheroic world of the screwball film, combining fast, witty dialogue with the often neglected slapstick nature of the genre. In *The Miracle of Morgan Creek* (1944) Sturges successfully blends a war backdrop and a screwball comedy, largely through the genius of focusing on an antiheroic "4-Fer" (someone not subject to the military draft for physical or mental reasons), perfectly cast with diminutive Eddie Bracken.

Two additional screwball comedies from the early 1940s merit special acknowledgment. Like *The Miracle of Morgan's Creek* they were able to utilize a distant war-related backdrop without fumbling the laughs: Billy Wilder's aforementioned *The Major and the Minor* (1942) and George Stevens's *The More the Merrier* (1943).

The latter film finds Jean Arthur, Joel McCrea, and Charles Coburn in a story revolving around the housing shortage in wartime Washington, D.C. It's a delightful variation on the genre with nearly musical chairs for guidelines as the three leads share one apartment. But 1940s war-related screwball comedies such as these were the exception.

The war years had other profound effects on American films. The chaos of the period forever dampened America's love affair with the crackerbarrel figure; the "Catch-22" nature of the contemporary world made it harder and harder to relate to such a capable figure. In Capra's *It's a Wonderful Life* (1946), a former archetype of this character nearly commits suicide and the storyline must introduce a deus ex machina in the form of a second-class angel sent to preserve order. It was as if Capra had taken a suggestion from the influx of fantasy into screwball comedy in the late 1930s, when ghosts and spirits proved to be a new source of eccentricity for the genre. As screwball comedy investigated the supernatural with films like *Topper* and *Here Comes Mr. Jordan* (1941), the capable comedy figure also either had found help in the heavens, as in *A Guy Named Joe* (1943), where Spencer Tracy and Lionel Barrymore are literally guardian angels for the Air Force, or had returned to an earlier America where he was not out of place, as in *Meet Me in St. Louis* (1944), *Life with Father* (1947), and *Cheaper by the Dozen* (1950). Even in the latter situation, the male figures were given some antiheroic traits, as if the filmmakers were displaying the roots of this figure of frustration.

By the mid-1940s the antihero had become dominant in American humor. The five antiheroic characteristics—abundant leisure time, childlike nature, urban setting, nonpolitical activity, and frustration—represented a major transition in American humor and served as a foundation of a frequently neglected film genre: screwball comedy.

NOTES

1. Herb Stone, *I Married A Witch* review, *Rob Wagner's Script* (December 19, 1942), in *Selected Film Criticism, 1941-1950*, ed. Anthony Slide (Metuchen, New Jersey: The Scarecrow Press, 1983), p. 85.

2. Douglas W. Churchill, "Laughter At So Much Per Tickle," *New York Times* February 6, 1938, Section 10, p. 5.

3. Leo McCarey, "Comedy and a Touch of the Cuckoo," *Extension,* November 1944, p. 34.

4. *Holiday* review, *Time* magazine, June 13, 1938, p. 23.

5. Pete Martin, "Going His Way," *Saturday Evening Post,* November 30, 1946, p. 70.

6. McCarey's *Bells of St. Mary's* includes the observation: "We should never get too far away from our childhood."

7. Henri Bergson, "Laughter" (1910), in *Comedy*, ed. Wylie Sypher (Garden City, New York: Doubleday & Company, 1956), p. 175.

8. Robin Wood, *Howard Hawks* (1968; rpt. London: British Film Institute, 1981), p. 70.

9. Thorne Smith, *Topper,* in *The Thorne Smith 3-Bagger* (Garden City, New York: Sun Dial Press, 1945), p. 682.

10. Molly Haskell, *From Reverance to Rape: The Treatment of Women in the Movies* (Baltimore: Penguin Books, 1974), p. 131.

11. E. H. Gombrich, *The Story of Art* (London: Phaidon Press, 1972), p. 470.

12. Matthew Baigell, *The American Scene: American Painting of the 1930s* (New York: Praeger Publishers, 1974), p. 55.

13. Gavin Lambert, Personal Interview, George Cukor Oral History, American Film Institute, Los Angeles, 1971.

14. Stanley Cavell, *Pursuits of Happiness: The Hollywood Comedy of Remarriage* (Cambridge, Massachusetts: Harvard University Press, 1981), p. 49.

15. Ibid., pp. 49-51. For Frye see both: *Anatomy of Criticism: Four Essays* (1957; rpt. Princeton, New Jersey: Princeton University Press, 1973), p. 183; and *A Natural Perspective* (New York: Columbia University Press, 1965), p. 128.

16. Cavell, *Pursuits of Happiness,* p. 49.

17. Ibid., p. 51; Frye, *A Natural Perspective*, p. 128.

18. Frye, *Anatomy of Criticism*, p. 182.

19. *Topper* review, *New York Times*, August 20, 1937, p. 21.

20. New York artist Anthony Garrity, a sketch contributor to *Esquire,* was brought in to design a "futuristic automobile." *Topper* file, Billy Rose Theatre Collection, New York Public Library at Lincoln Center.

21. *My Man Godfrey* review, *New York Times,* September 18, 1936, p. 18.

22. *My Man Godfrey* review, *Variety*, September 23, 1936, p. 16.

23. Andrew Bergman, *We're in the Money: Depression America and Its Films* (1971; rpt. New York: Harper & Row, 1972), pp. 132-48.

24. Richard Gertner, ed., *International Motion Picture Almanac, 1976*, (New York: Quigley Publishing Company, 1976), p. 51A.

25. Frank Capra, *The Name Above the Title* (New York: Macmillan Company, 1971), pp. 39-40.

26. Capra's close ties with crackerbarrel humor are examined in detail in Wes D. Gehring, "Frank Capra—In the Tradition of Will Rogers and Other Crackerbarrel Yankees," *Indiana Social Studies Quarterly*, Autumn 1981, pp. 49-56.

27. Jim Leach, "The Screwball Comedy," in *Film Genre: Theory and Criticism*, ed. Barry K. Grant (Metuchen, New Jersey: The Scarecrow Press, 1977), p. 82.

28. Ibid., pp. 82-83.

29. Raymond Durgnat, *The Crazy Mirror* (1970; rpt. New York: Dell Publishing Company, 1972); see especially the close of chapter 19 (p. 122) and chapter 20 (pp. 123-30). See also Durgnat's "Genre: Populism and Social Realism," *Film Comment,* July/August 1975, pp. 20-29, 63. I do not endorse all the film directors Durgnat includes in his Populist grouping, but there is agreement that Capra should be included in such a genre.

30. Wes D. Gehring, "McCarey vs. Capra: A Guide to American Film Comedy of the '30s," *The Journal of Popular Film and Television* 7, no. 1 (1978): 67-84.

31. Wes D. Gehring, Frank Capra letter to the author. December 10, 1979.

32. Wes D. Gehring, *Screwball Comedy: Defining a Film Genre* (Muncie, Indiana: Ball State University Press, 1983).

33. Robert Benchley, "An Interview with Mussolini," in *The Early Worm* (New York: Henry Holt and Company, 1927), p. 29.

34. Richard Schickel, editor/interviewer, "Frank Capra," in *The Man That Made the Movies* (New York: Atheneum, 1975), pp. 73-74.

35. Martin, "Going His Way," p. 48.

36. Joseph McBride and Michael Wilmington, " 'Do I Get to Play the Drunk This Time?': An Encounter with Howard Hawks," *Sight and Sound*, Spring 1971, p. 100.

37. James Curtis, *Between Flops: A Biography of Preston Sturges* (New York: Harcourt Brace Jovanovich, 1982), p. 152.

38. Andrew Sarris, "Preston Sturges," in *The National Society of Film Critics on Movie Comedy*, ed. Stuart Byron and Elisabeth Weis (New York: Penguin Books, 1977), p. 84.

39. Curtis, *Between Flops: A Biography of Preston Sturges,* p. 152.

40. William K. Everson, *Claudette Colbert* (New York: Pyramid Publications, 1976), pp. 78-79.

41. Molly Haskell, "Man's Favorite Sport? (Revisited)," in *Focus on Howard Hawks*, ed. Joseph McBride (Englewood Cliffs, New Jersey: Prentice-Hall, 1972), p. 136.

42. Ibid.

43. Ibid.

44. Cavell, *Pursuits of Happiness,* p. 119.

45. James Thurber and E. B. White, *Is Sex Necessary? Or, Why You Feel the Way You Do* (1929; rpt. New York: Harper & Row, 1975).

46. James Thurber, "The Car We Had to Push," in *My Life and Hard Times* (1933; rpt. New York: Bantam Books, 1947), p. 41.

47. *Turnabout* advertisement, *Photoplay*, July 1940, p. 5.

48. *I Married a Witch* file, Billy Rose Theatre Collection, New York Public Library at Lincoln Center.

49. Cavell, *Pursuits of Happiness,* p. 66.

50. Ibid.

51. *My Man Godfrey* review, *New York Times*, p. 18.

4.

THE DIRECTOR AS KEEPER OF THE SCREWBALL SANATORIUM

My Man Gregory was the keeper of the asylum in which the lunatics frolicked through *My Man Godfrey*.[1]
(Carole Lombard describing director Gregory La Cava.)

By 1941 even Alfred Hitchcock had officially joined screwball comedy ranks with *Mr. and Mrs. Smith* starring Carole Lombard (although Hitchcock's 1935 thriller *The 39 Steps* had revealed some characteristics of the genre). Thus, while not everyone directed a screwball comedy during the genre's 1934-44 heyday, a mere survey of directorial ranks would necessitate one of those coffee table-sized books—but without pictures! Ted Sennett's *Lunatics and Lovers* is the closest thing available to such a book, but it is a survey of the whole genre.[2] Though not without fascinating detail, its broadness tends to defeat one's understanding of just what the genre represents. Consequently, this chapter will limit itself to four of screwball comedy's most important directors, in order of importance: Howard Hawks, Leo McCarey, Preston Sturges, and Gregory La Cava. (An examination of, and the reasoning behind, exclusion of the great but more populist-oriented Frank Capra from this group is examined in detail in Chapter 3.)

An auteur approach, focusing on the director as author of the film, has been followed in this text, and most especially in this chapter, for four reasons. First, while the collective background of cinema production is not to be denied, the most standard approach to author in film study keys on director. Second, though auteurism is not without flaws, it does address a fundamental difference between film and theater. Unlike the latter, where the printed word is sacred, the movie script is merely a point of departure. Again, film study's orthodox canon credits the director with having the pivotal conception in film production. Third, while exceptions can be found to any standard, there is no question among film scholars that the focus directors in this study (Hawks, McCarey, Sturges, and La Cava) are true auteurs. Each demonstrated a consistency of comic theme over long, influential film careers. Fourth, because the majority of the films examined herein were done during the golden age of the American studio system (1930-45), a time when crossing craft lines was tantamount to heresy (a director was supposed to direct, a writer to write), the writing of pivotal screwball directors Hawks, McCarey, and La Cava is invariably absent from the credits. (Sturges was able to help establish a new precedent by being the credited director and writer.) Today they would have received cowriter credits. Even when a period screwball comedy film was adapted from a major success in another medium, such as Hawks's use of the Ben Hecht-Charles MacArthur play *The Front Page* as the foundation for *His Girl Friday* (1940; screenplay credited to Charles Lederer), these directors still managed to put their own (though uncredited) stamp upon the narratives. This was usually done through both daily rewrites and improvisation during production, phenomena which are thoroughly examined in this chapter. In the case of *His Girl Friday*, Hawks added the additional twist of changing a central *Front Page* character (Hildy Johnson) into a woman. This "simple" alteration, and the comic repercussions which automatically follow, are what make this adaptation a screwball-parody of a romance-comedy. This should not, of course, distract from the contributions made by writers, or others. And when pertinent, the text has not avoided such notations. See especially references to Billy Wilder and Charles Brackett, Claude Binyon (who worked so frequently with screwball director Wesley Ruggles), Preston Sturges (as screenwriter), and Ben Hecht and Charles MacArthur. But any study, short of an encyclopedia, needs a manageable leash with which to guide it. Auteurism is this study's leash. For those so inclined, however, further source material can be found in the detailed filmography of this volume's appendices. (Recognition of the director's significance might best be measured by the fact that two of the period's greatest screenwriters—Sturges and Wilder—went on to much greater recognition, both publicly and within the industry, when they were able to direct their work.)

Because part of the genre's comedy is self-conscious in nature—from in-house references to actors and earlier films to a content frequently reflecting directors's interests and inclinations—biographical material for the focus directors is included. Though it is obvious that all artists, to a certain degree, are influenced by real-life experiences, the screwball comedy is unique in its high degree of cross references for comic purposes. Biographical profiles of these directors also offer insights into why the genre has such a propensity for slapstick and a sense of the improvisational. Moreover, it offers reasons why these four directors could exercise such production control in *the* age of the studio.

Additional examination of many of these same subjects, as well as the working methods of other screwball comedy directors and writers, is explored further in Chapter 5 (on actors). As both this and Chapter 5 will reveal, screwball comedy, at least among its pantheon participants, was much more likely than other genres to reflect the backgrounds of those involved.

HOWARD HAWKS

Hawks once confessed, "Whenever I hear a story my first thought is how to make it into a comedy."[3] The statement would be more revealing had he said *screwball* comedy, because if one had to identify a single key director of the genre, the clear choice would be Hawks. No other director yielded as many screwball comedies of such consistently high quality over as prolonged a period. The list includes *Twentieth Century* (from the Hecht-MacArthur play, 1934, the genre's celebrated opening year), *Bringing Up Baby* (1938), *His Girl Friday* (from the Hecht-MacArthur play *The Front Page*, 1940), *Ball of Fire* (1941), *I Was a Male War Bride* (1949), *Monkey Business* (1952), and *Man's Favorite Sport?* (1964).

Hawks is also the most versatile film director among those listed, having made cinema classics in a number of genres besides screwball comedy. These include the gangster film (*Scarface*, 1932), the war film (*Air Force*, 1943), film noir (*The Big Sleep*, 1946), and the western (*Rio Bravo*, 1959). But he seems to have had the greatest impact on the screwball film—an appropriate development for someone whose first thoughts are of comedy. More specifically, his ties with screwball comedy stretch back to the beginning of the type, a statement not applicable to his other genre work. Furthermore, if one breaks down his filmography into the most definable genres, screwball comedy surfaces as the numerical winner.

Hawks's other genre work is not without interest for the student of screwball comedy, however, because his screwball films seem almost to parody it, as well as his life/style in general. As Chapter 3 has already demonstrated, the typical Hawksian screwball comedy male is an antiheroic, absent-minded professor who is literally overpowered by a female. Hawks himself probably described this characteristic of his comedy best and most to the point (as was his habit) with this simple reply to an interviewer's general question about dominant women in his comedies: "You take a professor, and you use the girl's part to knock his dignity down."[4]

In contrast, Hawks's dramas showcase capable men of adventure who constantly live their lives on the edge—stoically risking everything for their own private codes. In *The Big Sleep* Humphrey Bogart is Raymond Chandler detective Philip Marlowe, walking the film noir line between the corrupt establishment and those who do not even play at being nice. In *Rio Bravo* a small band of misfits (led by John Wayne) successfully holds out against great odds. In *Only Angels Have Wings* (1939) fliers in second-rate planes routinely risk everything to fly cargo over the Andes.

There are few women in these adventure films, and the rare female who sticks must make it on the most macho of male terms. She might best be exemplified by Lauren Bacall, who debuted in Hawks's adaptation of Ernest Hemingway's *To Have and Have Not* (1944), and later starred in *The Big Sleep*. This Hawksian protégée was decidedly at ease among men, even approaching sexuality with stereotyped male directness. (Hollywood legend even credits Hawks with creating Bacall's husky voice—having her go on extended shouting bouts long before shooting started on *To Have and To Have Not*.)

All this is not to say there are not ties between the Hawks screwball comedy and the drama. Both worlds showcase dedicated professionals (see chapter 6 for an examination of comic rigidity in the absent-minded professor). It is just that a comic look at the professional academic takes a decidedly different turn from a professional who packs a gun. Moreover, Hawks's comedy professional is generally distracted from his goal by the strong woman; in the drama her strong nature merely enables her to be one of the boys and help take part in a strived for or continuously dangerous endeavor.

Both worlds are also frequently claustrophobic enclosures set apart from normal human byways. Here again comic academic haunts produce a different response than a film noir Los Angeles or a beseiged western jail. All in all, screwball comedies allow the viewer the added pleasure of knowing the artist had a sense of humor, as well as complimenting the genre's propensity for in-house humor (at the expense of themselves and others within the American film industry).

Examining the artist's real life merely makes this knowledge more insightful, even expanding the sense of self-parody. Hawks did not just make films about macho male adventurers; he lived that life-style, too. Born in Indiana, he raced automobiles professionally as a teenager and later helped design a car which won the 1936 Indianapolis 500. (Hawks's *The Crowd Roars*, 1932, and *Red Line 7000*, 1965, both deal with race car drivers.)

During World War I he served with the United States Army Air Corps, and in future years there would be many films about flying and World War I (*The Dawn Patrol*, 1930; *Ceiling Zone*, 1936; *The Road to Glory*, 1936; *Sergeant York*, 1941). While his Hollywood ties predate the war, his film career would begin to escalate after the conflict. Yet there would always be time for planes, race cars (and motorcycles), and big game fishing and hunting, often with friends whose very names—Ernest Hemingway and Gary Cooper—once personified American maleness.

Howard Hawks, professional film director, also personified approaches to comedy and film production which frequently reappear in the work patterns of other pivotal screwball directors. Chief among these characteristics were a propensity for physical comedy, sometimes with direct homage to classic silent screen material and/or performers; a tendency to improvise, with a relaxed, frequently fun atmosphere to the production; Hollywood in-house humor, with actors sometimes playing variations of themselves, even to the point of self-parody; and a greater degree of production control than was the norm during the studio era.

First, it is important to keep in mind that screwball comedy, evolving early in the first decade after sound, owed much of its success to the marriage of visual/physical comedy and the spoken word. There is no denying the sometimes biting dialogue of the genre (though revisionist criticism like Pauline Kael's "Raising Kane" essay overemphasizes it[5]), but just as frequently the comedy is expressed in a totally visual manner. Film critic John Belton's comments on the physical action in the Hawks film, seemingly most relevant to his screwball comedies, are applicable to a significant number of other films in the genre (especially those of Leo McCarey):

> Hawks roots his films in physical action, shaping his plots around events rather than ideas, and building his characters around concrete gestures and mannerisms rather than abstract inner motivations . . . the expressiveness of the characters' physical actions [show] how they feel and what they are thinking. They do not need to explain themselves in words.[6]

Hawks received early directing experience in silent film comedy, including short subjects with Monty Banks (who eventually went on to feature-length thrill comedies, à la Harold Lloyd[7]). Hawks, who credits himself with the Americanization of Banks's original Italian name (Mario Bianchi), eventually graduated to silent comedy features such as *Fig Leaves* (1926) and *The Cradle Snatchers* (1927).[8] In fact, *Fig Leaves* is not without some screwball comedy roots: "After a prologue in Eden, with Eve telling Adam that she has 'nothing to wear,' the same actors appear as a modern New York couple . . . who stray to other partners but are reunited in the end.[9]

Hawks's silent comedy background and genuine fondness for the greats ("I like Keaton's [films]. But Chaplin is the best of 'em all."[10]) is apparent throughout his screwball comedies. On the set of *Bringing Up Baby* he even explained his views on "the great clowns" to stars Cary Grant and Katharine Hepburn: "Keaton, Chaplin, Lloyd, simply weren't out there making funny faces, they were serious, sad, solemn, and the humor sprang from what happened to them. They'd do funny things in a completely quiet, somber deadpan way."[11] Moreover, Grant was told to model himself after Lloyd—a model he almost came to resemble during the production, not unaided by his professorial, Lloyd-like glasses.[12]

Appropriately, the film frequently celebrates silent comedy. For example, Grant finds himself on all fours following George the dog, trying to find where the pooch buried Grant's rare dinosaur bone. At one point he is even moved to help George dig, dog-style. Among other visual scenes is the now classic ripped dress routine in the restaurant, where Grant keeps popping his hat onto Hepburn's exposed backside, before she knows it is exposed, and then their eventual exit as one unit, Grant covering their retreat. But most wonderful of all is the Grant-Hepburn leopard hunt in the woods, which features a smorgasbord of silent comedy, from the seemingly bottomless stream which appears so shallow until one takes a step (variations of which were especially popular with Laurel & Hardy) to Grant's feigned attempt at strangling the frustrating Hepburn (who has just caught his head in her butterfly net), so reminiscent of a similar action (comparably motivated) by Buster Keaton in *The General* (1926).

Grant and Hepburn's romantic battle royal showcases countless other mime scenes and sight gags, including Grant's wild ride on the running board of a Hepburn-driven auto at the opening of the film and a close that features probably the biggest pratfall in slapstick history: Hepburn causes the brontosaurus skeleton Grant is working on to collapse.

This emphasis on visual comedy continued in Hawks's post-World War II screwball films, especially the following high points from Grant's performance in *I Was a Male War Bride*: his receiving a ride to remember on the handlebars of a runaway motorcycle (patterned after a similar ride by Buster Keaton in *Sherlock, Jr.,* 1923); his being hung up on a railroad crossing arm; his being a comic victim of the old out-of-the-way wet paint sign, "after" he has climbed the pole in question (again most evocative of Laurel & Hardy); his being forced to hide on the most shaky of window awnings and, once discovered, having to defend himself on an even shakier awning; finally, his being wardrobed first with undersized male clothing, only to have it later replaced with equally undersized female clothing.

A second important commonality between Hawks and other pivotal screwball comedy directors is the tendency to improvise:

> Hawks believes that the best gags are spontaneous. "You can't always put them into a prepared script. They just happen. We start out in the morning [on *Man's Favorite Sport?*] playing with the props. By mid-afternoon we had developed a completely different approach to the scene."[13]

A good Hawksian example of the "they just happen" phenomenon occurs in *Bringing Up Baby*. Hawks, praising Hepburn's improvisational skills, stated: "In one scene [during the leopard hunt in the woods] she broke the heel of a shoe. She was right on camera, and without fluffing a line, she said, as she limped, 'I was born on the side of a hill!' "[14]

Other Hawks performers relate similar stories. In her autobiography Rosalind Russell states:

> Hawks was a terrific director [on *His Girl Friday*]; he encour-
> aged us [the performers] and let us go . . . once Cary [Grant]
> looked straight out of a scene and said to Hawks (about
> something I was trying), "Is she going to do that?" and Hawks
> left the moment in the picture—Cary's right there on film asking
> an unseen director about my plans.[15]

Hawks's critical biographer Gerald Mast has observed that while Hawks would have a guideline script, the director "constantly reworked his ideas on the set and at home, as his filmed narration took shape, until he reached a narrative conclusion that frequently bore no relationship at all to the one in the script with which he began shooting."[16]

Hawks's improvisational set was also a relaxed, happy set. Fritz Feld, the comic psychiatrist in *Bringing Up Baby*, remembers:

> Often in the morning Howard Hawks would come in and say,
> "It's a nice day today. Let's go to the races." And we'd pack up
> and *go* to the races. Kate continued her custom of serving tea on
> the set. We all laughed and laughed, and were very happy.[17]

Hand in hand with improvisational fun is commonality number three—Hollywood in-house humor, with performers often encouraged to play their characters close to themselves.

> Once Hawks had effected the perfect synthesis of star
> personality and fictional character he could (and would)
> eliminate or revise whole passages and events in the written
> script, so that the story that resulted remained true to the
> character-personality as well as to its original structural logic.
> Character inevitably produces credibility in stories, and for
> Hawks these credible star personalities were the characters.[18]

Though Mast's observations are generally insightful, there is a qualifier when one considers Hawks as screwball comedy director. Just as Hawks's films in this genre parody his adventure work, there at times appears to be a tendency for him to use a star's screen persona for comic effect, such as making romantic leading man Cary Grant into an absent-minded professor. Thus, while there is still need to be aware of a screen persona, by turning this persona on its ear, the comedy is enhanced all the more, as is the sense of film industry self-parody so typical of the genre.

Moreover, just as Hawks would get dialogue "to fit the actor rather than the actor to fit the words,"[19] it is still frequently more fruitful to consider the person over the personality. For example, when Lombard made *Twentieth Century*, she was not a real star; consequently there was no star personality to manipulate. Moreover, as Larry Swindell's excellent Lombard biography notes, her casting was a result of her offscreen image as "a good-time girl—generous, uninhibited, delightful in all her excesses" (which would be consistent with her part as Lily Garland).[20] Hawks himself stated: "Lombard played herself—dizzy and quite touching—for me in *Twentieth Century*."[21]

A more flamboyant example of the "fictional" character being more than similar to the person being cast involves John Barrymore's part in *Twentieth Century:* "Hawks wanted Barrymore for the Oscar Jaffe role because he *was* Jaffe: histrionic, preening, ego-driven almost to clownishness, outrageous and yet persuasive."[22] While not generally known at the time, the Jaffe character had been "conceived for the stage in the Barrymore image, though played by Moffat Johnston on Broadway."[23] (Hecht and MacArthur, authors of the Broadway production of *Twentieth Century*—which was based on Charles Bruce Milholland's play *Napoleon on Broadway*—also receive the screenplay credit on the Hawks production.)

Naturally, Barrymore is outstanding in the adaptation, and finds himself the subject of the greatest scene of self-parody in the genre. Barrymore has just slipped onto the train *Twentieth Century*, thanks to a disguise which includes a putty nose. Safely aboard, Barrymore begins to play with this putty nose, and soon the man known the cultured world over as "the great profile" most resembles Pinocchio. But even this has a parody topper: "the great profile" then picks that Pinocchio-sized proboscis.

Naturally, to become involved in such self-parody was to enjoy the part, and Barrymore very much enjoyed the part: "I've never done anything I like as well . . . a role that comes once in an actor's lifetime."[24] And the critics were equally pleased, from *Variety*'s "Give Barrymore a chance to go off his nut . . . and it's a pleasure," to Mordaunt Hall of the *New York Times* observing, "Barrymore acts with such imagination and zest that he never fails to keep the picture thoroughly alive. . . . Oscar Jaffe's [Barrymore's character] imperiousness is enough to rattle the brains of anybody working for him."[25]

There are numerous other celebrated examples of cinema self-parody in Hawks's screwball comedies—especially when it involved fellow improvisor Cary Grant. For example, Grant's character in *His Girl Friday* tells a story about an Archie Leach (Grant's real name) getting his throat cut; later he describes one character as a mock turtle (Grant's role in *Alice in Wonderland*, 1933), and another as looking like that "guy in the movies,"

Ralph Bellamy, the character's real name. In *Bringing Up Baby* Grant's character is given the title of "Jerry the Nipper," a nickname that first appeared in McCarey's *The Awful Truth* (1937). Grant even footnotes this when he says of co-star Hepburn, who has reintroduced the name, "She's merely making it up out of motion pictures she's seen."

Hepburn's role in *Bringing Up Baby* as screwball Connecticut heroine Susan Vance has been drawn both from her own background and from a cross section of genre heroine characteristics (more of the genre drawing upon itself). Hawks said her "part in *Bringing Up Baby* was her; she *was* a Connecticut heiress, she *was* full of opinions, she *was* inventive and certain about everything."[26] Hawks likened her to Carole Lombard: "She might run around like a tomboy, but she had beauty and the ability to wear clothes and to look like a lady."[27] But there are footnotes in Hepburn's role to other genre heroines. For example, her imitation of a gun moll during the jail scene would seem to have been inspired by Jean Arthur's comically similar gun-moll scene in *The Whole Town's Talking* (1935). Moreover, Hepburn's comically high-pitched, self-conscious laugh (which occurs whenever someone does not have a prayer of a chance against her) was no doubt borrowed from Irene Dunne, who had already employed it in two popular screwball films, *Theodora Goes Wild* (1936) and *The Awful Truth*, earning her two Best Actress Academy nominations for her roles.

The fourth and final commonality was the greater degree of production control exercised by Hawks and several other screwball directors. Again, it is a natural extension of such earlier points as improvisation and the use of self-parody. Hawks was not under long-term contract to any studio during the sound era, and continually negotiated different contracts for different projects; frequently he acted as his own producer. His production control was probably greater than any other director in the genre. Moreover, as one final safeguard, Hawks shot very little extra footage. This meant that regardless of who edited it, there could be little variation in construction. Thus, while Hawks's first thought about a story focuses on how to make it into a comedy, his final on the set action guarantees comedy control. Like the generally uncredited off-screen voice (spoken by Hawks) which comically baits Cary Grant at the beginning of *Monkey Business*, Hawks seems all pervasive.

LEO McCAREY

After Hawks the most central screwball comedy director is Leo McCarey, whose teaming and molding of Laurel & Hardy represents an early articulation of the antihero in American film. More importantly, he was instrumental in easing the phenomenon now known as screwball comedy into feature films.[28] Like Hawks, McCarey's screwball comedy work covers a long period. Early sound films like *Part-Time Wife* (1930) and *Indiscreet*

(1931) predate the traditional 1934 starting point yet fulfill the genre conventions. In fact, as McCarey noted in his American Film Institute Oral History, "there are several scenes in *The Awful Truth* that are paraphrases of identical scenes in *Part-Time Wife*."[29] Unfortunately, the quasi-screwball nature of his *Six of a Kind* (1934) was obscured by a personality comedian cast which includes W. C. Fields, Charles Ruggles, and George Burns and Gracie Allen—though Burns and Allen were the ultimate screwball couple. In 1935 McCarey does what is essentially a screwball comedy in period costume—*Ruggles of Red Gap* (1935). While not without some populist conventions, its antiheroic nature ties it much more logically to the screwball comedy camp.[30]

In 1937 McCarey received an Academy Award for his direction of one of screwball comedy's central works, *The Awful Truth*, which continues to accommodate the high praise *Variety*'s period review promised—"Film will live up to the expectations of the filmgoers no matter how much theatres promise the pic will deliver."[31] More recently, Charles Silvers, head of the Film Study Center at the Museum of Modern Art in New York City, described *The Awful Truth* as "one of the nicest of screwball comedies, certainly the best outside of Hawks. It marks something of a synthesis between McCarey's slapstick beginnings and his now-mature romanticism."[32]

In 1940 McCarey reunited his screwball couple from *The Awful Truth* (Cary Grant and Irene Dunne) in another classic of the genre: *My Favorite Wife*. With many parallels between the two (*New Republic* film critic Otis Ferguson even called *My Favorite Wife* a "nonsense-sequel to *The Awful Truth*"[33]), the movie was a major critical and commercial success.

While McCarey both produced and coauthored the story for *My Favorite Wife*, an automobile accident kept him from technically receiving directing credit. Yet, he held production conferences in the hospital before shooting began and was back on the set within "two or three weeks" of the starting date.[34] Thus, the McCarey touch is rather obvious. Bosley Crowther's *New York Times* review of *My Favorite Wife* even spends considerable time on the McCarey nature of the film.[35]

In 1942 McCarey again teamed with Cary Grant to make *Once Upon a Honeymoon*, which co-stars Ginger Rogers. Unfortunately, what begins as a delightful screwball comedy, with Grant and Rogers reworking some tape measure shenanigans, previously used by McCarey in the Laurel & Hardy short subject *Putting Pants on Philip* (1927), soon is bogged down by political questions involving the war.

Late in his career McCarey returned to the genre one final time for *Rally 'Round the Flag Boys!* (1958). While not on a par with his earlier classics, the film is an entertaining look at one post-World War II development in the genre, an attempt to move much of the action to the suburbs. As with Hawks's *Man's Favorite Sport?* (originally planned for Cary Grant but

8. Leo McCarey (left), Irene Dunne, and Alex D'Arcy on the set of *The Awful Truth* (1937). (Photograph courtesy of the Museum of Modern Art/Film Stills Archive.)

ending up with Rock Hudson), McCarey's film is hurt by miscasting (Paul Newman and Joanne Woodward play the central couple). Political intrusions upon the antiheroic world are largely defused, however, by way of reducing them to cartoon-like situations, such as any scene which involves Jack Carson as an army officer.

Like Hawks, McCarey's career showcased his skills in a number of genres, but they were generally in the comedy camp. Besides screwball comedy, he did populist comedy (winning directing and original story Academy Awards for *Going My Way*, 1944), and personality comedy (including the Marx Brothers's greatest and seemingly *only* directed film—*Duck Soup*, 1933). Even when nominally outside the comedy genre camp, as with the still moving melodrama *Make Way for Tomorrow* (1937), or his late career melodramatic love story *An Affair to Remember* (1958, a remake of his *Love Affair*, 1939), McCarey's comic touch was invariably there. (Only in the unfortunate *My Son John*, 1952, was it found wanting.)

Besides never straying far from comedy, McCarey has an antiheroic thread which runs through both his career and his personal life. Unlike Hawks, whose screwball films were a complete parody flip-flop of his adventuresome real life, McCarey's pioneer antiheroic artistry would seem to have been drawn from a very antiheroic real life—a link between life's experiences and one's art which he shared with fellow antiheroic creator James Thurber. (Thurber also wrote a short story which refers to McCarey, although not by name, called "The Man who Corrupted Moonbaum."[36] In fact, three significant antiheroic parallels can be drawn from a comparison of Thurber and McCarey.

First, both artists draw from domestic frustrations with their wives. Of all the antihero creators, Thurber is best known for these "battle of the sexes" portrayals. Thus, his career is a celebration of marital disharmony best showcased in the Mr. and Mrs. Monroe stories:

> Thurber wrote . . . devastating pieces based on his own marriage. He and Althea [the first Mrs. Thurber] were Mr. and Mrs. Monroe, in a series of eight stories published in the *New Yorker* during 1928 and 1929. Every Monroe story was founded on a real incident of their waspish life together. As Thurber wrote his Columbus friend Herman Miller: "The Monroe stories were transcripts, one or two of them varying less than an inch from the actual happenings."[37]

The comic antiheroes in the film work of Leo McCarey suffer the same female frustration that plagues the Thurber male. In McCarey's Laurel & Hardy shorts of the 1920s, and then continuing into his 1930s features, the wife is a definite liability with regard to household harmony. And as with Thurber's real source, McCarey drew this world from personal experience.

Thus, when Peter Bogdanovich interviewed McCarey for the American film Institute's oral history collection, the following comments were made about *The Awful Truth*, a prime example of McCarey's "battle of the sexes":

> *Bogdanovich:* Do you remember how you got the idea for *The Awful Truth*? Was it based on some experiences you'd had with your wife?
>
> *McCarey:* Yes.
>
> *Bogdanovich:* Misunderstandings?
>
> *McCarey:* Yes. It told, in a way, the story of my life, though the few scenes about infidelity, I hasten to add, were *not* auto-biographical—they were imagination only.[38]

Taking the above comparison a step further (female domination), it would seem quite appropriate that both Thurber and McCarey should also have derived their sense of comedy from dominant female family members. Thurber gave his mother "all the credit for everything he was or became, especially his sense of humor."[39] In McCarey's case, it was an aunt—"Sister Mary Benedict, my father's sister, who made a great impression on my life, had a wonderfully rich sense of humor. We were close friends, and I learned from her the magic of a smile."[40] As a final bit of topping to the fact that the comic antihero's world is dominated by women, it seems quite appropriate that Leo McCarey was named for his mother, Leona.[41]

A second trait characteristic of both Thurber and McCarey, as well as of the comic antihero, is general failure at almost every task, be it leisure- or career-oriented. If it had not been for fiction and film, both gentlemen could most likely have looked forward to less than celebrated lives. Thurber underlines this in a letter he wrote a friend, early in his career:

> I write mostly soi-disant humor since I haven't brains enough to write more solid articles and wouldn't if I could. I often worry about my future since I am no doctor and at best but a mean scrivener, but out of all the things one does, from pipe fitting to testing seamless leather belting and from ceramics to statesman-ship, I can do only one thing, even passably, and that is make words and space them between punctuation points.[42]

McCarey suffered under the same type of handicap. He failed in the nightclub business, in a law practice, and in songwriting; by 1946 he had "written more than 1,000 songs, all of them monumental failures—unless you count one mild success, 'Why Do You Sit on Your Patio?,' which netted him two dollars and fifty cents."[43] But the item that buried the law career is easily the most popular antihero story circulating on McCarey; it seems to appear in any McCarey article of any length and goes something like this:

> Months dragged by with no cases. Then one day a big burly fellow walked in. His wife was suing him for a divorce, and he wanted to contest it to avoid paying alimony. She mistreated him, he said unhappily. Leo's heart went out to the big fellow. He took the case.
>
> They were sitting in the courtroom when the wife came in, trailing behind her a bunch of half-starved children. "She came to the stand first," says Leo, reliving it, "and one eye was closed. A little wasp of a woman who looked like Lillian Gish. She told the judge, 'Pardon my halting speech, your honor, but my husband kicked me in the teeth and broke my ribs.' Her children looked at papa and screamed. After about ten minutes of this, the judge looked up frostily and asked, 'Who is defending this guy?' I got up, very dignified, and said, 'Your honor, I would like to ask for a recess so this rat can get another lawyer!' Then I got out of there fast, my client right behind me. I passed the Times Building, running like hell. 'What are you doing, Leo?' a friend yelled. 'Practicing law!' I yelled back, without losing a step."[44]

This has become the stuff of legends; Peter Bogdanovich (who did the McCarey oral history) even extrapolated the scene to open his film on early Hollywood—*Nickelodeon* (1976). The Leo McCarey figure (Ryan O'Neal) even states, "My name is Hal Harrigan but you can call me Leo." Thus, he receives an Irish surname, as well as Leo for a nickname. Bogdanovich closes this episode with "Leo" literally running from court (and an upset client) into a film situation: an independent film company during the Trust War with the Motion Picture Patents Company. Other versions of this story have closed with similar law-to-film runs.

The third analogy between Thurber and McCarey (as well as the comic antihero) is that they are victims of absentmindedness (see also Chapter 6 on absentmindedness and comedy theory) and accidents. Both men seemed to revel in this disjointed state, becoming nearly as famous for these characteristics as their antihero creations. Thurber's accident-proneness might be excused by his poor eyesight (and eventual blindness), but there was no alibi for his absentmindedness: "He tended to wallow in his absentminded dishabille, referring to himself, in print, as looking 'like a slightly ill professor of botany who is also lost.' "[45]

There seem to be no excuses for McCarey. After an apparently normal upbringing, the adult McCarey biography suddenly starts to rank with the best story of any jinxed antihero this side of a State Farm casualty report. Few available articles on McCarey neglect to deal with this character trait. Thus, Pete Martin called him "the film industry's leading physical Humpty Dumpty,"[46] while Sidney Carroll wrote an article entitled "Everything Happens to McCarey: During those sparse times when he isn't breaking his valuable neck, Leo McCarey does direct some extraordinary pictures."[47]

Among those accident-prone and absent-minded McCarey stories, two are consistently repeated. Both are well on their way to achieving the legendary status that the McCarey courtroom scene has now achieved. The first example, which Carroll calls "the beginning of his experiments in the field of self destruction"[48] took place in the late teens, when McCarey had just entered law school. On his way to class, he walked into what he assumed was an elevator. In actuality it was merely an elevator shaft, and he took a rather nasty fall, breaking both his legs. However, McCarey was to achieve more compensation here than he usually granted his future antiheroes: his $5,000 insurance policy put him through law school.

The second often-quoted McCarey story, and almost the ultimate McCarey accident, was to occur many years later in 1940. It was the aforementioned automobile accident prior to the production of *My Favorite Wife* and best exemplifies the Sidney Carroll description of McCarey "as an artist in the art of self-demolition."[49] Out driving with his friend and writer Gene Fowler,

> McCarey made a wrong turn and turned the car on top of Fowler and himself. When they were found, thus bedded down under a couple of fenders, the rescue party took one look at McCarey and decided that an ambulance would be an unnecessary expense to his about-to-be-bereaved family. They phoned for a more suitable vehicle. McCarey rode to the hospital in that more suitable vehicle—a hearse.
>
> He and Fowler are whole again now, after two years of recuperation, but a short time after the surgeons had reassembled McCarey in much the same manner that one puts together a prefabricated house, they discovered that they had screwed one of his arms on the wrong way. McCarey had to go back to the hospital for what he called "re-takes on the left arm."[50]

Beyond these parallels with fellow antiheroic artist Thurber, McCarey managed to add still another real tie between the private person and his public art. That is, as Chapter 3 demonstrated, the big city—inevitably New York City—was a danger zone which both contributed to and symbolized many of the frustrations of the antihero. Celebrated antiheroic humorist and close McCarey friend H. Allen Smith (author of such books as *Low Man on a Totem Pole* and *Life in a Putty Knife Factory*) has chronicled the director's "contemptuous attitude toward New York City" and the "McCareyesque [antiheroic] method of demonstrating that contempt."[51] Allen describes a McCarey who, by utilizing Grand Central Station, underground taxistands, and basement entrances to his hotel (where he would then stay put), would never be technically outside in New York City. This is hardly unlike the classic Thurber essay, "A Box to Hide In," whose title so nicely describes one alternative to the antiheroic dilemma.[52]

McCarey followed a similar approach with Hawks to comedy and film production. First, there was the propensity for physical comedy, sometimes drawing from the silent comedy material he constructed for Charlie Chase and Laurel & Hardy (as well as his own slapstick-conscious private life). Late in life he observed: "My experience in silent films influenced me very much."[53] Chaplin was his comedy idol, as well as a good friend. "One of the most precious souvenirs I have is a fan letter Chaplin sent me in which he congratulates me on my work with Laurel & Hardy and predicts a beautiful future for me."[54] Thus, whether it is the Laurel & Hardy-like escapades of a very drunken Charles Laughton and Charles Ruggles in *Ruggles of Red Gap*, as they attempt to sneak quietly into the house past a domineering wife, or Cary Grant's *The Awful Truth* problems with inanimate objects, such as an oversized hat, a sometimes upright chair, and a slammed door, McCarey's silent comedy roots are constantly on display. Not surprisingly, "McCarey doesn't count on words to put a scene over, and he uses as few of them in a movie as he possibly can. 'Do it visually' is his motto."[55] Thus, even though he usually worked on every script (credited or uncredited), as was the case with Hawks, McCarey's visual approach to screen comedy took precedence over the verbal. For example, *New York Times* critic Bosley Crowther's ecstatic review of *The Awful Truth* observes:

> Its comedy is almost purely physical . . . with only here and there a lone gag to interrupt the pure poetry of motion, yet its unapologetic return to the fundamentals of comedy seems, we repeat, original and daring . . . a comedy in which speech is subsidiary . . . a picture liberally strewn with authentic audience laughs which appear to be just as they were in the days of Fatty Arbuckle.[56]

Second, McCarey also tended to improvise while shooting and was probably Hollywood's most celebrated example of this approach during the sound era. Thus, film critic and historian Andrew Sarris stated: "Leo McCarey came to represent a principle of improvisation in the history of American film," while film critic Robin Wood entitled his revisionist essay on *Once Upon a Honeymoon*—"Democracy and Shpontanuity."[57]

This improvisational approach was no doubt aided by McCarey's ability to enthuse his performers with his on-the-set storytelling, establishing an improvised situation. McCarey himself noted the significance of these story sessions: "I spent a lot of time discussing the scene with the people."[58] This ability was not hurt by the fact he was a delightful man with whom to work. Ingrid Bergman found him "a terribly funny man—the jokes that went on, and the gaiety! He always had a piano on the set; he used to play the piano while people were changing the lights or rehearsing. He was a very easy-going man."[59] Irene Dunne called him a "dear, sweet man" who deserves more recognition.[60] Before the production of *The Awful Truth* a concerned Ralph Bellamy (who would receive an Academy Award nomination for his supporting role) approached the director about the absence of a script:

> When I went to Leo's house, he met me with his perpetual gleeful grin and dancing eyes. . . . He said nothing much about the story or the part. He just joshed and said not to worry—we'd have lots of fun, but there wasn't any script. . . . There never was a script. Each morning Leo would appear with a small piece of brown wrapping paper more often than not, and throw us lines and business. . . . We were quickly won over to him and had the fun he'd promise. And we made the film in six weeks, a record for that kind of picture.[61]

McCarey's storytelling (this on-the-set seeding of an improvisational setting) went well beyond being merely fun with which to work. He seems to have been pleasantly overpowering with his storytelling mix of both verbal and mime skills:

> McCarey had a habit of dominating every film he directed, in ways that were spontaneous, graceful, and various. Sometimes he did so much improvising at the rehearsal stage and even on the sound stage that the actors were never sure exactly what was happening. Sometimes his constant pantomimes in the course of his conversation were infectious enough to show up on film being performed by the actors. (Many of Stan Laurel's familiar mannerisms, in fact, were originally familiar mannerisms of McCarey's. The director had a "Let's go have a beer" gesture and an "Anybody want to play tennis?" gesture that friends and associates haven't shaken even yet.)[62]

H. Allen Smith remembers one visit with McCarey when the storytelling was so diverting that the identity of another visitor was hardly noted. Later Smith realized he had missed talking to Ingrid Bergman![63]

There is no doubt some off-the-cuff shooting occurred (the oral history is somewhat contradictory on this point, probably due to the director's poor health).[64] But the essential McCarey method would seem best described in a

Bogdanovich summary (a respiratory disease made speech difficult for McCarey): "What you would do is work with the actors on the side, run through the scene and add things as you went along [writing it down]."[65] That is, the improvisation generally would take place just prior to the shooting.

Third, improvisation plays right into Hollywood in-house humor and actors drawing upon themselves, and McCarey was no exception. One of the more celebrated scenes in *The Awful Truth* provides an illustration of improvisation and exposure of the real person rather than the actor. McCarey, after discovering Irene Dunne was a mediocre piano player (he had come upon her sitting at a piano on the set attempting to read "Home on the Range" sheet music) and Ralph Bellamy was a poor singer (though he knew the lyrics of "Home on the Range"), the director requested:

> "Irene, play it just the way you're doing it now. And Ralph, you belt it out with loud Oklahoma pride. It's a comedy, you know."
>
> The camera was set up . . . Leo said "Roll it," and "Action!" and Irene hammered out the sheet music and I [Bellamy] threw back my head and slaughtered "Home on the Range."
>
> We finished and no one said "Cut!"
>
> Irene and I looked up and Leo was under the camera, so doubled up with laughter he couldn't speak. Finally he said, "Print it!"
>
> After several similar episodes in which dialogue was by Leo, seemingly out of the air, we finished the [first] day.[66]

Fourth, McCarey was able to exercise tight control over his productions in four ways. First, his improvisational philosophy always had granted him a great deal of freedom. Second, coupled with this (like Hawks), he shot very little coverage of each scene, preferring to "edit" in the camera, leaving few alternate ways for the footage to be assembled. Third, his reputation as a master of comedy allowed him to become an independent in the 1930s, sometimes resulting in nearly carte blanche situations. For example, Columbia studio (producers of *The Awful Truth*) head Harry Cohn "had no idea how the story had developed . . . [but] he had complete confidence in Leo. Leo had that kind of respect and record in the business."[67] Fourth, McCarey was also capable of using trickery to maintain control. When the rigid line of craft demarcation would raise its head in the studio period, McCarey would continue his multiple tasks but neglect to take credit for them.[68]

Trickery could, of course, take additional courses. For example, writer/director Garson Kanin (credited with direction for *My Favorite*

Wife) has described at length McCarey's mesmerizing verbal control not of actors but rather of producers and studio chiefs to accept his project ideas:

> McCarey possessed a rare comic intelligence. He could create hilarious situations, and imaginatively, almost inexhaustibly, develop those situations. He was not a writer, but he was a superlative talker, and in a time and place [Hollywood of the 1930s] where there was a paucity of readers and a plethora of listeners, talkers were more effective (and more successful than writers).[69]

Bing Crosby and David Butler expand further on both McCarey's storytelling abilities and production trickery. And while the film in question is not a screwball comedy, the comments flesh out the Kanin story and display just how typical this sort of McCarey action was:

> He was tremendously inventive—a great storyteller—and in those days when the director had an idea for a picture, he'd have to tell it to the heads of the studios and get their approval. The story he told the studio heads for *Going My Way* bore no resemblance whatever to the story he finally shot. . . . The production department always demanded 20 or 30 written pages in advance of shooting. So Leo would dictate reams of stuff which he had no intention of using.[70]

McCarey the man would seem to have been every bit as entertaining as the antiheroic figures he gave to the world of film. Moreover, the title of a rare McCarey excursion into the realm of essays (an article largely taken up with finding an ending for *The Awful Truth*) might double as a McCareyesque definition of screwball comedy: "Comedy and a Touch of Cuckoo."[71]

PRESTON STURGES

While Hawks and McCarey were both groundbreakers and perpetuators of screwball comedy, creating examples of the genre over many years, Preston Sturges made several classic screwball comedies at the close of the genre's initial movement (early 1940s), examples which in many ways stretched the basics to the comic maximum. These basics include strong women, antiheroic men (and a matching comically absurd world based on chance), a propensity for slapstick, and in-house parody of both self and Hollywood.

The background Sturges brought to screwball comedy also represented an overview of the genre. Screwball comedy, as mentioned earlier, sometimes represented a marriage of the silent comedy director and the eastern scriptwriter (whose background was often the newspaper world or writing for Broadway, such as that of Ben Hecht who excelled at both). While the director remained dominant in the genre and frequently greatly assisted in script preparation (without credit), the spoken word was not to be denied. And its greatest genre showcase is the work of Sturges, an eastern playwright who was also a student of silent film comedy. This resulted in Sturges being a pioneer in the then-unique situation of being both the credited writer and the director of a film.

Sturges's biography was schizophrenically appropriate for his position as a leader in the art of screwball comedy. He divided much of his youth between a European-based bohemian mother (the follower and friend of Isadora Duncan who gifted the dancer with the infamous scarf) and a Midwestern-based father of a decidedly business background. After the divorce, Sturges's mother would provide him with an eclectic series of stepfathers and a "wandering expatriate childhood that gave him an early taste of life's instability."[72] Sturges frequently found this cultured world rather smothering, but it left an indelible mark on his later films, interspersing frantic wanderings, eccentric characters, and dominate females. The practical, stable home of his father was generally preferred by the boy. This, too, is reflected in his films, where traditional, even Capra-like, values are sometimes spouted—though only to be quickly satirized.

Like McCarey, Sturges's life was rather antiheroic in nature. In fact, James Curtis's excellent biography of the director is even entitled *Between Flops*, a self-description once penned by Sturges.[73] Also like McCarey, his frustrations still had a decidedly comic side. For example, he too was a frustrated songwriter, having penned such "classics" as "Asia Minor Blues"—certainly on a par with McCarey's "Why Do You Sit on Your Patio?" His eclectic interests ranged from designing a flying machine (part helicopter, part airplane), to inventing a kissproof lipstick. Every great success, such as his one early hit Broadway play, *Strictly Dishonorable*, would be matched by several failures. His film-directing career followed the same pattern, meteoric rise and fall.

After the early comedy successes of *The Great McGinty* (1940) and *Christmas in July* (1940), Sturges made one of the greatest screwball comedies of all time—*The Lady Eve* (1941), which topped the *New York Times* "Ten Best" list for the year. In the next three years he would make five more films, two of which were major screwball comedy additions: *The Palm Beach Story* (1942) and *The Miracle of Morgan Creek* (1944). A third film, *Sullivan's Travels* (1942), eventually falls from the category because of its ultimate message nature. Sturges would make several more films in the next few years, including the radically different yet quasi-screwball comedies, *The Sin of Harold Diddlebock* (1947) and *Unfaithfully Yours* (1949). But an unfortunate partnership with fellow eclectically minded Howard Hughes and film subject choices "remote from the tastes of their time" all but negated any contemporary impact of his post-1944 work.[74]

The four commonalities applied to Hawks and McCarey are generally true of Sturges, too, with the exception of improvisation. First, physical comedy was extremely important to him. At the height of his career Bosley Crowther analyzed Sturges's work in a *New York Times* article entitled "When Satire and Slapstick Meet." Film critic and scriptwriter Frank Nugent's 1945 *Variety* essay interpretation of Sturges was entitled "Genius with a Slapstick."[75]

More importantly, the Nugent piece includes Sturges's own laws of what govern film box office, a list composed in 1934—a year now considered the starting point of screwball comedy—in the director's early Hollywood days:

> 1. A pretty girl is better than an ugly one. 2. A leg is better than an arm. 3. A bedroom is better than a living room. 4. An arrival is better than a departure. 5. A birth is better than a death. 6. A chase is better than a chat. 7. A dog is better than a landscape. 8. A kitten is better than a dog. 9. A baby is better than a kitten. 10. A kiss is better than a baby. 11. A pratfall is better than anything.[76]

Author Nugent immediately concluded at this point that "Sturges owes all his success, or nearly all, to his strict observance of Law 11.[77] While this is an overstatement (no one wrote wittier dialogue), Sturges had such a gift for orchestrating physical comedy with verbal humor that playwright Alexander King aptly called him "The Toscanini of the pratfall."[78]

Sturges's dialogue, which he once defined as "the bright things you would like to have said except that you didn't think of them in time,"[79] is, however, more apt to operate independently of the visual than in Hawks. That is, Hawks once observed, "I don't use funny lines. They're not funny unless you see them."[80] For example, in *Bringing Up Baby* Professor Grant finds himself all but kidnapped to a Connecticut estate by madcap Hepburn. Once there his clothes are removed and he is forced to explore the setting in a lacy nightgown. Cornered for an explanation, the frustrated and feminine-attired Grant suddenly leaps into the air, explaining, "I went gay all of a sudden." Grant's observation is not intrinsically funny, but coupled with the visual it is hilarious. (For McCarey, the accent was even more on the visual.)

In Sturges's work, dialogue is more likely to be funny (as the quotes which open several chapters of this book demonstrate) regardless of the visual. And conversely, the Sturges comic visuals exist just as independently, such as the honeymoon scene in *The Lady Eve*, the land yacht chase in *Sullivan's Travels*, and the opening race to the church in *The Palm Beach Story*.

Though dialogue is probably of more importance to a Sturges screwball comedy than to one by Hawks or McCarey, there is no denying the significance in his work of both slapstick and the revitalization he brought to an old tradition. For example, in 1944 the *New York Times* credited him with restoring "to the art of the cinema a certain graphic velocity which it has missed since the turmoils of Mack Sennett's zanies went out with the talking film."[81] (Sturges's stock company of regulars included silent comedy veteran Chester Conklin, an original member of Sennett's Keystone Kops and early supporting player to Charlie Chaplin. His later featured roles included the mechanic in Chaplin's *Modern Times*, 1936.) Moreover, Sturges forever footnoted his interest in silent comedy in a big way when he opened *The Sin of Harold Diddleback* (starring Harold Lloyd) with the closing climactic football game from Lloyd's 1925 classic *The Freshman*. The rest of the film focused, in part, on exploring Lloyd's 1920s go-getter character twenty-odd years later.

Celebrated film critic Manny Farber has even further tied Sturges to silent comedy by metaphorically linking his dialogue to the fast pacing of an earlier era. In his "Preston Sturges: Success in the Movies" essay, written with W. S. Poster, he observes:

> Sturges perversely thought up a new type of dialogue by which the audience is fairly showered with words. The result was paradoxically to speed up his movies rather than slow them down, because he concocted a special, jerky, spluttering form of talk that is the analogue of the old, silent-picture firecracker tempo.[82]

Farber further expands the hypothesis that Sturges's work represents the spirit and summation of what had preceded him both in silent comedy, as well as improving on earlier sound comedy: "Sturges was the only legitimate heir of the early American film, combining its various methods, adding new perspectives and developing the whole in a form suitable to a talking picture."[83]

The Farber position is a brilliant reading of the comically juggernaut speed of the Sturges film. It is remiss only in not noting other earlier precedents, especially those by Howard Hawks and Gregory LaCava. Sturges quite often took the phenomenon to its ultimate comic extreme, but Hawks and LaCava sped up things considerably in such films as *His Girl Friday* and *My Man Godfrey*. In both cases there are even direct dialogue references to this speed. For example, at one point in *His Girl Friday* Cary Grant speaks so rapidly that Rosalind Russell begins to verbalize the accelerated mumble-jumble associated with an auctioneer, topping this speed-speaking diatribe with "Sold American." In fact, Hawks is generally credited today with the concept of overlapping dialogue. Thus, while Farber's stance is most appropriate for Sturges, it is also applicable to a number of other screwball comedy artists.

Second, while Sturges did not improvise, as did many of his screwball comedy directing peers, his then unique status as the credited writer/director eliminated some of the need; the original script was already one hundred percent his own. He also had a standing stock company of players for whom he wrote similar parts in picture after picture. (Sturges character actors also received more screen time than the typical supporting player.) Moreover, as early Sturges biographer James Ursini noted, some of the Sturges stock company had ties with the director stretching back to his 1930s scriptwriting days.[84] For example, Sturges regulars William Demarest, Franklin Pangborn, and Luis Alberni were all in the screwball *Easy Living* (1937), which was scripted by Sturges but directed by Mitchell Leisen. Indeed, Sturges films were constantly populated with familiar screwball players, from regulars like Pangborn and Eric Blore, to the special casting of a Demarest in *The Lady Eve*, or a Diana Lynn in *The Miracle of Morgan Creek* (whose role was similar to one she had in Billy Wilder's *The Major and the Minor*, 1942). Consequently, this further accented the summing up nature of Sturges's association with the genre and made improvisation less necessary.

Still, as with earlier screwball comedy sets, a party-like atmosphere frequently prevailed:

> Sturges never closed his stages. He welcomed visitors, anyone interested in watching him work. Between shots [on *The Lady Eve*], he kept Harry Rosenthal off to one side playing the piano. The noisier and more confused the environment, the better he seemed to like it.[85]

Joel McCrea (*Sullivan's Travels* and *The Palm Beach Story*) observed, "I never worked with one [director] where I had so much fun. I really felt like I'd do it for nothing."[86] And while Sturges had a propensity for keeping his dialogue as written, script changes were not unheard of:

> I agreed with very few directors when I was merely writing. They argued tremendously, and sometimes they lost out. I look upon them now as brave fellows who went down with their colors flying. I don't, as a director, film a scene exactly as the writer—who was myself—wrote it.[87]

In fact, *Miracle of Morgan Creek* star Eddie Bracken revealed to this author at least one moment of classic set looseness when he surprised Sturges by directing for two days (Sturges was tied up in meetings). This included the pivotal "morning after" shot of Trudy Kockenlocker (Betty Hutton) returning to pick up poor Norval Jones (Bracken), who is waiting huddled in the theater entrance.[88] Sturges liked what he saw (especially the one-shot take of the aforementioned scene), and kept it in the finished film.

Third, Sturges's screwball comedies are frequently full of Hollywood in-house humor, with actors often playing variations of themselves and/or the director (as already demonstrated with Hawks and McCarey). This can be taken even to the point of parody—parody which can even address the genre itself, such as Sturges's examination of the screwball comedy's happy ending by beginning *The Palm Beach Story* with just such an ending (see Chapter 6).

As McCarey and Hawks parodied the romantic leading man image of Grant, Sturges parodied the screen personas of Henry Fonda and Joel McCrea:

> as with Fonda, Sturges played with the screen image of McCrea—that of the strong, silent, muscular, and uncompromising hero. The result is that the self-righteous poses he strikes, coupled with his innocence, seem all the more humorous.[89]

(In a Capra populist film these same values, which apply equally to a Capra favorite like Gary Cooper, would eventually be used for a serious message. Screwball comedy, however, maintains a focus on the humorous.)

Other examples of Sturges's Hollywood in-house humor would include using Toto as a name for Sig Arno's pet-dog-like character in *The Palm Beach Story* (see Chapter 3), or having Brian Donlevy play the cameo role of Governor McGinty in *The Miracle of Morgan's Creek*. (Donlevy had played the title role of the sometimes governor in Sturges's earlier *The Great McGinty*.)

Sturges's delineation of character has a richness which can be read carefully at several levels. For example, the fundamental outline of McCrea's role in *The Palm Beach Story* is full of the antiheroic frustrations expected in the screwball comedy male, such as being a victim both of society and a strong woman. Then, with the tailored casting of McCrea, the aforementioned parody effect doubles the comedy to which a diminutive Mr. Peepers type would have been limited. Finally, Sturges still manages to personalize parody by creating a character which seems to have many biographical ties to the director. Sturges's biographer Ursini hypothesized that McCrea's part, the frustrated inventor Tom Jeffers, possibly represented the director "commenting on the impracticality of some of his own designs and inventions. . . . Tom does represent another facet of Sturges and may indicate what the director was like during his years of idle invention in the late '20s."[90] Moreover, Tom's inability to support his wife in the style to which she was accustomed is more than just a little reminiscent of Sturges's relationship to second wife Eleanor Post Hutton, heiress to the C. W. Post cereal fortune. Also, the sexual skirmishes Tom has with Mary Astor's free-spirited character and her circling comic effect of a foreign husband (Sig Arno) are also similar to the life and lifestyle of Sturges's own mother.

Richness of character delineation does not need, however, to limit itself to seemingly obscure information (the director's background). *The Palm Beach Story* character of John D. Hackensacker III (played by Rudy Vallee) is a case in point. Vallee was the hit of the film, a hit seemingly based upon two factors. First, as was typical, Sturges tailored the role to the performer.[91] Thus, much of the humor plays off the natural pomposity which is Rudy Vallee. Or, as Sturges observed when he witnessed Vallee get unintentional laughs in a minor "relatively straight" film role: "This guy is funny and doesn't know it!"[92]

In addition to the parody Sturges was able to generate just by tapping the Vallee presence, additional comedy was provoked by making his character a wealthy romantic who sings (Vallee originally won fame and fortune crooning such songs as "I'm Just a Vagabond Lover"), who is tight with his money (synonymous with Vallee) and who mixes a special interest in women with old-fashioned ideas (another character tie to Vallee). The humor becomes more tongue-in-cheek when Claudette Colbert observes: "Oh, you have a nice little voice." (His voice had once been the rage of the nation.) And Vallee's response continues in the same comic understated vein: "Thank you. I used to sing in college." (While attending Yale, Vallee had been a member of the Yale Collegians which toured vaudeville, though his specialty was the saxophone.) When Colbert next asks if he had sung with a mandolin, Vallee comically replies, "I couldn't play it around the house." (While the mandolin was not his instrument, it is still closely tied to the 1920s collegiate image with which Vallee remains closely identified.)

The Vallee comedy topper of toppers, however, and perhaps the greatest parody of the man, arrives with his moonlight serenade of Colbert. There is Vallee on the lawn—with as much musical accompaniment as his old orchestra days—singing "Good Night Sweetheart," an old Vallee hit song which he actually introduced to America. Unbeknownst to Vallee, Colbert's estranged husband McCrea is already in her room making much better use of Vallee's music. What a comic affront to a former "vagabond lover"!

The Vallee role is popular for a second reason: John D. Hackensacker is a parody of John D. Rockefeller. They have similar names, bank accounts, sources of wealth (oil), and ties with a dime (Hackensacker limits his tips to that amount; Rockefeller was famous for giving dimes to strangers).

Fourth, Sturges also had a greater degree of production control than was the norm during the studio era. His status as a credited writer/director was unique and saved him from the kind of production mischief in which McCarey needed to involve himself. Sturges's trailblazer status here cannot be underestimated. Calling him a crusader, Frank Nugent observed:

> What he is trying to overthrow—using slapstick instead of a lance—is the old Hollywood theory that picture-making is a collective business, that a dozen minds all bumping together are necessarily better than one good one working alone.[93]

Sturges's production life at Paramount, his home studio since the early 1930s, was not without friction. When B. G. "Buddy" DeSylva replaced William LeBaron as head of production at the studio in 1941, potential storm clouds were being seeded. LeBaron was a relaxed former writer who had been producing for years. He also knew comedy and how to work with eccentric comedy geniuses. (He was a friend of W. C. Fields—no small task in and of itself—and produced a number of Fields's films.)[94] He was also the man who broke precedent to give Sturges his chance at directing. In contrast, DeSylva ran a more disciplined operation (discipline seldom being a term connected with comedy), with production experience primarily in musicals, and his personality was not quite as genial as LeBaron's.[95] Sturges was established, however, and continued success kept him safe for a time. But by late 1943 differences had mounted, and Sturges attempted to negotiate "the closest he could come to final cut [a film's final edited version—how it will appear in commercial release] in the days when such an agreement was unheard of."[96] It was unsuccessful and Sturges left Paramount for the more profitable open market.

Ironically, Sturges's move to greater freedom, unlike moves previously taken by Hawks and McCarey, would be a failure. Initially he formed a partnership with Howard Hughes, but they had critical differences over *The Sin of Harold Diddlebock*, which was briefly released in 1947 only to be pulled from distribution by Hughes. The film was re-released in 1950 as *Mad Wednesday* after Hughes had reedited and shortened it. As might be expected, several other Sturges-Hughes projects never even came close to fruition.

Interestingly enough, both Hawks and McCarey had had previous critical differences with Hughes on joint projects. Hawks had left the production of the controversial Jane Russell sex western, *The Outlaw* (1943, but filmed in 1941). McCarey's experience, anticipating Sturges's much more closely, resulted in McCarey being largely inactive between his productions of *My Favorite Wife* (1940) and *Once Upon a Honeymoon* (1942). However, both Hawks and McCarey went on to additional critical and commercial successes, while Sturges did not, though *Unfaithfully Yours* (written, directed, and produced by Sturges for Twentieth Century-Fox) is now considered a masterpiece. (At the time the film had no box office, although some reviews praised it.) A combination black comedy/screwball comedy, it chronicles the murderous fantasies of a jealous, older husband—largely inspired by Sturges's own jealousy of his much younger mistress Frances Ramsden (who played Harold Lloyd's much younger girlfriend/wife in *The Sin of Harold Diddlebock*). Moreover, the husband's part was "that of Sturges himself. The mannerisms, the endearments, the phrases, the attitudes, the rages—they all were his."[97]

While the late 1940s audience was not yet ready for such a dark screwball comedy, it was a valuable genre work, and the 1984 remake of the same name was much more commercially successful. Directed by Howard Zieff and starring Dudley Moore (Rex Harrison had played the lead in the original), the accent was more screwball than black: the original had three fantasy murders of the wife, the remake only one. Moreover, Moore's style here is in the broader, more physical comedy of a half-pint Cary Grant, from Moore's phenomenal range of facial expressions, to a gait which moved *Time* film critic Richard Schickel to suggest "the Ministry of Silly Walks should declare him a national treasure."[98]

Sturges's undoing was no doubt as much a result of his unique individualism as was his success. Notable filmmaker René Clair, director of the fantasy screwball comedy classic *I Married a Witch* (1942), which Sturges produced, observed: "Preston is like a man from the Italian Renaissance: he wants to do everything at once. If he could slow down, he would be great; he has an enormous gift, and he should be one of our leading creators."[99] Ironically, like so many of his antiheroic heroes, his ultimate career undoing might simply be explained through "Sturges's fatalism, or more specifically, his repeated emphasis on the importance of 'Chance . . .' " in his film stories.[100] Just as Sturges was the only screwball comedy director to make a movie about a film director, the helter-skelter speed at which his and other stories in the genre unfold seems close to his personal life-style. And while movies are forever, everyday flesh is not.

GREGORY LA CAVA

Gregory La Cava follows next as an outstanding screwball comedy director, largely through the significance of *My Man Godfrey* (1936). Though associated with a number of screwball or quasi-screwball comedies (*She Married Her Boss*, 1935; *Fifth Avenue Girl*, 1939; *Unfinished Business*, 1941; *Lady in a Jam*, 1942), it is *My Man Godfrey* which rates the special kudos. As noted in Chapter 1, during the 1930s this was the film sometimes seen as the starting point of screwball comedy. And though the genre's roots are now pushed back to 1934, nothing produced that year can match the sheer madcap exuberance of *Godfrey*.

After McCarey's silent comedy creation of Laurel & Hardy, no other screwball comedy director has stronger antiheroic film roots than La Cava. He was one of two cartoonists at America's first cartoon studio, Raoul Barré.[101] The studio's first work, produced and released by Edison (1915-16), is now celebrated for its surrealism.[102] La Cava was soon hired by newspaper magnate William Randolph Hearst for his pioneer animation company International Film Service, a firm gauged both to capitalize on and to publicize Hearst's many popular comic strips. La Cava was made production chief of the studio and animated films of such classic newspaper comic strips as *Krazy Kat, Happy Hooligan,* and *The Katzenjammer Kids* were the result.

Strips such as these were in the forefront of the American popular culture evolution of the comic antihero.[103] Prior to this unique work in early animation, La Cava had also been an art student under "Robert Henry, who . . . was one of the forerunners of modern art."[104] Thus, the antiheroic traits La Cava would later bring to screwball comedy were well grounded in two vanguard experiences in twentieth-century change.

Besides the general antiheroic spirit which pervades his screwball comedies, there are occasional footnotes to these pivotal comic strips. For example, it is difficult to watch the delightfully comic brat of a child in *She Married Her Boss* (Edith Fellows) and not be reminded of Rudolph Dirks's comically outrageous *Katzenjammer Kids*, which La Cava first brought to the screen in 1917. Like her comic strip predecessors, Fellows's performance is cartoon-like, from kicking a toy piano to biting her father (Melvyn Douglas). Moreover, the same comically brattish child can be found in Carole Lombard's *My Man Godfrey* role the following year. Though older, Lombard forever plays the wacky child, with her out-of-control bed-jumping and her tuneful rendition of "Godfrey Loves Me." In *Lady in a Jam* Jane Garland plays another tough nut of a child—the world-weary little cowgirl "Strawberry," forever taking bribes to leave when Ralph Bellamy attempts to court Irene Dunne. And *Unfinished Business* finds another adult playing the child in the guise of Robert Montgomery's frequently inebriated Tommy Duncan. Though softer than the previously highlighted cartoon-like children, Tommy is just as surreal: he hides under the bed from "purple things" (more conventional drunks would have pink elephants), and he has a toy black cat on wheels named Tobie that he keeps in a cabinet.

Another not-to-be-avoided cartoon footnote is the comic close highlight of *She Married Her Boss*, where several characters throw bricks at symbols of rigidity—store window mannequins. Throwing bricks was the comedy cornerstone of George Herriman's Krazy Kat (see Chapter 2), which La Cava also brought to the screen in the teens. The ongoing Krazy Kat premise had Kat loving Ignatz Mouse, while Mouse forever rejected this romance by creasing Krazy's head with a brick. But Kat never gets Ignatz's "hint." In fact, Kat reads the action as a sign of affection! (In *My Man Godfrey* another store-window-breaking scene is described as having taken place the night of the scavenger hunt. Moreover, Lombard's *My Man Godfrey* ability to interpret a William Powell-administered socking as a declaration of love is very much in the tunnel-love tradition of Krazy Kat—only Lombard eventually claims her prize.) In the 1920s La Cava worked on two-reel comedies for Johnny Hines, a silent comedian whose films are now remembered for their speed and a "certain appetite for the whimsically improbable."[105] While La Cava had not seriously planned to enter motion pictures, the Hines work seems an appropriate transition to live action film.

In 1924 La Cava moved to Famous Players (Paramount) and was eventually given the opportunity to direct features by William Le Baron.[106] This is the same Le Baron who later allowed Preston Sturges the then-unique opportunity to be a credited writer-director.

La Cava later directed and produced the W. C. Fields films *So's Your Old Man* (1926) and *Running Wild* (1927, from a story by La Cava). This La Cava-Fields contact is important for three reasons. First, the two men were kindred spirits. The comedian's grandson, Ronald J. Fields, observed of the friends: "The two loved playing golf together and gambling, but most of all they loved drinking and arguing [over comedy]."[107] It is this type of friendship and life-style, so important to the making of his later screwball comedies, which inspired the description of La Cava: "He is said to love the 'screwball type' both in life and on the screen."[108]

Second, though La Cava and Fields argued about humor, both their basic approaches to what would now be labeled comedy theory had strong roots in antiheroic comedy and the comic strips, from the aforementioned La Cava material to Fields's pivotal association with J. P. McEvoy's stage production of *The Comic Supplement*. In fact, the comic strip is the ongoing focus of *The Comic Supplement*—which is, after all, what the title is taken from.

The Comic Supplement of 1925 (originally copyrighted in 1924) seems to showcase strongly Fields's influence. It also retains the special-effect, light-show transition of the family (with Fields as the father) to cartoonland.[109] But now, instead of an immediate meeting of the family, the review opens with a fast-dancing chorus in brilliant comic strip colors: "suddenly turning their backs to the audience are discovered to be a chorus of well known comic supplement characters, Mutt and Jeff, Barney Google, Jiggs [of *Bringing Up Father*], etc."[110] These were additional comics in the vanguard of the evolving antiheroic movement. Not surprisingly, La Cava had drawn "some of the early Mutt and Jeff [animated] cartoons."[111]

The joint work of La Cava and Fields displays nicely their comic strip common ground (as well as the antiheroic tendencies of Fields's own copyrighted stage material), with its difficult wives and bratty children. Fields's position in *Running Wild* was not unlike, however, the role of der Captain in *The Katzenjammer Kids*, in that he had to play surrogate father to an unruly youngster as well as avoid the rolling-pin philosophy of a wife not far removed from die Mama. (Fields's view of his own long-estranged wife was hardly positive, either.)

Like Fields, La Cava's solo work is full of comically warring married couples, from the cartoon-like relationship of Mr. and Mrs. Bullock (Alice Brady and Eugene Pallette) in *My Man Godfrey* to the auto camp couple encountered by Irene Dunne and Patric Knowles in *Lady in a Jam*. (The latter film also has the ultimate man-eating female, Cactus Kate [Queenie Vassar], who pulls a shotgun as quickly as Maggie of *Bringing Up Father* pulls a rolling pin.) *Unfinished Business* has a veritable parade of such couples marching by Irene Dunne and Robert Montgomery. When the same film occasionally showcases an apparently counterbalancing happy couple, La Cava cannot resist the comic qualifier. For example, when a happy husband explains, "Marriage is a game," Montgomery asks, "What do you play it with?"

Third, like Fields, La Cava was fiercely independent and did not easily take supervision. During the late 1920s and early 1930s this meant La Cava frequently moved from one studio to another, though there was no question that he was a good filmmaker. But recognition of his cinema greatness, as with Fields's, would finally arrive later in the 1930s. In fact, period criticism sometimes credited Frank Capra and La Cava as being the greatest directors of the time.[112]

Earlier in the decade, however, La Cava had found himself visiting a psychiatrist.[113] Marital problems, disinterest in work, extra partying—all led to his seeking help. Analysis was a revelation for La Cava. He found his problems were based in a childhood "inferiority complex," when his hair was kept in "long blond curls and he was dressed very tastily in what they then called a Lord Fauntleroy suit."[114] (After his recovery, it was LeBaron who again gave him the opportunity to direct.)

These decidedly antiheroic revelations by a director now associated with the most antiheroic of genres forever sold La Cava on being a student of psychiatry. Thus, as the Lombard quote which opens the chapter proclaims, as well as inspiring the chapter title—"My Man Gregory was the keeper of the asylum in which the lunatics frolicked through *My Man Godfrey*."[115] But this job description could well be applied to all his screwball comedies. The sign which Claudette Colbert hung on the back of his *She Married Her Boss* director's chair—"Dr. Lucius La Cava, Dangerous Ward"[116]—soon became part of his identity. (Lombard would later relate how "He always has the name 'Dr. Lucius La Cava' printed on the back of his director's chair."[117]

La Cava had a definite psychiatric approach to his film work. That is, when Lombard observed that "Gregory went around psycho-analyzing people like me," she was not describing an occasional act by the director.[118] Numerous period articles refer to his interest in the subject, and a La Cava-authored story on Claudette Colbert actually lists his battery of thirty introvert/extrovert questions.[119] Nothing would seem more appropriate for a genre which often focuses on both mental eccentricity (including psychiatrists) and the personal idiosyncrasies of its players. Fittingly, La Cava's last screwball comedy, *Lady in a Jam*, has a psychiatrist (Patric Knowles) trying to cure Irene Dunne of her zaniness. And even more fittingly, the female patient ends up driving the male doctor bonkers.

The four commonalities applied to Hawks, McCarey, and Sturges are generally applicable to La Cava, too. First, as already noted, his films and film characters frequently assumed a cartoon-strip physical comedy intensity. Not as pronounced as in the work of Hawke and McCarey, La Cava's work was in the slapstick punctuation tradition for which Sturges later became famous. Bits of sharp dialogue would be followed by wild slapstick, such as Mischa Auer's extended monkey imitation in *My Man Godfrey* or Melvyn Douglas's kidnapping hoax in *She Married Her Boss*, the latter of which features both the brick-throwing sequence and a speeded-up car chase. Moreover, La Cava's sense of the film frame, no doubt a carryover from his work as an animator (and newspaper cartoonist), anticipates deep focus, for comic effect. For example, on more than one occasion the monkey-like Auer ends up climbing some latticework in the extreme background of the scene while related comedy takes place in the frame foreground. One such incident has the perennially antiheroic Eugene Pallette (as the father) complaining about the expense of maintaining such a wacky family (which always disgusts the freeloading Auer into a chorus of "money, money, money"). The scene then achieves a black comedy dimension when Auer assumes the hanging position of a crucifix (still in the extreme background), a parody of his overreaction to a minor inconvenience—a small-change Calvary.

Second, La Cava was an improvisational director in the sense that the story developed on a day-to-day basis as it was shot—in the tradition of silent comedy. He sometimes brought in bits and pieces of writing, but was more likely to compose each day on the set. Once this had been done, La Cava told the actors "the gist of the scenes at the last moment, in order to keep some sort of spontaneity in the proceedings."[120] La Cava's reasoning for this approach was that unlike the sustained theatre performance, cinema acting was done piecemeal, and no actor could maintain the correct mood for weeks on end. His acting would go flat as scenes were repeated over a sustained period. But:

> By making up things as we go along and writing dialogue on the spur of the moment, I think perhaps we're able to catch some of that sparkle and that verve which always have been among the theater's great assets.[121]

Also, as with so many other screwball comedy directors, La Cava's actors were given "full freedom to suggest additions or changes in action and dialogue."[122] Appropriately, La Cava's greatest work within the genre, *My Man Godfrey*, is now celebrated as the most informal, improvisational of his productions. An open bar was maintained on the set, and filming proceeded at the most leisurely of paces.[123] This author discussed La Cava's drinking with the director's later producer, the award-winning Pandro S. Berman, who stated it helped, not hindered, La Cava's work.[124] Ironically, Berman noted that late in La Cava's career, when the director was

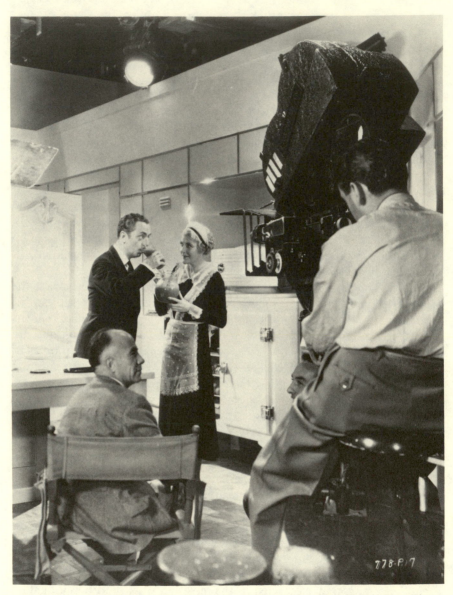

9. Gregory La Cava (seated in director's chair), William Powell, and Jean Dixon on the set of *My Man Godfrey* (1936). (Photograph courtesy of the Museum of Modern Art/Film Stills Archive.)

abstaining from alcohol, his work seemed to suffer. Aptly, La Cava films sometimes showcase a drunken scene as pivotal to the plot. There are two extended drinking scenes in *She Married Her Boss*, where first Colbert gains insight and then Douglas loses his rigidity. *My Man Godfrey* also has two pivotal scenes which focus on alcohol, one in which Powell administers to the tipsy, and another when he joins their ranks. La Cava's ultimate comic tribute to inebriation comes in *Unfinished Business*, in which Robert Montgomery is constantly under the influence. (His favorite drink is the Whiz Boom—"You can hear the whiz but you never feel the boom.") Montgomery also offers the ultimate black comedy axiom for the drinker warned about ruining his health—"Health is like money, it's no good unless you spend it."

It would not seem inappropriate to add that La Cava's fellow screwball comedy director Leo McCarey was also a hard drinker who sometimes spotlighted the subject in his work: the Laurel & Hardy film *Blotto* (1930, story by McCarey); the pivotal drunk scene in *Ruggles of Red Gap*, where the formerly rigid Laughton is finally, unequivocally, loosened up; the all-out chandelier-swinging drunk of Paul Newman and Joan Collins in *Rally 'Round the Flag Boys!* Moreover, La Cava and McCarey were both close friends of America's greatest native-born comedian and most celebrated drinker—W. C. Fields—whose films constantly revolved around the bottle. Finally, it should go without saying that the screwball genre frequently floats on alcohol's ability to either loosen the rigid or to encourage the childlike, from the *Topper* scenes to Dudley Moore's hilarious showcase of insobriety in *Arthur*.

Improvisation was, moreover, not just a key ingredient of the working methods of pivotal screwball comedy directors. Screenwriters with whom they worked frequently followed a similar credo. For example, Billy Wilder and Charles Brackett, the credited screenwriters on such screwball comedies as Hawks's *Ball of Fire,* Ernst Lubitsch's *Bluebeard's Eighth Wife,* Mitchell Leisen's *Midnight*, and Wilder's own *The Major and the Minor* (his first American directing credit) were equally informal artists. Thus, "The team made a practice of leaving their scenarios unfinished until actual production was underway, preferring to see how they 'played' before deciding how to complete them."[125]

Third, the Hollywood in-house humor nature of La Cava's screwball comedies is almost entirely tied to actors playing themselves. Berman described to the author La Cava's need to get his key actors on the set:

> he would go into action and as he would talk to these people and get to know them and let them talk to each other—he would learn what their real personalities were. This was the secret of everything La Cava ever did—to capture on film the basic personality of the person he was using, and that's when he would

function, and when he could crystalize on what he wanted to do
and when he would create.[126]

Just this message was a key thrust of the appropriately titled La Cava
article, "Give Me REAL People," which appeared in the March 26, 1938,
issue of *Colliers*. La Cava observes: "Give me real people to work with,
people like Bill Powell and Carole Lombard. . . . When I direct them I tell
them to use their own personalities, not to assume someone else's."[127]
Another essay from the previous year, focused on *Stage Door*, then in
production, for which La Cava would win the prestigious New York Film
Critic's Best Director award, 1937. The author observed, "La Cava has
only one principle in pictures: 'Acting has no place on the screen.' "[128]
Again, the message was the same—mold the role around the real personality
of the *actor*—a term which here becomes a misnomer.

As has been the case with the other highlighted directors in this chapter,
La Cava has sometimes seemed to showcase an in-film alter ego. In *My Man
Godfrey* it is most definitely Carole Lombard whose warm and comically
insightful article "My Man Gregory" both describes the director and draws
parallels between them. Early in the article, after establishing her extremely
extroverted nature according to the La Cava testing method, she declares
"as Carole Lombard, M.P.Ph.D. (Doctor of Motion Picture Psychology) I
am selecting My Man Gregory as the subject of this intensive analysis of a
guy whom I consider a genius."[129] She quickly establishes La Cava's
extroverted nature: "My Man Gregory wouldn't know an inhibition,
himself, if it socked him in the eye, or dropped from Mars right on his
devoted head, which has become slightly bald from thinking."[130]

Reaching beyond La Cava's need to psychoanalyze his players, Lombard
reveals the director's wish to get close to them, right down to applying
nicknames. Thus, she notes La Cava's then-famous christening of the
French-born Colbert as "The Fretting Frog," the action which had
precipitated her nicknaming him "Dr. Lucius La Cava." Eventually
Lombard states:

> As I'm a soprano, mostly lacking in inhibitions, I can and do
> yell louder than My Man Gregory. Maybe this is why he is for
> me a 100 per cent. It isn't love, it's admiration. He claims that I
> am his female counterpart.[131]

Fourth, La Cava also had more production control than the norm during
the studio period. Besides the control his day-to-day approach allowed, he,
too, did as much in-the-camera "editing" as possible. In fact, he avoided
retakes, frequently acting as producer of his films, which was the case with
My Man Godfrey.

La Cava's control through rewriting was true regardless of the property.
Thus, even the celebrated Edna Ferber-George Kaufman play *Stage Door*

was rewritten by La Cava. When this more than loose adaptation appeared, Kaufman good-humoredly observed, "La Cava should have called it *Screen Door*."[132] The film was often considered better than the original play, although *Colliers* author Quentin Reynolds was probably closer when he opined, "it wasn't better. It was different. It was another story with the same title."[133]

La Cava's control could also be seen in comically eccentric ways, such as his eventual power to dictate personal contracts sixty pages in length, which provided for every possible action. For example, it was said in Hollywood, "If La Cava suddenly decided that the sound stages should be painted a lurid green, an obscure clause in his contract would be found giving him the right . . . at the studio's expense."[134] It is the type of comic distrust for which his close friend W. C. Fields is still known. In fact, another comically ironic Hollywood statement about La Cava sounds positively Fieldsian: he should shoot his contract instead of a script.[135]

In the beginning La Cava's refusal to compromise threatened his film career. But eventually word of mouth told an entirely different story—a story equally applicable to Hawks, McCarey, and Sturges: "He's got something. If you let him alone he'll make you a picture."[136]

NOTES

1. Carole Lombard, "My Man Gregory," *Screenbook* magazine, February 1937, p. 38.

2. Ted Sennett, *Lunatics and Lovers* (New Rochelle, New York: Arlington House, 1973).

3. Andrew Sarris, ed., *Interviews with Film Directors* (1967; rpt. New York: Avon Books, 1972), p. 237.

4. Joseph McBride, ed., *Hawks on Hawks* (Los Angeles: University of California Press, 1982), p. 69.

5. Pauline Kael, "Raising Kane," in *The Citizen Kane Book* (Boston: Little, Brown and Company, 1971), pp. 3-84.

6. John Belton, *The Hollywood Professionals: Howard Hawks, Frank Borzage, and Edgar G. Ulmer*, vol. 3 (New York: A. S. Barnes & Co., 1974), p. 11.

7. Walter Kerr, *The Silent Clowns* (New York: Alfred A. Knopf, 1975), p. 292.

8. McBride, *Hawks on Hawks*, p. 14.

9. Ibid., p. 162.

10. Ibid., p. 66.

11. Charles Higham, *Kate: The Life of Katharine Hepburn* (New York: W. W. Norton & Company, 1975), p. 88.

12. Ibid., p. 87.

13. "Howard Hawks Talks About Broad Farce Comedy in 'Man's Favorite Sport,' " in *Man's Favorite Sport? Press Book* (Los Angeles: Universal Pictures, 1963), p. 5.

14. Higham, *Kate: The Life of Katharine Hepburn*, p. 90.

15. Rosaline Russell and Chris Chase, *Life Is a Banquet* (New York: Random House, 1977), pp. 89-90.

16. Gerald Mast, *Howard Hawks, Storyteller* (New York: Oxford University Press, 1982), pp. 54-55.

17. Higham, *Kate: The Life of Katharine Hepburn,* p. 89.

18. Mast, *Howard Hawks, Storyteller*, p. 54.

19. Ibid.

20. Larry Swindell, *Screwball: The Life of Carole Lombard* (New York: William Morrow and Company, 1975), p. 141.

21. Higham, *Kate: The Life of Katharine Hepburn,* pp. 87-88.

22. Swindell, *Screwball: The Life of Carole Lombard*, p. 141.

23. Ibid.

24. *20th Century* review, *Variety,* May 8, 1934, p. 14.

25. Ibid.; *20th Century* review, *New York Times,* May 4, 1934, p. 24.

26. Higham, *Kate: The Life of Katharine Hepburn,* p. 87.

27. Ibid.

28. See Wes D. Gehring, *Leo McCarey and the Comic Anti-Hero in American Film* (New York: Arno Press, 1980), pp. 88-149.

29. Peter Bogdanovich, "Leo McCarey Oral History" (Los Angeles: American Film Institute, 1972), p. 53.

30. See Wes D. Gehring, "McCarey vs. Capra: A Guide to American Film Comedy of the '30's," *The Journal of Popular Film and Television* 7, no. 1 (1978): 67-84.

31. *The Awful Truth* review, *Variety,* October 20, 1937, p. 12.

32. Charles Silver, "Leo McCarey: from Marx to McCarthy," *Film Comment,* September 1973, p. 10.

33. Donald Deschner, *The Films of Cary Grant* (Secaucus, New Jersey: The Citadel Press, 1973), p. 140.

34. Bogdanovich, "Leo McCarey Oral History," p. 99.

35. Bosley Crowther, *My Favorite Wife* review, *New York Times,* May 31, 1940, p. 15.

36. Burton Bernstein, *Thurber: A Biography* (New York: Ballantine Books, 1976), pp. 438-439; James Thurber, "The Man Who Hated Moonbaum," in *My World—And Welcome To It* (New York: Harcourt, Brace and Company, 1942), pp. 59-67.

37. Bernstein, *Thurber: A Biography,* p. 238.

38. Bogdanovich, "Leo McCarey Oral History," p. 83. (The 1920s Arthur Richman play from which *The Awful Truth* is said to be adapted bears little resemblance to the 1937 film. See a rare print copy of the play at The Library of Congress: *The Awful Truth* [New York: Co-National Plays, Inc., 1930; shelf no. 79344].)

39. Bernstein, *Thurber: A Biography,* p. 31.

40. Leo McCarey, "Comedy and a Touch of Cuckoo," *Extension,* November 1944, p. 34.

41. William H. Mooring, "What McCarey Forgot to Tell . . . ," *Extension,* November 1944, p. 5.

42. Bernstein, *Thurber: A Biography,* p. 205.

43. Peter Bogdanovich, "Hollywood," *Esquire,* February 1972, p. 8.

44. Ibid.

45. Bernstein, *Thurber: A Biography*, p. 289. See Chapters 3 and 6 for more on

the significance of Thurber's having referred to himself as looking "like a slightly ill professor."

46. Pete Martin, "Going His Way," *Saturday Evening Post*, November 30, 1946, p. 65.

47. Sidney Carroll, "Everything Happens to McCarey: During those sparse times when he isn't breaking his valuable neck, Leo McCarey does direct some extraordinary pictures," *Esquire*, May 1943, pp. 43, 57.

48. Ibid., p. 43.

49. Ibid., p. 57.

50. Ibid.

51. H. Allen Smith, "A Session with McCarey," *Variety*, January 7, 1970, p. 23.

52. James Thurber, "A Box to Hide In," in *The Middle-Aged Man on the Flying Trapeze* (1935; rpt. New York: Harper & Row, 1976), pp. 224-27.

53. Bogdanovich, "Leo McCarey Oral History," p. 66.

54. Ibid., pp. 29-30.

55. Martin, "Going His Way," p. 70.

56. Bosley Browther, *The Awful Truth* review, *New York Times,* November 5, 1937, p. 19.

57. Andrew Sarris, *The American Cinema: Directors and Directions, 1929-1968* (New York: E. P. Dutton & Co., 1968), p. 99; Robin Wood, "Democracy and Shpontanuity," *Film Comment*, January-February 1976, pp. 6-15.

58. Bogdanovich, "Leo McCarey Oral History," p. 114.

59. Robin Wood, "Ingrid Berman on Rossellini," *Film Comment*, July-August 1974, p. 14.

60. Wes Gehring, Telephone Conversation with Irene Dunne (Los Angeles, August 23, 1979).

61. Ralph Bellamy, *When the Smoke Hit the Fan* (Garden City, New York: Doubleday & Company, 1979), pp. 129-130.

62. Joe Adamson, *Groucho, Harpo, Chico and Sometimes Zeppo* (New York: Simon and Schuster, 1973), p. 209.

63. Smith, "A Session with McCarey," p. 23.

64. Bogdanovich, "Leo McCarey Oral History," pp. 46, 85.

65. Ibid., p. 46.

66. Bellamy, *When the Smoke Hit the Fan*, p. 130.

67. Ibid., p. 129.

68. Bogdanovich, "Leo McCarey Oral History," p. 60.

69. Garson Kanin, *Hollywood* (New York: Viking Press, 1976), p. 90.

70. Bing Crosby and David Butler, "Remembering Leo McCarey," *Action*, September-October 1967, p. 12.

71. McCarey, "Comedy and a Touch of Cuckoo," pp. 5, 34.

72. David Williams, "Sturges the Great," *Newsweek,* July 26, 1982, p. 72.

73. James Curtis, *Between Flops: A Biography of Preston Sturges* (New York: Harcourt Brace Jovanovich, 1982), p. x.

74. Sarris, *The American Cinema: Directors and Directions, 1929-1968,* p. 116.

75. Bosley Crowther, "When Satire and Slapstick Meet," *New York Times Magazine*, August 27, 1944, pp. 14-15, 37; Frank Nugent, "Genius with a Slapstick," *Variety*, February 7, 1945, pp. 2, 23.

76. Nugent, "Genius with a Slapstick," p. 23.

77. Ibid.

78. "Preston Sturges," *Look,* October 3, 1944, p. 64.

79. Maxine Block, ed., "Preston Sturges," in *Current Biography 1941* (New York: H. W. Wilson Co., 1942), p. 845.

80. McBride, *Hawks on Hawks*, p. 67.

81. Crowther, "When Satire and Slapstick Meet," p. 14.

82. Manny Farber and W. S. Poster, "Preston Sturges: Success in the Movies" (1954), in *Negative Space* (New York: Frederick Praeger, 1972), p. 96.

83. Ibid., p. 94.

84. James Ursini, *Preston Sturges: An American Dreamer* (New York: Curtis Books, 1973), pp. 43-44.

85. Curtis, *Between Flops: A Biography of Preston Sturges*, p. 146.

86. Ibid., p. 156.

87. Ibid., p. 183.

88. Wes Gehring, Conversation with Eddie Bracken after a performance of *Sugar Babies*, in which Bracken was touring (Muncie, Indiana, October 5, 1982).

89. Ursini, *Preston Sturges: An American Dreamer*, p. 113.

90. Ibid.

91. Curtis, *Between Flops: A Biography of Preston Sturges*, p. 162.

92. Rudy Vallee (with Gil McKean), *My Time Is Your Time* (New York: Ivan Obolensky, 1962), p. 178; Curtis, *Between Flops: A Biography of Preston Sturges,* p. 160.

93. Nugent, "Genius with a Slapstick," p. 23.

94. See Wes D. Gehring, *W. C. Fields: A Bio-Bibliography* (Westport, Connecticut: Greenwood Press, 1984).

95. Curtis, *Between Flops: A Biography of Preston Sturges,* p. 150.

96. Ibid., p. 188.

97. Ibid., p. 230.

98. Richard Schickel, *Unfaithfully Yours* review, *Time,* February 20, 1984, p. 82.

99. Farber, "Preston Sturges," p. 90.

100. Ursini, *Preston Sturges: An American Dreamer*, p. 64.

101. Leonard Maltin, *Of Mice and Magic: A History of American Animated Cartoons* (New York: New American Library, 1980), p. 12.

102. Ibid.

103. See Gehring, *W. C. Fields: A Bio-Bibliography.*

104. Quentin Reynolds, "Give Me REAL People," Colliers, March 26, 1938, p. 52.

105. Walter Kerr, *The Silent Clowns* (New York: Alfred A. Knopf, 1975), p. 290.

106. Reynolds, "Give Me REAL People," p. 53.

107. Ronald J. Fields, *W. C. Fields: A Life on Film* (New York: St. Martin's Press, 1984), p. 45. See also Gehring, *W. C. Fields: A Bio-Bibliography.*

108. Maxine Block, ed., "Gregory La Cava," in *Current Biography 1941* (New York: H. W. Wilson Co., 1942), p. 484.

109. J. P. McEvoy, *The Comic Supplement* (1924), Library of Congress Copyright Department (Madison Building); J. P. McEvoy, *The Comic Supplement* (1925), Billy Rose Theatre Collection, New York Public Library at Lincoln Center.

110. McEvoy, *The Comic Supplement* (1925), unnumbered page preceding p. 1.

111. Block, "Gregory La Cava," p. 483.

112. Reynolds, "Give Me REAL People," p. 53; Block, "Gregory La Cava," p. 484.

113. Reynolds, "Give Me REAL People," pp. 52, 53.

114. Ibid., p. 52.

115. Lombard, "My Man Gregory," p. 38.

116. Gregory La Cava, "The Fretting Frog: The Story of Claudette Colbert's New Leap to Fame," *Photoplay,* November 1935, p. 99.

117. Lombard, "My Man Gregory," p. 38.

118. Ibid.

119. La Cava, "The Fretting Frog," p. 100.

120. "Cuff System Adapted By La Cava," *Hollywood Citizen News,* March 6, 1941, n.p., in the "Gregory La Cava File," The Academy of Motion Picture Arts and Sciences Library (Los Angeles).

121. "Cuff System Adapted By La Cava."

122. Block, "Gregory La Cava," p. 484.

123. Robert Lewis Taylor, *W. C. Fields: His Follies and Fortunes* (Garden City, New York: Doubleday & Company, 1949), pp. 200-201.

124. Wes Gehring, "Pandro S. Berman on Hollywood During the 1930s: An Interview," *Paper Cinema* (Boston: Geoffrey H. Mahfuz, forthcoming.).

125. Anna Rothe, ed., "Billy Wilder," in *Current Biography 1951* (New York: H. H. Wilson Company, 1952), p. 658.

126. Gehring, "Pandro S. Berman."

127. Reynolds, "Give Me REAL People," p. 53.

128. Sally Jefferson, "The Lowdown on that Ginger Rogers-Katharine Hepburn Merger," *Movie Mirror,* October 1937, p. 29.

129. Lombard, "My Man Gregory," p. 38.

130. Ibid.

131. Ibid., p. 90.

132. Reynolds, "Give Me REAL People," p. 18.

133. Ibid.

134. Block, "Gregory La Cava," p. 483.

135. Ibid.

136. Reynolds, "Give Me REAL People," p. 53.

5.

SCREWBALL PLAYERS—THE RIGHT KIND OF PEOPLE

When someone likens the *My Man Godfrey* scavenger hunt gathering to an asylum, Alexander Bullock (Eugene Pallette) observes: "All you need is an empty room and the right kind of people."

By the time Hollywood teamed James Cagney and Bette Davis in *The Bride Came C.O.D.*, a 1941 version of *It Happened One Night* (1934), it would seem that every major American film star had been cast in a screwball or quasi-screwball comedy. However, the money people had evidently forgotten Pallette's qualifier for the do-it-yourself asylum—an empty room with the *right kind* of people. This chapter will examine some key screwball comedy players—players, to borrow a popular contemporary variation of Pallette's phrase, with the right stuff.

If in-depth film scholarship has generally minimized its attention to screwball comedy, it should come as no surprise that serious study of stellar performers within the genre has been even more neglected. On the rare occasion when a performer is isolated, it is inevitably the madcap heroine, with the greatest attention given to the often-acknowledged queen of the genre, Carole Lombard. But even this notice is usually only a passing footnote, a point of departure before an author moves onto her dramatically fascinating personal life, including her marriage to Clark Gable and her tragic death in a plane crash.

This chapter is an outgrowth of the recent recognition that certain performers who have appeared numerous times in one particular genre often have helped shape the evolution of that genre itself. Colin McArthur, in his excellent *Underworld USA*, makes just such an argument concerning the continuing impact of James Cagney and Edward G. Robinson on the gangster film since the 1930s and Humphrey Bogart in the 1940s thriller:

> Men such as Cagney, Robinson, and Bogart seem to gather within themselves the qualities of the genres they appear in so that the violence, suffering and *angst* of the films is [sic] restated in their faces, physical presence, movement, and speech.[1]

Andrew Sarris, among others, has drawn the same genre-performer analogy in writing of John Wayne and the western.[2] The list could extend indefinitely and include Fred Astaire and Gene Kelly in the musical, Boris Karloff and Vincent Price in the horror film. The unique performer is even now being considered along broader auteur lines, as in Patrick McGilligan's provocative *Cagney: The Actor As Auteur*, an "authorship" delineation generally reserved only for certain directors.[3]

Ironically, film theorist Béla Balázs had laid the groundwork for the actor/genre analogy years earlier with his writing on the true personalities of the screen, performers whose persona remain popularly consistent whatever the role.[4] More recently, film historian Gerald Mast has drawn attention to the unique observation of art historian Erwin Panofsky on the special ties between the film character and the actor:

> Othello or Nora are definite, substantial figures created by the playwright. They can be played well or badly, and they can be "interpreted" in one way or another; but they must definitely exist, no matter who plays them or even whether they are played at all. The character in a film, however, lives and dies with the actor.[5]

These words are all the more prophetic for screwball comedy, a genre which is often uniquely self-conscious (for comic effect) about the background of its directors (see Chapter 4) and/or actors, as well as frequently embracing improvisation or near improvisation production techniques.

This chapter will focus upon eight screwball comedy performers: Cary Grant, Carole Lombard, Irene Dunne, Claudette Colbert, Katharine Hepburn, Jean Arthur, Melvyn Douglas, and Fred MacMurray. Grant, Lombard, and Dunne, because of their unique significance to the genre, will receive special attention.

CARY GRANT

Howard Hawks, screwball comedy's premier director, has said of Cary Grant, "It's pretty hard to think of anybody but Cary Grant in that type of stuff [screwball comedy]. He was so far the best that there isn't anybody to be compared to him.''[6] Besides appearing in seven screwball comedies by the genre's two top-ranking directors Hawks and Leo McCarey (see Chapter 4), such as *The Awful Truth* (1937) and *Bringing Up Baby* (1938), he starred in a host of other significant genre pieces. Among these include roles as the amiable ghost George Kerby in the Hal Roach-produced *Topper* (1937) and the vacation-bound Johnny Case of the George Cukor-directed *Holiday* (1938).

In those screwball comedies made outside the traditional time boundaries of the genre, 1934 through the early 1940s, Grant continues to appear in the most important examples, such as French army captain Henri Rochard, who becomes a "bride" in *I Was A Male War Bride* (1949) and absent-minded professor Barnaby Fulton in *Monkey Business* (1952).

Grant bolstered this association with screwball comedy by recreating for *The Lux Radio Theatre* some of his classic roles in the genre; he even starred in radio productions of celebrated screwball comedies in which he had not originally appeared, such as *Theodora Goes Wild* and *Here Comes Mr. Jordan*.[7] Probably his greatest film role in the genre, as Jerry Warriner in *The Awful Truth*, also proved to be the most popular on radio, where it was done three times, with Grant starring twice.[8]

Grant's presence is so strongly linked to the screwball comedy that when film critic-director Peter Bogdanovich did his 1972 salute to the genre, *What's Up, Doc?*, male lead Ryan O'Neal is made to do a feature-length imitation of Grant, largely drawn from *Bringing Up Baby*, upon which the Bogdanovich film is unofficially based. The same thing already had occurred in the screwball second half of Billy Wilder's classic *Some Like It Hot* (1959), when Tony Curtis pursued an eccentric comic romance with Marilyn Monroe, using an ongoing Grant impersonation. (In the Bogdanovich production, *Bringing Up Baby* was shown before shooting began.)

More recently, "good ol' boy" film star Burt Reynolds has methodically mapped out plans to enter the light comedy world of films like *A Touch of Class* (1973, a contemporary adult screwball comedy in which a frustrated George Segal must choose between two women, somewhat reminiscent of *My Favorite Wife*).[9] But the comedic leading man Reynolds is basing his transition on is none other that Cary Grant.[10] In Reynolds's 1978 film *Starting Over*, he very much captures Grant's vulnerable screwball comedy antihero, and again the story of the film necessitates choosing between two women.

Finally, the excellent contemporary screwball comedy *Seems Like Old Times* (1980) found Chevy Chase also emulating the Grant model, especially in his talent for mixing the pratfall with the non sequitur. Chase himself seemed to underline this by the significance he placed on a Grant telegram welcoming him to the world of screwball comedy.[11]

Comedy theorist Henri Bergson (see also Chapter 6) would have defined this Grant phenomenon and the additional humor it provokes (reinforcing screwball comedy's underlying self-conscious nature) in the following manner: "What is most comic of all is to become a category oneself into which others will fall, as into a ready-made frame; it is to crystallize into a stock character."[12] Grant has very much become a screwball comedy "category."

The Grant screwball comedy persona is a product of his ability to combine great physical/visual comedic skills with the more traditional characteristics of the leading man. Here was something unique: a visual comedian who was also tall, dark, and handsome, and who had a pleasant speaking voice. Screwball comedy helped bring about this new type. In a 1955 interview, director Howard Hawks addressed the uniqueness of this change and its meaning for his first screwball comedy, *Twentieth Century*:

> It was the first time the dramatic leads, instead of secondary comics, played for laughs. I mean we got the fun out of John Barrymore and Carole Lombard. It was two or three years ahead of its time.[13]

Grant soon would become both *the* Hawks leading man in this comedy/drama metamorphosis, as well as occupying the same honored status for the genre itself.

Grant was completely at home in the slapstick milieu; he had a gift for visual/physical comedy. It is a generally ignored fact that the boy Archie Leach (Cary Grant) began his entertainment career as an acrobatic comic in the music halls and variety theaters of England, where he was born. He spent most of his teen years with Robert Pender's celebrated collection of knockabout boy comedians and their completely visual routines. It was one of Britain's top acts and toured continuously, eventually bringing Grant to the United States in the early 1920s. Grant's background mirrors the Karno music hall tours and training of cinema's greatest visual/physical comedian, Charlie Chaplin, a special favorite of Grant's. (In fact, Grant's first wife was Chaplin's former leading lady from *City Lights*, 1931, Virginia Cherrill, who played the blind girl.)

Grant, who has revealed that the high point of a frequently unhappy childhood was attending silent film comedy (from Chaplin to John Bunny[14]) observed of his experience with the Pender troupe:

> I grew to appreciate the fine art of pantomime. No dialogue was used in our act and each day, on a bare stage, we learned . . . how to convey a mood or meaning without words . . . how best immediately and precisely to effect an emotional response—a laugh or, sometimes, a tear.[15]

Long-time Grant friend and associate Don Barclay, having observed Grant take some unnecessary falls in the mud for a film, said it would seem that these bits of slapstick were his favorite requirement for a cinema role.[16] And Pete Martin, *The Saturday Evening Post*'s legendary movie chronicler, credited Grant with having lifted some silent comedy basics to a "high plane."[17]

Grant incorporates this propensity for visual/physical comedy in all of his screwball films. For example, in *The Awful Truth*, he mimes most effectively a McCarey hat routine centering on a huge derby which the director originally patented first for Charlie Chase and then Laurel & Hardy in the silent era. In addition, Grant has several vigorous romps with the dog Asta; he doubles as a mechanical figure on a cuckoo clock,[18] reminiscent of Chaplin becoming a mechanical figure in a giant clockface-like setting during *The Circus* (1928). He spends considerable time in a delightfully silent reconciliation attempt which necessitates being down on all fours to compete with an uncooperative cat, a doubly stubborn woman, and an overly airy nightshirt. (For other examples of Grant's mime skills, especially in the work of Hawks and McCarey, see Chapters 3 and 4.)

Balancing Grant's slapstick talents, which were not cinematically showcased until his screwball comedies, were his impeccable leading-man credentials. He had been a critically and commercially successful romantic lead on Broadway and had even toured with equal success as a musical comedy star. Before his comedy arrival in screwball films he had starred romantically opposite many of the most beautiful women in Hollywood, including two that were almost equated with open sexuality: Mae West and Marlene Dietrich.

It is important to pause briefly upon "sexuality"; while this author does not embrace the premise that the main stimulant in the development of screwball comedy was the suppression of sexuality in 1930s films, a consequence of the implementation of the Motion Picture Production Code in 1934 (see Chapters 1 and 7), romanticism is still part of the genre. That romanticism is what separates antiheroic screwball comedy from the broader base of pioneer antiheroic personality comedians like Laurel & Hardy and W. C. Fields (when Fields was not portraying the con man).

Paramount, Grant's home company before his screwball-comedy free-lance days, had been pointing Grant in a romantic direction since his 1932 screen debut. That first year he starred opposite Dietrich in *Blonde Venus*, probably the most sexually erotic of the seven controversial films the actress did under the tutelage of director Josef von Sternberg between 1929 and 1935. Grant essays the part of wealthy playboy Nick Townsend; Dietrich is his mistress. Though the film did not do as well as Paramount had hoped, the Dietrich-von Sternberg relationship always generated a great deal of publicity. Moreover, critics and public alike had been impressed with

Grant. Because of this, Paramount even considered starring him in a remake of Valentino's *Blood and Sand* (1922), possibly with Dietrich as the Killer Vamp.[19]

The following year he starred opposite Mae West in two history-making films—*She Done Him Wrong* and *I'm No Angel*. Containing West's not yet censored sexual innuendo, they were two of the most controversial films of the era. Consequently, she is often given sole credit (or blame) for the creation of the censorship code the following year. But because of this sexuality, the films were two of the greatest box-office hits of the 1930s, and often have been credited with pulling their parent studio, Paramount, out of depression receivership.

In both films Grant would receive top billing after West, who had handpicked him to be her leading man. Though the focus of sexuality was West, she had constructed Grant's roles for a certain degree of sexuality, even eroticism. For example, in *She Done Him Wrong* Grant plays a government undercover agent, something the audience is unaware of until the end of the film. His "cover" throughout the film is that of Captain Cummings from the nearby church mission. Cummings's inability to resist Lady Lou (West), even when the audience finally knows his real identity, creates the added titillation that a man of the cloth has fallen. The closing dialogue merely underlines that fact: Grant approvingly calls West "You bad girl"; she answers, "You'll find out."

In both cases the real focus was on West, as it had been on Dietrich *Blonde Venus*. But Grant's recurring presence in these films worked toward creating a film persona keyed to 1930s sexuality, if for no other reason than sex by association.

Film critic Pauline Kael has observed he was not quite *the* Cary Grant at this point, for he had not "learned to project his feelings of absurdity through his characters and to make a style out of their feeling silly."[20] But West's sexually provocative evaluation of Grant—"You can be had" (*She Done Him Wrong*)—with which Kael opens her lengthy Grant essay, does create a tie (along with sexuality) between his early work and his later films. This Grant vulnerability is most apparent in his screwball comedies, several of which Kael mentions at this point in her Grant piece.[21] (Film critic Richard Schickel politely disagrees with Kael's "You can be had" premise as too simplistic, but neither Schickel nor Kael seems cognizant of the fact that her image of the later Grant seems largely tied to his screwball comedy appearances.[22])

Coupled with Grant's eventual screwball ability to balance an equal dichotomy of slapstick and sexuality (*Bringing Up Baby* nonstop co-star Katharine Hepburn is not above pausing to observe just how handsome he is, even as the absent-minded professor) is a decided gift for improvisation. Biographer Albert Govoni notes the actor had this talent for improvisation from the beginning of his career, as a teenager.[23] But as presented in

Chapter 4, these gifts were never showcased effectively until Grant worked for McCarey and Hawks. Without belaboring the subject further (see previous chapter), it should be noted that Grant later grouped directors George Stevens and George Cukor with McCarey and Hawks in this area of creative freedom.

In terms of screwball comedy, Cukor directed him in *Holiday* and *The Philadelphia Story*, (1940, both from Philip Barry plays) though the latter has periods of melodramatic talkativeness. Stevens, who did such non-Grant screwball comedies as *Vivacious Lady* (1938) and *The More the Merrier* (1943; Grant starred in the 1966 remake, *Walk, Don't Run*), directed Grant in a populist comedy with screwball overtones (*The Talk of the Town*, 1942), and a melodrama (*Penny Serenade*, 1941) whose comic caring-for-baby scenes with co-star Irene Dunne anticipated the post-World War II developments of the genre once it moved to the suburbs.

A third key factor in Grant's screwball comedy success (after improvisation and an ability to mix slapstick and sexiness) was his independent business acumen, paralleling that of the genre's frequently independent directors. Grant knew the type of film character best suited to him, as well as how to market that character. Not surprisingly, he was one of Hollywood's earliest (1937) free-lance performers; Grant bills himself as the first.[24] This was at the height of the Hollywood studio system, when the vast majority in the film industry picked up their assignments on Monday morning. Thus, it was no accident of random studio production that brought him these celebrated screwball comedy roles.

His first year as an unattached property saw Grant's initial entry into the genre. The results were two classic screwball comedies: *Topper* and *The Awful Truth*. (In fact, *The Awful Truth* was director McCarey's first independent project after breaking with Paramount.) Back-to-back after *The Awful Truth* came *Bringing Up Baby* and *Holiday*. Grant saw his strength in these comedies very early.

As already demonstrated with Grant (among others) in Chapter 4, screwball comedy often uses the real-life identity and/or screen persona of the performer for comic effect. For Grant this has included everything from an in-film reference to his original name (Archie Leach) to a general screwball comedy identity of frustration which parodies his celebrated romantic leading-man credentials. More pointedly, the screwball comedy Grant is generally eaten alive by his female co-star. It is the antiheroic child versus the dominate, even motherly, female.

As the scientist-professor of *Bringing Up Baby* he is completely overpowered—even hunted down—by Katharine Hepburn, while the professor of *Monkey Business* carries that state into a heavily female-dominated marriage, a natural extension of *Baby*'s crazy courtship. In both *My Favorite Wife* and *The Awful Truth* wife Irene Dunne manages to reduce Grant to the most gelatin of little boys by the final reel. (Moreover, he is dominated for most of *My Favorite Wife* by two wives!) In *Topper*, even as a spirit, he does not get all the respect one would expect from a wife, let alone a fellow spirit. And he gets even less respect in those roles where he must appear in wifely garb, such as *Bringing Up Baby, My Favorite Wife,* and the so aptly titled *I Was a Male War Bride.* The marginal screwball comedies continue this superbly comic male frustration. For example, in *Arsenic and Old Lace*, wife problems add to the difficulties that emanate from his sweet but lethal maiden aunts, who benevolently poison sad, old gentlemen.

Grant brought such inspiration to this female-frustrated male that it is reminiscent of realist film theorist André Bazin's observations on "transposed autobiography," where an actor brings such intensity to a role, or a series of roles, that the performance goes leagues beyond merely assuming a character.[25] However, it was not until late in Grant's career that the true vulnerability of his real life began to be revealed.

In Grant's three-part 1963 autobiography in *Ladies Home Journal* (see footnote 14), simply entitled "Archie Leach," he describes the sometimes shattered fragility of a childhood shaped by a dominate mother and a submissive father. When Grant was ten, his mother was forever removed from his childhood when she was committed to a mental institution.

Next is the rather provocative 1977 *New York Times* interview with Grant so appropriately entitled, "Cary Grant: No Lady's Man."[26] It took place eleven years after his retirement from films. Grant was especially candid, considering that during his career he had been overly guarded about his personal life. (In fact, interviewer/author Warren Hoge found most of Grant's earlier interviews all sounding alike.) As the title suggests, this revealing session was dominated by the present focus of interest, his relationship with women.

Grant's personal interaction with women was found to be just like that of his screwball comedy antihero persona, only darker. Hoge best summarized the situation by noting that Grant "has spent most of his life afraid of women, made positively miserable by them, starting with his often confining mother and continuing on through relationships in and out of marriage."[27] Grant also noted that in real life he was constantly looking for a substitute mother. The performer then summarizes this section of the interview with a most striking metaphor drawn from the world of insects: "Once the female has used the male for procreation, she turns on him and literally devours him."[28] Grant's female-dominated screwball comedy character could not have phrased it any better.

The interview also examines Grant's feelings of rejection after the institutionalization of his mother—the first woman to "desert" him:

> I was making the mistake of thinking that each of my wives [he had had four at that time] was my mother. . . . I had even found myself being attracted to people who looked like my

mother. Of course, at the same time I was getting a person with her emotional make-up, too.[29]

With the 1983 publication of Geoffrey Wansell's *Haunted Idol: The Story of the Real Cary Grant*, a lifetime of the darkly antiheroic is further exposed. Much more is revealed of the claustrophobic childhood, the extremely dominant mother, and her removal. His mother seems to have scarred Grant's future relationships with women in two ways. First, there was the overly devoted attention, as if "she wanted a doll, a dependent being who would be unable to exist without her love and affection."[30] Second, when she was suddenly removed from his childhood, Grant began to suffer the ongoing distrust of women that has already been suggested.

Such antiheroic revelations thus destroy the once-popular notion that the romantic sophisticate of so many films was merely playing himself. *But* the revelations reinforce the ties between the real Grant and the antiheroic genre of screwball comedy. Ironically, this continues to be ignored in the literature on the actor. The image of the romantic Grant remains dominant, no doubt helping to explain why he can comically suffer through so much screwball silliness and slapstick and still remain a romantic prize worth claiming by the genre's dominate women.

Andrew Sarris once noted, in the most fleeting of asides, that Grant was "the most gifted light comedian in the history of cinema."[31] What he failed to add was that this honored status was based largely on performances in that neglected genre called screwball comedy. Just as Cagney and Robinson have become icons of the gangster, or Bogart of the thriller, Grant has put an undeniable stamp on the screwball genre.

An appropriate close is a Grant anecdote about Hollywood. The story also draws upon Chaplin's *Pay Day* (1922), a rare example of the comedian as a henpecked husband—an interesting choice for Grant to have made in light of the present subject matter. This anecdote, a silent comedy metaphor, is constantly unfurled as Grant's philosophy of life, and makes an analogy between Hollywood success and riding a streetcar.[32] The streetcar has only so much room, and every time someone climbs aboard, someone else falls out the back or is pushed. Even if you manage to stay on the streetcar, it never takes you anywhere; you just go in circles. Grant's view of his position on this "ride" is extremely tenuous—he does not have a seat and he must stand in the aisle and hold on to one of the leather ceiling straps. This is a world view with which any Walter Mitty-like screwball male would be most familiar.

CAROLE LOMBARD • IRENE DUNNE

While Grant best essayed screwball comedy's antiheroic male, Carole Lombard and Irene Dunne represent *the* two variations on the eccentric heroine. That is, Lombard is dizzy from the opening minutes of each film;

Dunne generally assumes an eccentric cover midway into the film. Lombard's screwball heroine can be termed character comedy, for it begins with her past. In role after role she showcases a nonstop (almost stream-of-consciousness) daffiness that became the Lombard trademark. Her zaniness is a given of the story, with no real reason presented, though critics tended to offer suggestions—such as that she had been dropped on her head when young.[33] In fact, through the years Lombard's craziness was explained with everything from the comic pun "a one-track mind with grass growing over its rails" (*My Man Godfrey*, 1936) to the more direct "she hasn't a brain in her head" (*Mr. and Mrs. Smith*, 1941).[34]

In contrast, to paraphrase the title of Dunne's first screwball comedy film—Dunne Goes Wild for a specific purpose. Consequently, her comedy is situational in its composition. When necessary she becomes the most comically uninhibited of sophisticates (*Theodora Goes Wild*); at other times she essays an equally uninhibited but decidedly unsophisticated Southern belle (*The Awful Truth, My Favorite Wife*).

Both character and situational heroines abound in the genre but Lombard and Dunne are the pivotal models, with 1936 being the equally pivotal starting point for both (Lombard's role in *Twentieth Century* notwithstanding). That year matched the off-the-wall craziness of Lombard's Irene Bullock (*My Man Godfrey*) against the calculated zaniness of Dunne's Theodora Lynn (*Theodora Goes Wild*). Both women won Academy nominations in the Best Actress category.

Screwball purists might prefer the character type, but unless one has a Lombard with which to sustain it, utilization of the situational approach, at least in part, would seem to offer more possible creative variations. Certainly, this was the case when many elements of 1930s and 1940s screwball comedy began to appear in television situation comedy of the 1950s and 1960s. In fact, screwball comedy frequently offers elements of both, such as the inherently eccentric characters which populate *The Palm Beach Story*, with Claudette Colbert being a situational heroine capable of profiting from her position. Television saw these elements best combined in the *I Love Lucy* show; Lucille Ball was at once a zany and a comic victim of countless situations.

Further examination of Lombard and Dunne merely accents the uniqueness of their character versus situation split, right down to their approaches to comedy theory. Dunne, who had played in few comedies before *Theodora Goes Wild*, believed, "The best way to be funny is to be cold-blooded and purely mental about it."[35] Conversely, Lombard accepted film director Eddie Cline's comedy advice (at a time both were working for silent comedy master Mack Sennett) that to be comically effective she must "Just act everything the same way you behave normally."[36]

Much of Lombard's pre-screwball comedy success seems to have prepared her for the genre. Like Grant, she had had previous slapstick/mime training with a major figure in the art. Lombard's teacher was Mack Sennett, for whom she made a number of silent two-reeler comedies in the late 1920s. Also, like Grant, Lombard began using these talents again when she entered screwball comedy. Beginning with *Twentieth Century* (1934), "she tapped the legacy Mack Sennett had given."[37]

Not surprisingly, her comedy is easily the most physical of any heroine in the genre. In fact, her screwball comedies seem to have followed a major Sennett axiom on comedy: get someone soaking wet, preferably at the close of the film. Thus, Lombard frequently finds herself comically drenched (though her storylines better integrate this water slapstick than did Sennett's). In *My Man Godfrey* when she plays possum with William Powell (a former husband in real life with whom she was still on good terms), she ends up in the shower; in *Mr. and Mrs. Smith* she weathers a torrential downpour while stranded on a giant ferris wheel. And in both *Nothing Sacred* and *True Confession* she fakes watery dilemmas at the more Sennett-minded conclusions. In the former film she ends up saving the antiheroic male "rescuer" (Fredric March), while she "allows" her *True Confession* husband (Fred MacMurray) to play it more conventionally in the latter vehicle.

All these scenes are funny not because there is any surprise and/or loss of dignity involved, the standard comedy theory definition for this type of action (such as Dunne's sudden fall into the pool in *My Favorite Wife*). They are funny because they hardly faze Lombard. For example,

> She does not emerge [from the *Nothing Sacred* soaking] with her hair perfectly curled nor do her clothes miraculously become pressed in the next scene. Carole is realistic when she goes after the laughs. Her hair hangs in stringy wisps and her clothes are soggy. She doesn't care.[38]

She proceeds as before. Like the title of one of her Sennett shorts, *Run Girl Run* (1928, in which Lombard plays a star runner at Sunnydale School, where the three R's are "Romeos, Roadsters, and Roller skates"), Lombard keeps coming. Thus, in *My Man Godfrey* her unplanned shower upsets her for no more than a split second; she then proceeds to bounce on the bed in celebrations—Godfrey's action has been interpreted as a left-handed declaration of love. Lombard is neither logical nor stopable.

Lombard's physical comedy is also most apparent in her battles with screwball comedy males. Though she is a stunning beauty, her tendency to throw punches and assorted inanimate objects places her much closer to those physically intimidating women in earlier antiheroic showcases, such as the rolling-pin-toting Maggie of the newspaper cartoon strip *Bringing Up Father* (1913) or the equally formidable wives "gracing" Laurel & Hardy in the 1920s.

10. William Wellman waters Carole Lombard, while Fredric March watches, on the set of *Nothing Sacred* (1937). (Photograph courtesy of the Museum of Modern Art/Film Stills Archive.)

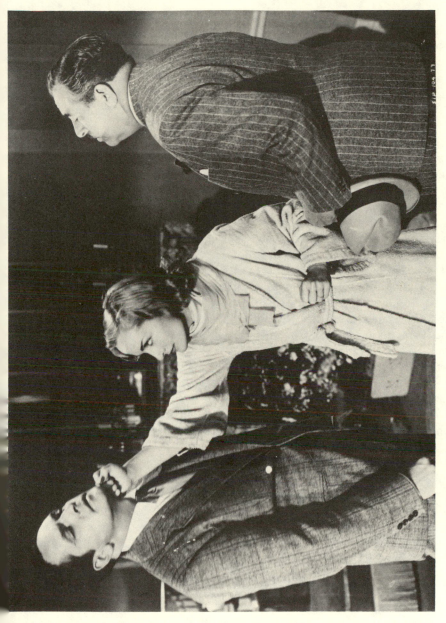

11. Carole Lombard uses Fredric March's face for target practice, while Walter Connolly watches, in *Nothing Sacred* (1937). (Photograph courtesy of the Museum of Modern Art/Film Stills Archive.)

Lombard's most famous screwball combat occurs in *Nothing Sacred,* when she and co-star Fredric March take turns K.O.ing each other. But while March's delivery of a knockout is to help protect the hoax that Lombard is deathly ill (people are seldom at their best unconscious), Lombard's return "favor" is more in the line of sweet revenge, done with a certain feminine modesty. As *Times* magazine described it, "When Hazel [Lombard] comes to, she smiles sweetly, [and] K.O.'s Wally (March).[39]

The film was a major critical and commercial success, with *Variety* calling the fight routine "one of the best laugh scenes ever put on the screen."[40] The film also rated additional attention because of the screwball antics associated with its production. Director William "Wild Bill" Wellman, seemingly having taken a lesson from Gregory La Cava's party-style direction of the previous year's influential *My Man Godfrey* (see Chapter 4), was described by *Life* magazine as believing "the way to get a cast into the spirit of a farce is to create the general atmosphere of a lunatic asylum."[41] Lombard and Wellman did everything between scenes from playing baseball to shooting out floodlights. In the same spirit, Lombard and March gifted Wellman with a strait jacket at the production's close.[42]

As Lombard had written earlier in the year, La Cava "informed me that he had decided, after mentally pulling me apart for a sort of jewel count, that I was an incurable extrovert!"[43] This "incurable extrovert"—on screen and off—had had more than just Sennett's training to prepare her for screwball comedy.

Thirties author Jean Farge Guignol observed that before finally achieving film success in screwball comedy, Lombard was "well known as a vivacious, exciting and excitable girl off the screen. The life of the party. . . . The zest of Hollywood. On the screen she was just another glamour girl."[44] It was because of this personality that Howard Hawks gave her the career break to essentially play herself in *Twentieth Century* (see Chapter 4).

While Lombard had been born in Indiana (and was sometimes referred to as "the Hoosier tornado"), most of her childhood was spent in the film colony itself.[45] Reared by a strong-willed feminist mother long separated from Carole's father, Lombard was the classic tomboy, interested in both athletics and competing with two older brothers. In fact, the actress who would later K.O. Fredric March received boxing lessons as a child (as did one brother) from lightweight boxing champion Benny Leonard![46] Not surprisingly, she was soon able to beat her boxing brother in the ring. As if foreshadowing a future in film, one of her early childhood bouts was observed by pioneer director Allan Dwan.[47] The result was a small part in Dwan's *A Perfect Crime* (1921). The girl who wanted to be a movie star had thus already been in a film by the age of twelve.

A film career did not then suddenly blossom, but Charlie Chaplin did give her a screen test for what would eventually become *The Gold Rush* (1925). Fox films signed Lombard to her first movie contract in 1924.[48]

Again there were ups and downs in the following years, but for "the Hoosier Tornado," who had first found herself in Los Angeles during the pivotal 1910s—the birth years of American film as a Hollywood product—movies would become her way of life.

The eventual apprenticeship in slapstick also provided another important influence: Sennett "insisted on his actors knowing the business from the ground up, so Carole learned how a camera operated, monkeyed around with sets and lights and was encouraged to bean a director who mangled a scene."[49] Her later famous extroverted comaraderie with every level of the Hollywood production team, especially on the set, was an outgrowth of both her personality and her interest in filmmaking. Like film director and friend Gregory La Cava, who directed her in *My Man Godfrey*, she was very strong in her support of the Hollywood rank and file. Not surprisingly, she was also later well-known for being on the set even when the scene(s) did not require her presence—hardly the Hollywood norm. A later *Colliers* overview of her career was appropriately entitled "Fun in Flickers."[50] Besides being a natural description of her movie involvement, it also reflects the more casual approach to filmmaking she knew in both silent film and screwball comedy.

All this is not to say Lombard simply partied herself into a film career; the masculine-willed screwball heroine she and so many other women brought to the genre was just as apparent in her private life. Period articles like "Carole Lombard Tells: 'How I Live By a Man's Code' " and "She Gets Away with Murder" chronicled just that fact.[51] In the piece "Luck—and Lombard," which was more interview than article, she observed, "Determination and tenacity are the important things [in a career]."[52] These characteristics are also central to the screwball heroine, whether it is Irene's (Lombard's) ceaseless pursuit of Godfrey in *My Man Godfrey* or Susan's (Katharine Hepburn's) equally tenacious pursuance of a professor in *Bringing Up Baby*.

Lombard's famous screwball angers had everything but obscenities—something, of course, the 1934 Production Code would not allow. But her cussing was anything but nonexistent off the screen. "The legendary blue talk . . . began as self-defense."[53] The language kept wolves at a distance and later evolved as part of the relaxed Lombard style. "Her flair for the raunchy squelch would work into the folklore of Hollywood."[54] In fact, when this author interviewed William Wellman years later, the director offered his own observations on the subject, without any prompting: "Lombard *did* say dirty words, but not all the time. And when she did say them, for some reason or another, they didn't sound like dirty words. There was a poetic something about her."[55] Lombard's free-spirited, one-of-the-boys charisma was true on screen and off.

Irene Dunne, while equally charismatic, was a decidedly different screwball presence and private person from Lombard. Thus, the contrasting canvases of their already delineated character-versus-situation approach to screwball comedy were based in one broad difference. Lombard was a free-spirited eccentric whose private life was frequently public. Dunne was forever the lady on screen and off (excepting, of course, those moments of screwball comedy truth, when she went "wild"). Nicknamed Lady from birth, her private life was called "one of Hollywood's chief enigmas."[56]

Recognition of Dunne's inherent ladylike manner is not, however, some recent revelation of a revisionist film historian. Period literature grants her number one lady status on screen and off. For example, syndicated columnist and media personality Elsa Maxwell placed Dunne first in her list of "The 10 Great Ladies of the Contemporary World," while *Movie Mirror*'s "Youth Forum" observed: "The Forum had all heard that Irene Dunne was known as Hollywood's Perfect Lady and . . . they found out you can be a perfect lady and a perfectly friendly, warm personality, too."[57] This issue of *Movie Mirror* (March 1940) then introduced Dunne as the month's "Guest Conductor"—leader of a regular body of individuals advising youngsters who had written the "Forum." *American Magazine* later entitled a Dunne biography "Lady Irene," and *Current Biography* would describe her late 1930s position in filmland as the "First Lady of Hollywood."[58]

Columnist and later television personality Ed Sullivan described Dunne as "the most ladylike lady of the screen" when he chronicled a behind-the-scenes look at her *My Favorite Wife* fall into the pool.[59] This dignity-losing comic fall was unusual for Dunne, who normally controls any comic shedding of proper decorum. Of course, the unusualness of the event was indirectly noted by both the fact it was news and that Producer Leo McCarey qualified the fall's comic damage by deciding it would be (in the words of Ed Sullivan) "much funnier if her hair does not get mussed."[60]

Because it is important that Dunne's lady make a conscious, controlled switch to comedy, her *My Favorite Wife* fall does not generate the laughs one would expect in an otherwise nearly flawless film. This same principle also explains why Dunne's screwball comedy *Joy of Living* (1938) did not live up to expectations. Dunne's lady in this film is too much pursued by the romantically aggressive Douglas Fairbanks, Jr.

Much of the humor in a Dunne screwball comedy is based in the contrast between her proper persona and the slightly unhinged person she decides to let out. It is not, however, that she needs thawing, as is the case with Katharine Hepburn in *The Philadelphia Story* (1940) and *Woman of the Year* (1942). Dunne is most often likably normal from the start of each movie. Though her films showcase a wealthy life-style undoubtedly attractive to their initial depression audiences, things seem more realistic and easier to identify with. No small part of this is based in Dunne's motherly manner. As women film historian Marjorie Rosen (*Popcorn Venus*, 1973) observes, basing her analysis upon *The Awful Truth, My*

Favorite Husband, and *Penny Serenade*, "she was essentially a matronly, warm comic personality."[61] Dunne herself once comically threatened, borrowing from Owen Wister's *The Virginian*, "when I am called 'dignified,' I feel like saying to the accuser, 'When you say that, smile!' "[62]

Besides Dunne's frequent mothering of the antiheroic Grant (see Chapter 3), her screwball comedy films are more likely to include a child than those of any other heroine in the genre. Thus, the presence of a baby in *Theodora Goes Wild* represents a key plot development at the film's close. While *The Awful Truth* substitutes a Scottish terrier named Mr. Smith for a child, two children were included in *My Favorite Wife*. And if there was ever any doubt as to which wife would be chosen, the mutual admiration between Dunne and the children, versus wife number two's coolness, told the viewer all it was necessary to know. The screwball scenes in the generally melodramatic *Penny Serenade* (Dunne felt it had more laughs than most comedies) center on the comic baby-rearing dilemmas in which rookie parents become involved.[63] In Dunne's *Unfinished Business* (1941), a mixture of screwball comedy and melodrama, the whole story keys upon the film closing realization that she has a baby. And *Lady in a Jam* (1942) builds a close relationship between Dunne and child actor/supporting player Jane Garland. Importantly, Dunne's more family-oriented screwball comedies anticipate the post-World War II developments of the genre as it attempted to move to suburbia. Not surprisingly, Dunne would later excel in the title role of the non-screwball comedy *I Remember Mama* (1948), as well as being the spirited mother in *Life with Father* (1947).

In real life, "It's distinctly understood among her few intimates that Irene Dunne is meant when one asks after the Mother Hen. 'Well, what's Mother Hen about today?' "[64] By all accounts, Dunne's personal life-style has always been caring but distinctly quiet. As *Photoplay* writer Sean Hamilton revealed, in an article entitled "This Is Really Irene Dunne" (Hamilton includes a Dunne thank you note verifying the authenticity of the author's comments):

> I can promise you nothing sensational. For Irene Dunne is not a sensational woman [in terms of the public star]. I can guarantee no juicy bits of intimate gossip. For I know of none. Unless, perhaps she lies awake nights heartsick about the kitchen sink in her new home. She's afraid it's too near the door. Or would you call that juicy? No? No. I thought not.[65]

While Lombard had truly movie-star marriages to first William Powell and then Clark Gable (no Hollywood courtship and marriage was more closely followed), Dunne was married quietly to former New York dentist Francis Griffin for nearly forty years (he died in 1965). While Lombard's social circle was decidedly composed of film people whose off-screen

12. Irene Dunne displays her "Theodora" smile at the premiere of *Penny Serenade* (1941). (Photograph courtesy of the Museum of Modern Art/Film Stills Archive.)

activities frequently received as much ink as their film appearances, Dunne's circle was smaller and was centered outside the entertainment profession. Moreover, much of "Mother Hen's" time was taken up with an adopted daughter, which no doubt later attracted her to the adoption-focused story *Penny Serenade*. In fact, Dunne observed of this film: "I don't think I've felt as close to any picture. It's very much the scheme of my own personal life."[66] When once asked why she had always been so ultrareticent about her private life, she responded, "I didn't realize I was, but, if so, it must be because I consider it so simple I don't see how it can interest anyone."[67]

The Lady Dunne-Loony Lombard dichotomy is also reflected in the relationship between their screwball comedies and their films outside the genre. Dunne had already achieved great success in musicals, melodramas, and the western *Cimarron*—the Academy Award-winning Best Picture for 1930-31, for which she won her first nomination for Best Actress. In fact, Dunne was so impressive in *Cimarron*, especially her character's speech when elected to Congress, that Will Rogers, who disapproved of women entering politics, was moved to observe: "If women like Irene Dunne would run for Congress, I'd vote for them."[68] Among her other pivotal non-screwball comedies were the melodrama *Back Street* (1932) and the musical *Show Boat* (1936; she had also starred in the stage version).

Film theorist Stanley Cavell underlines the importance of Dunne's musical background to her screwball comedy identity when he suggests that Ralph Bellamy is immediately telegraphed as a loser in *The Awful Truth* after the Dunne-Bellamy "Home, Home on the Range" duet. Cavell bases this view on Bellamy's question to Dunne as to whether she has had lessons. (Despite having butchered the song, Bellamy is proud of not having had the luxury.) Cavell states that the

> exchange about lessons is a gag based on the knowledge that Irene Dunne is a singer, a piece of knowledge no one who knew anything about her could have failed to know. The initial point of the gag is its satisfaction of the demand of the genre that each member of it declare the identity of the flesh and blood actress who plays its central female character.[69]

Cavell goes on to compare Dunne's modest but pleased acceptance of her great gift of song (as opposed to Bellamy's pride with no gift) to Fred Astaire's equally balanced ego toward his gift of dance. Appropriately, Cavell defines this balance as "sophistication."[70] For Dunne, this is just another way of calling her lady.

Lady Dunne's ties to the musical are reinforced frequently in her screwball comedies (as well as drawing from her life), starting with her first, *Theodora Goes Wild*, in which she both sings in her small-town church (as Dunne really did as a youngster) and at home—to quiet the non-musical singing of Melvyn Douglas. The latter example is quite ingenious, especially Dunne's use of the song "Be Still My Heart," with the accent on the title's first two words. It is a serenade and accompanying musical reply, screwball comedy style—meaning it is full of comic irritation.

A musical Dunne is also central to *The Awful Truth*. Early on Cary Grant suspects Dunne of having made more than one kind of music with handsome voice instructor Alexander D'Arcy. Later Grant appears at what he thinks is a Dunne-D'Arcy rendezvous; it turns out to be a recital. And the only thing Grant breaks up is Dunne's singing voice; when he tips over his chair as he listens to her sing, her voice breaks into the most delightful laugh. Again, song has defined a screwball comedy relationship in Dunne's favor.

In both *The Awful Truth* and *My Favorite Wife*, music is also tied to Dunne's going wild scenes. That is, in the former film when she "becomes" Grant's zany, heavily Southern-accented sister (Dunne was born in Louisville, Kentucky, and once had a very thick Southern-accent), her repertoire of comic ways to embarrass Grant (who has become involved with someone else) includes doing a nightclub number, "Gone with the Wind," performed earlier by the heavily Southern-accented Dixie Belle Lee (Joyce Compton). In *My Favorite Wife* Dunne returns again as a Southern eccentric with an accent. While she does not sing, she plays the sympathetic music-appreciating mother to a young daughter (Mary Lou Harrington) whose piano skills might best be described as torturing. (One of the first things Santa brought Dunne's real-life daughter was a piano.[71])

In *Joy of Living* Dunne is actually cast as a theatrical musical comedy star (which she was in the 1920s) whose family pushes her career for meal-ticket reasons. While Dunne was not similarly used by her family, in later years she expressed displeasure with their emphasis on music study: "Lessons, that's all I remember of my childhood. My parents wanted me to be a singer. Whenever I wanted to play with the neighborhood children I had to practice. There were lessons, lessons, always lessons."[72]

Unfinished Business, part screwball comedy and part melodrama, revolves around Dunne and music. It opens with her singing at a small-town wedding before leaving for an unsuccessful try at the New York Opera. (Dunne had followed a similar course in real life.) She next finds work singing messages over the phone, eventually graduating to happy birthday numbers in a nightclub—where she meets both a past lover and a future husband (Robert Montgomery). Much later, after a separation from Montgomery, the couple chance to meet at the opera, where Dunne is now in the chorus. Thus, *Unfinished Business* has come full circle, with a musical Dunne forever central to the film.

Lady in a Jam, Dunne's last screwball comedy, even recycles some variations on earlier musical moments in the genre. For example, when she returns to a calculated zaniness (uncharacteristically, the film had opened with her in an eccentric state), she again uses song to express her methodical madness. Moreover, a singing Bellamy—dressed as a cowboy, no less—returns to do even greater violence to music that he did in *The Awful Truth*. This time around no dumb question by Bellamy is necessary, if ever it was (see the Cavell position examined earlier in this chapter), to understand Dunne and Bellamy are not right for each other. With Bellamy's voice, one would not even wish him on Cactus Kate (Queenie Vassar), Dunne's shotgun-toting grandmother in the film.

Not everything musical in *Lady in a Jam* has been recycled, however. The film's most ingenious gag has an Indian chorus (on horseback) singing "Here Comes the Bride" in dialect to Dunne. Predating Mel Brooks's *Blazing Saddles* (1974) by thirty-two years, the comic surprise it generates brings to mind two scenes from that film: the black workers singing "I Get a Kick Out of You" (with Temptations-like choreography) and the Indians speaking Yiddish.

Dunne's Lady Irene status was thus firmly established before her screwball comedies by her involvement in other genres, the most important of which (the musical) as has been shown, frequently spotlighted in her screwball films. Moreover, the personalized/improvisational nature of screwball comedy, tied so closely to the real lives of its directors and stars, is also reinforced by knowledge of the significance of music in Dunne's personal life. In fact, Charles Silver, who directs the Museum of Modern Art's Film Study Program, credits Dunne and Grant in *The Awful Truth* as "giving two of the most superbly timed and improvised performances in all cinema."[73]

Amazement was at first expressed that Dunne could so successfully enter the screwball comedy realm. For example, 1930s *Motion Picture* author Sonia Lee stated Dunne had "given Hollywood the shock of its life" by revealing herself to be a "comedienne of the first rank as gaily erratic as a snow flurry in May."[74] Yet, besides the special screwball tailoring for Dunne, it must be remembered that both the musical and the melodrama (the non-screwball genres in which Dunne was most active), are sister genres to screwball comedy. That is, like screwball comedy, they are of indeterminate time and space—they can take place in any period or place (see Chapter 1). And characters must deal with compromise, since the action of all these genres is governed by the mores of a more conventional society. After all, that is how one knows certain players are screwball. Thus, unlike the determinate time and place western, there is never anything as neatly final as a shootout at the O.K. Corrall. Yet, as women film historian Ethan Mordden observed, "Dunne is so *lady* that when she becomes antic it's like a Quaker going to war: take it *very* seriously."[75]

In contrast to Dunne's already film-established Lady Irene rank (her last screwball comedy is even called *Lady in a Jam*), Lombard's status as a loony had less support from her pre-screwball comedy film career, outside of her association with Sennett. But this slapstick connection was used as both a metaphor for her screwball comedy work and her private life. Thus, *Life*'s feature article on *Nothing Sacred* noted some of Lombard's "scenes give scope for a notable talent at low comedy which she acquired during her early career as one of Mack Sennett's pie-throwing bathing girls."[76] And a 1941 article on her personal life is entitled "As a Star of Talkies She Retains Zest for Life of Mack Sennett Era," observing Lombard "has never quite outgrown those dear old custard-pie days and as an actress she loves to play in comedies."[77]

Other than the Sennett tie, Lombard's pre-screwball comedy film identity was like Cary Grant's—the attractive sex symbol, though she had appeared in nothing so box office as the Mae West-Grant films. Still, one period overview of her career broke it down into three stages: "(1) sexy; (2) screwy; (3) serious."[78] And like Grant's ability to project a certain sexuality even in the most antiheroic of postures, Lombard can be sexy in the most spaced-out of apogees.

Because, however, Lombard had not achieved the pre-screwball comedy film success of Lady Dunne, her personal eccentricities were much more central to her public persona; this was also the reason Howard Hawks had cast her in the all-important *Twentieth Century*. Moreover, the off-screen Lombard so matched the screwball comedy one that the public did not accept her post-screwball attempts at serious roles, even though her critical reviews were often positive. Thus, at the time of her tragic death she had returned home to screwball comedy, having made *Mr. and Mrs. Smith* and the not-yet-released screwball/black comedy *To Be or Not to Be* (1942).

Ironically, Dunne's last screwball comedy, *Lady in a Jam* also appeared in 1942 as if the two poles of the screwball heroine had to close their work jointly in this genre. Screwball comedy itself was winding down at this time, largely because of World War II. But just as it would surface with new strength in years to come, Lady Dunne and Loony Lombard would represent ongoing classic models of the screwball heroine.

CLAUDETTE COLBERT • KATHARINE HEPBURN • JEAN ARTHUR

Three additional screwball comedy heroines meriting further examination are Claudette Colbert, Katharine Hepburn, and Jean Arthur. Colbert, still best known for her Academy Award-winning Best Actress performance in *It Happened One Night* (1934), has yet to receive the recognition due for her body of work within screwball comedy. In fact two films—*Midnight* (1939, directed by Mitchell Leisen, from a Billy Wilder-Charles Brackett screenplay) and Preston Sturges's *The Palm Beach Story* (1942)—rank with the genre's best.

In *It Happened One Night* Colbert plays a runaway heiress, a near victim of a male gold digger. But the best of her subsequent screwball comedy roles placed her in the apparent gold-digger stance. This is especially true of *Bluebeard's Eighth Wife* (1938, where she out-bluebeards Bluebeard), *Midnight* (appropriately named Eve, she observes early: "No woman ever found peace in a taxi. I'm looking for a limousine."), and *The Palm Beach Story* (which would double as a graduate course in gold digging). In fact, *The Palm Beach Story* is packed with Colbert-Joel McCrea (as her estranged husband) dialogue such as:

> *Colbert:* "I might not get married again. I might become an adventuress."
>
> *McCrea:* "I can just see you starting for China on a twenty-six foot sailboat."
>
> *Colbert:* "You're thinking of an adventurer, dear. An adventuress never goes on anything under three hundred feet with a crew of eighty."

Not only does this exchange nicely demonstrate Colbert's gold-digger stance, it also reiterates the basic woman in control position of screwball comedy. Thus, Colbert flaunts her anticipated new "career" while giving McCrea an English lesson. Ironically, even when McCrea receives a rare chance to play teacher and correct a Colbert malapropism, her mistake (if it was a mistake) is decidedly on the money in comically describing their relationship. Colbert had observed: "I'm just a milestone around your neck." Though McCrea offers the correct word (millstone), for a frustrated inventor and his curvaceous wife, "milestone" is the antiheroic truth.

As if passing some gold-digger screening test, Colbert often finds herself starting her adventuress adventure with merely the clothes on her back. But unlike *It Happened One Night*, which also begins this way, the stakes are much higher. Consequently, in *Midnight* she first appears in possession of only the flimsiest of evening gowns. This disadvantage, if it is a disadvantage, is soon parlayed into a most comfortable existence as a European baroness. In *The Palm Beach Story* her clothing "handicap" becomes a pair of men's pajamas which soon make her an American baroness of sorts after meeting a Rockefellerish John D. Hackensacker III (Rudy Vallee). Because Hackensacker writes everything he buys in a little book, the viewer is even granted an overview to the new state of her wardrobe, which now includes everything from "12 pair of stockings" to "3 brassieres (fancy)," as well as two dozen other items.

Naturally, by the conclusion of her gold-digger films, especially the trilogy of *Bluebeard's Eighth Wife, Midnight,* and *The Palm Beach Story,* Colbert does the right non-gold-digger thing. She returns to Gary Cooper in *Bluebeard*, despite having literally driven him crazy as well as taking him for a $100,000-a-year divorce settlement. In *Midnight*, in spite of her early comment about taxis, she ends up with taxi driver Don Ameche. And in *The Palm Beach Story* she eventually returns to McCrea—though he will now be rich because of Vallee's backing.

Colbert's ability to play "America's most sophisticated sweetheart,"[79] a title she had even before the aforementioned trilogy, draws from both Colbert's real-life and her pre-screwball comedy roles. First, while hastening to add she was never a real-life gold digger, Colbert's French birth granted her a more worldly position on screen and off. As was the case with the sophisticated American film comedies of German-born director Ernst Lubitsch, American audiences seemed more accepting of adult fare from European-born artists. (Colbert had appeared in Lubitsch's non-screwball *The Smiling Lieutenant*, 1931, as well as *Bluebeard's Eighth Wife*; she had also starred with French great Maurice Chevalier in *The Big Pond*, 1930, winning the role because she was bilingual.[80] Early in the sound era foreign language versions were frequently made, instead of today's use of subtitles or dubbing.)

Born in Paris, she came to this country as a child, but she continued to maintain French ties and American journalists seldom forgot her European heritage. Notice of this background appeared frequently in Colbert articles (see especially the 1930 Colbert portrait from *Colliers* entitled "Woman from Paris"[81]). Moreover, it was accented all the more by the filmmakers with whom she worked. Gregory La Cava, who nicknamed her "The Fretting Frog,"[82] directed her in *She Married Her Boss*, where her desire to live in Paris is an important plot point. In *The Gilded Lily* (1935) Colbert goes to Europe as a nightclub singer to seek revenge on a titled Englishman (Ray Milland) she believes has wronged her. *I Met Him in Paris* (1937) should have been titled *I Met Them in Paris*, for she meets two possible Mr. Rights (Melvyn Douglas and Robert Young) there as she fulfills her character's dream of going to Paris. There is also an amusing turn with a French waiter who thinks he can speak English, too. *Bluebeard's Eighth Wife* casts her as a Parisian; the film is set in Paris and Czechoslovakia. *Midnight* also takes place in Paris and on an estate outside the city. Thus, the most wordly of screwball heroines regularly found her comedies set abroad, accenting both her foreign persona and the high life associated with the genre.

Colbert's pre-screwball comedy film career had frequently been composed of virtuous characters, but in 1932 she had successfully essayed the part of Poppaea—described as "the wickedest woman in the world"—in Cecil B. DeMille's *Sign of the Cross*. And the same year as *It Happened One Night*, she had returned to DeMille for the title role of another epic which mixed history and sexuality: *Cleopatra* (1934). Thus, like Cary Grant and Carole Lombard, she brought pre-packaged sensuality to a genre (screwball comedy) sometimes defined in suppressed sexuality terms.

While the role of Poppaea had been a calculated career move on Colbert's part (see *American Magazine*'s 1935 article, "She was *such* a Nice Girl"[83]), screwball films revealed her natural gift for comedy and allowed her to play someone very close to the independent career woman she was. While not without being worrisome (remember La Cava's "Fretting Frog" tag), author Kyle Crichton's "Career Girl" portrait of Colbert reported, "She insists that the way to get along is to have a superiority complex and work hard."[84]

While Loony Lombard and Lady Dunne got their men through special screwball variations of the dating game, Colbert generally won hers somewhat reluctantly. Her screwball heroines seemed more out for a good time, which is one of the key reasons they traveled so much. The other reason for all the travel was that Colbert's heroines were often trying to dodge possessive men: her father (Walter Connolly) in *It Happened One Night*, a romantic cabbie (Don Ameche) in *Midnight*, a husband (Joel McCrea) in *The Palm Beach Story*.

As is often the case in the genre, such characteristics were not alien to the performer. Colbert's independently unconventional living arrangement with first husband actor Norman Foster—they maintained separate residences—caused many a raised eyebrow in early 1930s Hollywood.[85] And twice during the decade she took career-risking extended holidays (of six and eight months, respectively) to travel, the first by tramp steamer. Before the second trip she observed, "Well, I'm young now. So's Jack [Pressman, her second husband]. In another ten years we'll forget how to be mad and impromptu about things. Careers or no careers, we'll go now while we can enjoy it."[86] Not only does this philosophy apply for several of her screwball heroines, it is very similar to her parting declaration to Joel McCrea in *The Palm Beach Story* before taking one more impromptu trip.

As with other key performers in the genre, Colbert's screwball comedies were frequently peppered with indirect references to her and scenes from earlier firms. An especially popular starting point is the critical and commercial success *She Married Her Boss*. Colbert plays a department store executive desirous of a trip to Paris but who is saddled with such decisions as: Can pajama outfits be broken up? In *I Met Him in Paris* Colbert plays a department store fashion designer who finally is realizing a long-desired Parisian holiday; *Bluebeard's Eighth Wife* begins with an extended sexually comic look at the controversy generated by trying to break up a pajama outfit in a department store.

She Married Her Boss would also be the first screwball comedy in which a character would accuse her of being a gold digger. And just as her role in the film involved loosening up a rigidly overworked leading man as well as her own character, Colbert confessed to director La Cava that she was involved in an ongoing breakdown of her own rigidity.[87] Since La Cava's working method was so dependent upon the personal identities of his players (see Chapter 4), this no doubt had an effect on the molding of her *She Married Her Boss* character. Moreover, though La Cava does not take credit for it, his aforementioned "Fretting Frog" article would seem to suggest that he was instrumental in tapping fundamental Colbert qualities not previously seen on the screen. (La Cava and Colbert were already friends who had just worked closely on the intense 1935 drama *Private Worlds*, about a mental institution.)

A key twist of the plot in *The Gilded Lily* has Colbert being publicized as "The No-Girl," someone who has turned down a titled foreigner. In 1927 the then-Broadway star had created a major stir when she confessed to liking her acting career so much that, "Why, I honestly think if the Prince of Wales should suddenly propose to me, I'd say, after the first faint, 'What! and give up my career?' I'm that earnest."[88] Much later it was revealed that as a youngster she not only had had the standard daydreams about marrying a prince, she had actually met the Prince of Wales at a special New York luncheon where she represented the French children in her school. She later reminded him of this early introduction when the two met as adults.[89] For Colbert, princes were more than just a random screwball subject.

Without turning this discussion into a game of Trivial Pursuit, one of the more interesting Colbertisms in the genre is based on the hitchhiking scene in *It Happened One Night*, where Colbert's exposed leg bests all the thumb moves thought possible by a very frustrated Clark Gable. Though director Frank Capra later revealed that she originally did not want to show her leg, the near use of a chorus girl's limb (for "doubling" purposes) made Colbert change her mind.[90] Though Capra makes no mention of it, her hesitancy was probably the result of the great deal of attention her legs had already attracted. In her late 1920s star-making Broadway role as the worldly Lou in *The Barker*, reviewers were fascinated by a sex appeal attached to "the best looking legs that have walked across a Broadway stage in many a moon."[91] In fact, "her shapely legs inspired a New York columnist to use the phrase, 'a swell pair of Colberts,' whenever he wanted to pay tribute to a lady's supporting attractions."[92] Thus, it was not for nothing that Capra remembered, "There are no more luscious gams in the world than Colbert's—not even Marlene's (Dietrich)."[93]

It should be noted, moreover, that Capra's production of *It Happened One Night* is very much in the ad lib, keep-it-moving, let-actors-play-themselves tradition examined in the chapter on directors. After the movie became one of the commercial and critical hits of all time, Capra would spend years on future projects with social themes. But *It Happened One Night* was shot on a short schedule with a tight budget. Capra observed, "Relieved from the onus of studio 'expectations,' we slammed through the film clowning, laughing, ad-libbing."[94] Indeed, Capra suggests Colbert's ongoing in-film hostility toward Clark Gable is merely a recycling of a real hostility toward the director (she was originally hesitant about the role).[95]

Appropriately the French girl at the beginning of screwball comedy also made the post-World War II *The Egg and I* (1947), an important transitional film in a genre which was then starting a move to the suburbs—or, in this case, to a chicken farm. Colbert, teamed a third time with Fred MacMurray (they had appeared together in *The Gilded Lily* and *The Bride Comes Home* in 1935), was far from being a gold digger here, but maybe that is why *The Egg and I* was such a commercial hit. After all, the greatest consistency of Colbert's career had been successful films. And as one 1930s film magazine closed a Colbert article: "She knows what she wants—how to get it and how to hold it."[96] For Colbert, things had not changed in the intervening years.

Unlike the heroines examined thus far, there is not the same uniformity of character in Katharine Hepburn's screwball comedy film roles. Coming later to the genre than did Lombard, Dunne, and Colbert, Hepburn is, however, the most forceful. Moreover, her greatest screwball role, as madcap heiress Susan Vance in *Bringing Up Baby,* is important both because it is extremely funny and because it represents "the final evolution of [the dizzy screwball heroine] . . . she's completely unhinged, so zany that at times she seems almost certifiably insane."[97] Hepburn biographer Gary Carey, from whom the preceding quote is drawn, oversimplifies the condition of screwball heroines, however, when he suggests most were "dizzy young creatures."[98] As already demonstrated with Dunne and Colbert, the nonstop loony was not every screwball heroine's approach.

As befits a frequently cinematically self-conscious genre, though, Hepburn's Susan Vance combines the zaniness of Lombard with the gone-wild side of Dunne (especially the latter's comically wicked laugh—forever implying to the male, "you don't have a chance.") And Hepburn's gun-moll imitation near the close of *Bringing Up Baby* harkens back to a similar Jean Arthur scene in *The Whole Town's Talking* (1935). But despite these footnotes to other heroines, Hepburn still manages to give the role her own special speed and authority—rather like a Bryn Mawr pep rally march played at 78 r.p.m.

Hepburn immediately followed *Baby* with the more restrained *Holiday*, where she does not so much rehabilitate a rigid Grant (as was the case in *Baby*) as save him from the elitist fossilization a marriage to her stuffy sister (Doris Nolan) would represent. Though Hepburn understudied the role on Broadway a decade earlier, her film rescue mission is somewhat reminiscent of Colbert's saving of Melvyn Douglas from another class-conscious sister (Katharine Alexander, Douglas's sister and surrogate wife) in *She Married Her Boss.*

Hepburn's performances in *Bringing Up Baby* and *Holiday* do have several parallels. In both cases they play upon the actress's own Connecticut background of privilege and independence (Connecticut being a favorite haven of the genre and the location of *Bringing Up Baby*). Moreover, each role celebrates her individualism. In the former her unrelenting unusual courtship wears Grant down; in *Holiday* she defends Grant's individualism and breaks with her materialistic family. *Baby* and *Holiday* also showcase the naturally athletic Hepburn, from an accomplished golf game to pratfalls and tumbling.

A final parallel between the two is that neither had more than marginal success at the box office, though Hepburn received good reviews. In fact, it was at this time that Harry Brandt, president of the Independent Theatre Owners of America, declared Hepburn and several other Hollywood film stars "box-office poison." The national press picked up on the "poison" claim and it proved to be very damaging.

After *Holiday*, the equally forceful real-life Hepburn (Carey appropriately subtitled his Hepburn biography *A Hollywood Yankee*) bought out her film contract and returned to the East. She would eventually star on Broadway in the critical and commercial hit *The Philadelphia Story*, written expressly for her by *Holiday* author Philip Barry. Buying the film rights, she would then return to Hollywood in triumph, with the film adaptation repeating the stage success.

The Philadelphia Story (1940) does not, however, celebrate Hepburn's individualism. Instead, it undercuts it. Hepburn forcefulness (which off screen had already "won" her the nickname of "Katharine of Arrogance") has turned to ice, and her character, appropriately named Tracy Lord, is in need of a rescue by former husband Cary Grant (whose relaxed manner matches his relaxed name—Haven). With the aid of Grant, whom she remarries, and reporter James Stewart (who would win the Academy Award as Best Actor for his role), Hepburn does not marry the socially rigid blue blood John Howard. But the "film tends to underline and overstress everything that worked in the play, including Tracy's comeuppance."[99]

Screwball comedy normally focuses on the remaking of the man—the breaking up of social and academic rigidity. Thus, the thrust of *The Philadelphia Story*, the humanizing of Hepburn, contradicts the traditional movement of the genre as well as Hepburn's previous two screwball outings, where in both cases she rescued Grant from rigidity.[100] This variation might be more palatable if it were less preachy: messages never mix well with madcap romance.

Women film historian Molly Haskell has observed that even in Hepburn's best films, "there was a cutting edge to her parts as written, a kind of ruthless, upper-class eccentricity, that was more a revenge on, than an expression of, her personality."[101] This is especially true in *The Philadelphia Story*. According to George Cukor, who directed her in numerous films besides the one in question, Hepburn's pre-*Philadelphia Story* unpopularity was because "She challenged the audience and that wasn't the fashion in those days. When people first saw her they saw something arrogant in her playing."[102]

While *The Philadelphia Story* goes against the screwball genre, it does point up the inherent conservative nature of the genre: female individualism is to be directed entirely at male conquest; it is not a commodity meant to exist outside of a romantic situation of "all's fair in love and war." Thus, in *The Philadelphia Story* and the subsequent social comedy *Woman of the Year* (1942), the battle to bring Hepburn into the camp of humanizing love at all costs is both intense and outside the norm of screwball heroines—because they had never left.

The opening of a 1937 *Motion Picture* magazine article on Hepburn describes this phenomenon in a more colloquial manner:

> You know those wooden dolls you slap down and then . . . they bob up again . . .? They were made to be slapped down. Katharine Hepburn reminds me of them. Reminds me of a bright challenge to the world to slap her down so that she can demonstrate her ability to bob up again. For Katharine's life has been a series of slappings-down and gettings-up.[103]

The article then chronicles a number of Hepburn biography facts long since a part of the popular culture awareness of the actress—facts which sound tailor-made for the dominate screwball comedy heroine. One example is the strong-willed parents (her mother was a pioneer feminist in national campaigns for suffrage and birth control) who instilled independence in their daughter. Another fact: tomboy Katharine was so disappointed that she was born a girl that she once had her hair severely cropped and put on boy's clothing in order not to be discriminated against in roughhouse play with her brothers. (Much later she would describe her life as having been "lived like a man."[104])

If one includes her real-life Connecticut connection, including Bryn Mawr trimmings, Hepburn seems born to the genre. Ironically, then, the most strong-willed screwball heroine on screen and off won her only box-office success in the genre with a film for which she seems to have been "made to be slapped down."

In contrast to the gold-digger characterization of Colbert or the extreme individualism of Hepburn, Jean Arthur is mild-mannered. Just as bad things seem to happen to the male comic antihero, so good things readily come Arthur's way. Paradoxically, Arthur is today probably most associated with the strong woman roles she played in Frank Capra's *Mr. Deeds Goes to Town* (1936) and *Mr. Smith Goes to Washington* (1939). But as noted in Chapter 3, these films are populist classics, not screwball comedy archetypes. Arthur's true screwball identity is much softer than her rival genre heroines.

When mainstream screwball Arthur works are examined—films like *Easy Living* (1937), *Too Many Husbands* (1940), and *The More the Merrier* (1943)—her heroine could be claimed as a first cousin to Harry Langdon's grace of God silent screen character. That is, like Langdon, she inevitably wins out, but frequently by events for which she is not responsible and often unaware. For example, her screwball signature role in *Easy Living* even opens with a gift which arrives as if from the gods of comedy. Arthur is riding down Fifth Avenue in an open-air bus when a mink coat descends from the heavens and chooses Arthur as its new owner. In reality, millionaire Edward Arnold has tossed it out a penthouse window as a lesson to the nonstop spending of his wife. But as the story continues, Arthur continues to be the innocent recipient of the most delightful gifts, including the genre's most decadent apartment, all because New York assumes her to be Arnold's mistress.

If screwball signature scenes from other genre heroines are juxtaposed with innocent Arthur's "heavenly" mink encounter, Arthur's softer screwball comedy presence is further accented. For example, Lombard would best be showcased punching out Fredric March in *Nothing Sacred*, while Dunne's genre hall-of-fame scene would be her first comic transformation in the self-explainingly titled *Theodora Goes Wild*. Colbert would naturally be associated with the hitchhiking scene in *It Happened One Night* in which she exposes one of her already famous Broadway legs. Yet, Colbert's comic diatribe against Joel McCrea early in *The Palm Beach Story* (1942), where she spouts something of a gold digger's "Bill of Rights," is a strong second. The overpowering Hepburn needed, of course, no "Bill of Rights"—normally doing just as she pleased, especially in *Bringing Up Baby*. And the most memorable Hepburn scene in that film is the symbolic conclusion, when she brings down both the brontosaurus skeleton and Cary Grant's last vestige of rigidity. A strong runner-up scene from *Baby* occurs on the golf course early in the film, where Hepburn first takes Grant's golf ball, then his automobile, then finally Grant himself.

It could be argued that Colbert, like Arthur, also has nice things suddenly happen to her, such as the Sugar Daddy benevolence of John Barrymore in *Midnight*, a film whose very title is a reference to the Cinderella story. In reality, however, the film is a very left-handed reference to both Cinderella and Arthur. Early in the film, as is the norm for all Colbert gold-digger stories, Colbert fully articulates her conscious decision to follow the most opportunistic of paths. In contrast, Arthur is nothing, if not innocent, in the most wide-eyed manner. This is demonstrated by the fact she even attempts to return the mink coat in *Easy Living*, something that never would occur to a Colbert character.

Arthur tends to be not only more innocent than her screwball comedy rivals, but also decidedly more normal. She is capable of playing the most delightful of madcaps. Her title role in the *Thin Man*-like *The Ex-Mrs. Bradford* (1936) even makes one wish the most cinematically blasphemous of thoughts—that Arthur, not Myrna Loy, had been teamed with William Powell in the series. But usually Arthur is closer to her role in *You Can't Take It With You* (1938), in which she is the only normal member of a very eccentric household.

Consequently, in *Too Many Husbands*, she is the wife who has not received adequate attention in two marriages. The return of husband number one, believed to have been lost at sea, allows her all the attention of a dual courtship, a situation she does not hurry to change. In *The More the Merrier*, two live-in men (Charles Coburn and Joel McCrea) are subletting her apartment in crowded Washington, D.C., something she had neither planned on nor wanted. But again Arthur falls heir to another romantic situation—largely the result of matchmaker Coburn. Thus, husky-voiced Arthur has the appeal of the shy girl next door.

As has been the case so often before for performers working in this genre, Arthur's shyness was innate to the real person. Articles from the period focused on this shyness, and Capra later chronicled the extreme trial it was for her to face the camera each and every time.[105] Not surprisingly, once she was able to fulfill her studio contract (she had less career control than any of the other screwball heroines examined), her film involvement quickly faded out. Eventually, those rare Arthur articles (she had never found it comfortable or necessary to talk to the press) said it all in their titles, such as *Cosmopolitan*'s 1953 "Disappearing Jean Arthur (though it did not address her fewer roles)," or *Life*'s 1960 "Seclusive Jean Arthur in her California Home."[106]

MELVYN DOUGLAS • FRED MacMURRAY

No other male comes close to screwball comedy centerpiece Cary Grant. The screen's greatest light comedian, Grant is a category unto himself. He was capable of exuding sexuality despite the most comic antiheroic posturing, and his physical comedy gifts were leagues beyond the competition. As film critic and historian Andrew Sarris has noted, Grant is the "only actor indispensable to the genre."[107] However, Grant could not be in every screwball comedy, despite compiling a sizable filmography in the genre. (Robert Montgomery, though without Grant's physical comedy skills, comes closest to Grant's mixture of comedic timing and sexual vulnerability.) Consequently, this section briefly examines two performers who represent broad general types in the genre—the worldly Melvyn Douglas and the American regular guy Fred MacMurray. Appropriately, the actors which Lewis Jacobs, dean of American film historians, finds "most representative" of the genre male, besides Grant, are MacMurray and Douglas.[108] (They are also the only ones Jacobs mentions in his brief writing on the genre during the period.)

The forever worldly Douglas showcased a great deal of versatility in the genre. He could be sophisticated with Greta Garbo (*Two-Faced Woman*, 1941; they had also starred in the non-screwball comedy *Ninotchka* in 1939 and the drama *As You Desire Me* in 1932), or he could mix sophistication and slapstick with Irene Dunne (*Theodora Goes Wild*). And he was also good at slipping into what might best be called the Ralph Bellamy sweet-but-square best-friend category, à la Bellamy's work in *The Awful Truth, His Girl Friday,* and *Lady in a Jam.* Douglas assumes this position for part of the time in *I Met Him in Paris* and all of it in *Too Many Husbands.* And like Bellamy, whose best second-fiddle roles supported Grant, Douglas does just the same in *Mr. Blandings Builds His Dream House* (1948). Interestingly enough, Bellamy and Douglas were "star students together in Douglas's first foray into drama school."[109]

While Douglas's versatility was always appreciated by his peers (William Powell had even suggested Douglas as a possible replacement for him in the "Thin Man" series when ill health threatened Powell's life.[110]), he received special peer recognition years later by being awarded two Best Supporting Actor Oscars (*Hud* in 1963 and *Being There* in 1979). But by then the actor had undergone such a physical change, from young leading man to the perennial aging father (also nominated in the Best Actor category for *I Never Sang for My Father* in 1970), that it is easy to forget that he is the same individual.

Even when essaying a Bellamy type, Douglas brought a worldliness to his role. In fact, one ad campaign for *I Met Him in Paris* had top-billed Colbert describing Douglas as "The man of the world who always has to cover up his emotions with a veneer of sophistication."[111] Thus, Douglas's screwball comedy roles often place him in rather chic positions or settings. *I Met Him in Paris* presents him as an expatriate American playwright living in the French capital. In *Good Girls Go to Paris* (1939) Douglas is a Parisian professor; in *Theodora Goes Wild* he is a New York artist; in *Too Many Husbands* he is a publisher.

Screenwriter Claude Binyon, who worked so often with screwball director Wesley Ruggles (an original member of the Keystone Cops) that *Time* magazine described him as Ruggles's "perpetual scriptor," said "Douglas was born to look casual."[112] Douglas starred in two of the best and most typical Ruggles-Binyon screwball comedies, *I Met Him in Paris* and *Too Many Husbands,* and was the subject of a Binyon article, "Memo on Melvyn," which describes Douglas as very much like his screen persona.[113] For example, the real-life Douglas has the same dry wit. After the completion of *Too Many Husbands,* in which he co-starred with Fred MacMurray, Douglas was to be interviewed on what it was like working with MacMurray. Keeping this in mind, Douglas then related to Binyon one possible comic direction the forthcoming interview might take:

> "I'll never forget," he said, "the moment that Fred MacMurray first walked on the set. He was much taller than he seems on the screen. I was quite disappointed to learn that he was married, and that his chin veers definitely to the left. He also has a dark beard which photographs in the afternoon."[114]

Not only is this amusing, it also brings to mind both the antiheroic spirit of Robert Benchley and the comic prissiness of screwball comedy supporting player Franklin Pangborn—forever the frustrated hotel or store manager.

While Douglas could and did project a certain sophisticated worldliness, not unlike the well-traveled activist he really was, Fred MacMurray represented another pivotal type for screwball comedy—the steady but unspectacular American boy next door. Years later he was still successfully projecting this image in the long-running situation comedy television series *My Three Sons* (1960-72). His greatest quality was dependability, both to his home studio of Paramount and in the program screwball comedies in which he often appeared.

He frequently gets the girl, despite such regular-guy liabilities as not having a European title (*The Gilded Lily*, opposite Colbert) and not having the fortune for which his family is famous (*Hands Across the Table* in 1935, opposite Lombard). Though without any semblance of sophistication (a characteristic generally alien to all-American types), he does project a certain athletic stick-to-it-iveness, not unlike a modest sound version of Harold Loyd. Thus, in *Too Many Husbands* it is MacMurray who instigates the chair-jumping competition with Melvyn Douglas—though true to his "average" title, he very quickly meets with antiheroic frustration and suffers a comic fall. But given the right situation, he could handle the entirely visual scene, whether it is chair-jumping or the lengthy silent spot in *Take a Letter, Darling* (1942, opposite Rosalind Russell) in which he is both introduced to and showcased for the romantic perusal of female office employees. Not surprisingly, Lombard (with whom he was frequently teamed) was an early, pivotal comedy teacher.

More often, however, MacMurray is merely less comically intrusive as the required male lead. Consequently, he "was the perfect foil for Lombard. Her intensity, hyperactivity, and complexity contrasted well with his simple, relaxed masculinity."[115] This is best demonstrated in *True Confession*, in which he is the exasperated, trying to be normal, husband married to an exceptionally zany Lombard.

Paramount did not, however, fully realize the sometimes vacuous decency MacMurray could project. For example, he would have made a delightful comically out-of-step academic—something the Disney studio rectified years later by casting him in the title role of *The Absent-Minded Professor* (1961).

MacMurray is so associated with the good guy that, ironically, probably his most memorable screen roles find him cast against type outside the genre, such as in Billy Wilder's *Double Indemnity* (1944). This film noir classic has him murdering for the love of the beautifully overpowering yet evil Barbara Stanwyck. Screwball comedy and the later noir both have manipulative women, moldable men, suppressed sexuality, an antiheroic world view, involvement of important screwball comedy people, and the overlapping time periods (1930s and 1940s) with which both genres are so heavily associated. Thus, noir might be read as the dark side of screwball comedy. Moreover, the casting of a MacMurray average guy in a noir film accented the sinister message that it is possible for the dark side to surface in anyone—precisely the chill upon which Alfred Hitchcock based many of his films.

The real MacMurray is, however, very close to that all-American type he played in so many screwball comedies and his later television show. Article after article, with titles like "Star Without Limousine," "Portrait of a Right Guy," and "Love Comes First for Fred MacMurray" showcase a practical, even boring, real-life identity.[116] A closer look at MacMurray's basic values is presented in the 1938 article "New Day for Fred MacMurray," which is largely an interview with the Wisconsin actor on the value to a youngster of the more normal Midwestern upbringing.[117] In fact, his hometown of Beaver Dam, Wisconsin, which sounds suspiciously like a Norman Rockwell setting, had, appropriately enough, been selected "Typical Small Town of America" for 1938.[118]

Screenwriter Claude Binyon adds what should be final proof of MacMurray's average guy tendencies, in a 1939 article entitled "'Long Shot' MacMurray," which refutes the old axiom "nice guys finish last."[119] MacMurray had been in a number of Ruggles-Binyon films, an involvement which would continue into the 1940s, and he and Binyon had become close friends. The article is composed largely of two stories about MacMurray's nice-guy antiheroic gullibility. The most comically informative story—and a pun upon the article's title, since it involves hunting—describes MacMurray's introduction to that sport by Binyon. Just prior to the opening of dove season and MacMurray's first hunting trip, the actor's doctor had expressed grave reservations about shooting "gentle birds." MacMurray was now having some second thoughts, which he shared with Binyon as they drove to the hunting site. Thus, after explaining how a dove dies of sadness when its mate is killed, MacMurray rubbed his eyes and continued, "The doctor said they're the most beautiful and gentle birds in the world. They borrow just enough grain from the farmer to fill their little craws and they wouldn't harm a living thing."[120]

Binyon's amusingly aggressive rebuttal, couched in comic overstatement, has parallels with Robert Benchley's delightful essay "Down with Pigeons"—the antihero driven to revenge.[121] Thus, Binyon replies,

> "Don't let him kid you. . . . Don't ever listen to a vegetarian. Doves are mean. They eat the farmer's grain and he has to mortgage the farm and then he loses it. They pick out children's eyes. I wouldn't trust a dove any further than I could throw Mount Whitney."[122]

Needless to say, MacMurray was won back to the hunting expedition. But his nice-guy gullibility has never been in danger.

Through laughter, antiheroes help us cope with this absurd modern world where our only good defense seems to be a humor founded in absurdity. The glossy window dressing of the 1930s screwball comedy helped make the first antihero feature film wave more palatable to an audience grounded in capable comedy characters. In today's "Catch-22" modern world, a genre devoted to topsyturvydom still seems to offer a number of valuable insights.

NOTES

1. Colin McArthur, *Underworld USA* (New York: The Viking Press, 1972), p. 24.

2. Andrew Sarris, *Confessions of a Cultist: On the Cinema, 1955/1969* (1970; rpt. New York: Simon and Schuster, 1971), p. 455.

3. Patrick McGilligan, *Cagney: The Actor As Auteur* (1975; rpt. New York: Da Capo Press, 1979).

4. Béla Balázs, *Theory of Film*, trans. Edith Bone (1952; rpt. New York: Dover Publications, 1970), pp. 284-87.

5. Gerald Mast, *Howard Hawks: Storyteller* (New York: Oxford University Press, 1982), p. 52. See also Erwin Panofsky, "Style and Medium in the Motion Pictures," in *Film Theory and Criticism*, ed. Gerald Mast and Marshall Cohen (New York: Oxford University Press, 1974), pp. 151-69.

6. Joseph McBride, *Hawks on Hawks* (Los Angeles: University of California Press, 1982), p. 69.

7. Donald Deschner, *The Films of Cary Grant* (Secaucus, New Jersey: The Citadel Press, 1973), pp. 273-74.

8. Ibid., p. 274.

9. Richard Schickel, "Hollywood's Honchos: Burt Reynolds and Clint Eastwood," *Time* (cover article), January 9, 1978, p. 54.

10. Ibid.

11. Larry Kent (interviewer), "Chevy Chase," *Chicago Tribune Arts & Fun/Books* magazine, August 10, 1980, pp. 6+

12. Henry Bergson, "Laughter," in *Comedy*, ed. Wylie Sypher (Garden City, New York: Doubleday & Comapny, 1956), pp. 157-58.

13. Andrew Sarris, *Interviews With Film Directors* (1967; rpt. New York: Avon Books, 1972), p. 233.

14. Cary Grant (with uncredited assistance of Joe Hyams), "Archie Leach," *Ladies Home Journal*, January/February 1963 (first of three-part series; see also March and April of 1963), p. 136.

15. Ibid., p. 142.

16. Pete Martin, "How Grant Took Hollywood," *Saturday Evening Post,* February 19, 1949, p. 59.

17. Ibid., p. 57.

18. For an interesting anecdote concerning this scene by the director, see Leo McCarey, "Comedy and a Touch of Cuckoo," *Extension*, November 1944, p. 5.

19. Jerry Vermilye, *Cary Grant* (New York: Pyramid Publications, 1973), p. 25.

20. Pauline Kael, "The Man from Dream City," in *When the Lights Go Down* (New York: Holt, Rinehart and Winston, 1980), p. 6.

21. Ibid., p. 3.

22. Richard Schickel, *Cary Grant: A Celebration* (Boston: Little, Brown and Company, 1983), p. 44.

23. Albert Govoni, *Cary Grant* (Chicago: Henry Regnery Company, 1971), pp. 37, 47.

24. Ibid., p. 109.

25. André Bazin, "The Grandeur of Limelight," in *What Is Cinema?*, vol. 2, selected and trans. Hugh Gray (1958; rpt. Los Angeles: University of California Press, 1967), p. 136.

26. Warren Hoge, "Cary Grant: No Lady's Man," *Des Moines Register* (*New York Times* copyright), July 6, 1977, pp. 1A, 8A.

27. Ibid., p. 1A.

28. Ibid.

29. Ibid., p. 8A.

30. Geoffrey Wansell, *Haunted Idol: The Story of the Real Cary Grant* (New York: William Morrow and Company, 1984), p. 27.

31. Andrew Sarris, "The World of Howard Hawks," in *Focus on Howard Hawks*, ed. Joseph McBride (Englewood Cliffs, New Jersey: Prentice-Hall, 1972), p. 62.

32. The best rendering of this is in the Pete Martin article, "How Grant Took Hollywood," p. 66.

33. *My Man Godfrey* review, *Variety*, September 23, 1936, p. 16.

34. *My Man Godfrey* review, *New York Times,* September 18, 1936, p. 18; *Mr. and Mrs. Smith* review, *New York Times*, February 21, 1941, p. 16.

35. Anna Rothe, ed., "Irene Dunne," in *Current Biography 1945* (New York: H. W. Wilson Company, 1946), p. 162.

36. Larry Swindell, *Screwball: The Life of Carole Lombard* (New York: William Morrow and Company, 1975), pp. 59-60.

37. Ibid., p. 143.

38. Jean Farge Guignol, "Intimate History of Carole Lombard," *Movie Mirror*, October 1937, p. 79.

39. *Nothing Sacred* review, *Time*, December 6, 1937, p. 49.

40. *Nothing Sacred* review, *Variety*, December 1, 1937, p. 14.

41. "Movie of the Week: *Nothing Sacred*," *Life,* December 6, 1937, p. 39.

42. Ibid.

43. Carole Lombard, "My Man Gregory," *Screenbook* magazine, February 1937, p. 38.

44. Guignol, "Intimate History of Carole Lombard," p. 44.

45. Carole Lombard file, Billy Rose Theatre Collection, New York Public Library at Lincoln Center.

46. Swindell, *Screwball,* pp. 30-31.

47. Ibid., p. 31.

48. Ibid.

49. Kyle Crichton, "Fun in Flickers," *Colliers,* February 24, 1940, p. 39.

50. Ibid., pp. 11, 39-40.

51. "Carole Lombard Tells 'How I Live By a Man's Code,'" *Photoplay*, June 1937, pp. 12-13, 78; Janet Bentley, "She Gets Away with Murder," *Photoplay*, March 1938, pp. 27, 88-89.

52. Virginia Wood, "Luck—and Lombard," *Screenland,* July 1937, p. 22.

53. Swindell, *Screwball*, p. 77.

54. Ibid.

55. Wes Gehring, "The Last William Wellman Interview," *Paper Cinema*, 1, no. 1 (1982): 13.

56. Caroline S. Hoyt, "Irene Dunne's True Life Story," *Modern Screen*, December 1938, p. 30 (continued in January issue); Jerome Beatty, "Lady Irene," *American Magazine*, November 1944, p. 29.

57. Irene Dunne File, Billy Rose Theatre Collection, New York Public Library at Lincoln Center (The Maxwell rating was referred to in a 1941 article from *The Boston Sunday Post.*); "Let's Talk It Out!" ("*Movie Mirror* Youth Forum"), *Movie Mirror*, March 1940, p. 58.

58. Beatty, "Lady Irene," pp. 28-29, 117-118; Roth, "Irene Dunne," p. 160.

59. Dunne File, Billy Rose Theatre Collection.

60. Ibid.

61. Majorie Rosen, *Popcorn Venus* (1973; rpt. New York: Avon, 1974), p. 189.

62. Irene Dunne, "Dignified," *American Magazine*, August 1942, p. 85.

63. Dunne File, Billy Rose Theatre Collection.

64. Sara Hamilton, "This Is Really Irene Dunne," *Photoplay*, April 1936, p. 27.

65. Ibid., p. 26.

66. Rothe, "Irene Dunne," p. 162.

67. Kay Proctor, "Play Truth and Consequences with Irene Dunne," *Photoplay*, July 1942, p. 84.

68. Beatty, "Lady Irene," p. 118.

69. Stanley Cavell, *Pursuits of Happiness: The Hollywood Comedy of Remarriage* (Cambridge, Massachusetts: Harvard University Press, 1981), pp. 246-47.

70. Ibid., p. 248.

71. Elizabeth Wilson, "The First True Story of Irene Dunne's Baby!" *Screenland*, June 1937, p. 20.

72. Ibid., p. 21.

73. Charles Silver, "Leo McCarey: from Marx to McCarthy," *Film Comment*, September 1973, p. 11.

74. Sonia Lee, "Discovering the Glamour in Irene Dunne," *Motion Picture*, March 1937, p. 39.

75. Ethan Mordden, *Movie Star: A Look at the Women Who Made Hollywood* (New York: St. Martin's Press, 1983), p. 101.

76. "Movie of the Week: *Nothing Sacred*," *Life*, p. 36.

77. Lombard file, Billy Rose Theatre Collection.

78. Ibid.

79. David Lee, "The Only Man in Claudette Colbert's Life," *Romantic Movie Stories*, January 1935, p. 32.

80. David Shipman, "Claudette Colbert," in *The Great Movie Stars: The Golden Years* (New York: Bonanza Books, 1970), p. 113.

81. John B. Kennedy, "Woman from Paris," *Colliers*, February 15, 1930, pp. 20-21, 60-61.

82. Gregory La Cava, "The Fretting Frog: The Story of Claudette Colbert," *Photoplay*, November 1935, pp. 26-27, 99-100.

83. Jerome Beatty, "She was *such* a Nice Girl," *American Magazine*, September 1935, pp. 58-59, 123-125.

84. Kyle Crichton, "Career Girl," *Colliers*, January 28, 1939, p. 64.

85. Lee, "The Only Man in Claudette Colbert's Life," p. 32.

86. Howard Sharpe, "The Romance of Claudette Colbert's Second Honeymoon," *Photoplay*, February 1938, p. 21.

87. La Cava, "The Fretting Frog: The Story of Claudette Colbert," p. 99.

88. Claudette Colbert file, Billy Rose Theatre Collection, New York Public Library at Lincoln Center.

89. "Play Truth and Consequences with Claudette Colbert," *Photoplay*, March 1939, p. 75.

90. Frank Capra, *The Name Above the Title* (New York: The Macmillan Company, 1971), p. 167.

91. Lee, "The Only Man in Claudette Colbert's Life," p. 86.

92. Frances Kish, "The Girl on the Cover," *Photoplay*, July 1931, p. 12.

93. Capra, *The Name Above the Title*, p. 167.

94. Ibid.

95. Capra, *The Name Above the Title*, p. 170.

96. Lee, "The Only Man in Claudette Colbert's Life," p. 86.

97. Gary Carey, *Katharine Hepburn: A Hollywood Yankee* (1975; revised and updated, New York: Dell Publishing Company, 1983), p. 98.

98. Ibid.

99. Ibid., p. 112.

100. Cavell, in contrast, sees the genre creating a "new woman" in his *Pursuits of Happiness* (p. 140). See Chapter 7 of this text.

101. Molly Haskell, *From Reverence to Rape: The Treatment of Women in the Movies* (New York: Penguin Books, 1974), pp. 181-82.

102. James Spada, *Hepburn: Her Life in Pictures* (Garden City, New York: Doubleday and Company, 1984), p. 82.

103. Gladys Hall, "She Who Gets Slapped," *Motion Picture,* December 1937, p. 26.

104. "The Great Kate Reviews Her Life with No Regrets," *U.S.A. Today,* November 6, 1984, p. 20.

105. For example, see George Pettit, "Now You'll Understand Jean Arthur," *Photoplay,* February 1937, pp. 56-57, 95; William F. French, "What Hollywood Thinks of Jean Arthur," *Photoplay*, September 1942, pp. 49, 98-100; Capra, *The Name Above the Title,* p. 184.

106. L. O. Parsons, "Disappearing Jean Arthur," *Cosmopolitan,* May 1953, p. 6-8, 10; "Seclusive Jean Arthur in Her California Home," *Life*, March 11, 1960, p. 59.

107. Andrew Sarris, "The Sex Comedy Without Sex," *American Film*, March 1978, p. 15.

108. Lewis Jacobs, "Significant Contemporary Film Content," in *The Rise of the American Film: A Critical History* (1939; rpt. New York: Teacher's College Press, 1971), p. 536.

109. Claude Binyon, "Memo on Melvyn," *Photoplay*, May 1940, p. 25.

110. Nancy Cole, "Thanks for the Memories," *Picture Play*, January 1939, p. 30.

111. Claudette Colbert, "Girls, Which Man Would You Choose?" (ad campaign for *I Met Him In Paris*), *Screenland* magazine, June 1937, p. 6.

112. *Too Many Husbands* review, *Time*, March 25, 1940, p. 93; Binyon, "Memo on Melvyn," p. 24.

113. Binyon, "Memo on Melvyn," pp. 24-25, 96.

114. Ibid., p. 96.

115. David Chierichetti, *Hollywood Director: The Career of Mitchell Leisen* (New York: Curtis Books, 1973), p. 93.

116. Kyle Crichton, "Star Without Limousine," *Colliers,* June 20, 1936, pp. 16, 48; Joseph Henry Steele, "Portrait of a Right Guy," *Photoplay*, February 1943, pp. 34, 92-93; Julie Lang Hunt, "Love Comes First for Fred MacMurray," *Photoplay,* September 1935, pp. 29, 96.

117. Howard Sharpe, "New Day for Fred MacMurray," *Photoplay*, June 1938, pp. 27, 87-88.

118. Ibid., p. 27.

119. Claude Binyon, "'Long Shot' MacMurrary," *Photoplay*, May 1939, pp. 20-21, 91.

120. Ibid., p. 91.

121. Robert Benchley, "Down with Pigeons," in *From Bed to Worse: or Comforting Thoughts About the Bison* (New York: Harper & Brothers, 1934), pp. 175-82.

122. Binyon, "'Long Shot' MacMurray," p. 91.

6.

THE SCREWBALL GENRE AND COMEDY THEORY

"[O]ne of the tragedies of this life [is] the men most in need of a beating up are always enormous."

> John D. Hackensacker III (Rudy Valley) to Gerry Jeffers (Claudette Colbert) in *The Palm Beach Story* (1942).

The screwball film title *Nothing Is Sacred* (1937) capsulizes nicely the comedy theory approach most applicable to the genre—superiority. Whether it is the destruction of a brontosaurus skeleton in the academic world (*Bringing Up Baby*, 1938), ghosts pestering the socially "stiff" of the real world (*Topper* series, starting 1937), or the traditional concept of romantic love, screwball comedy generally finds "nothing sacred."

Granted, several comedy theories are applicable to individual scenes in the genre. For example, the fact that screwball comedy often makes high society appear most eccentric, reducing the world of sophistication to silliness, could be dissected in terms of the theory of surprise. The incongruity approach might be applied to a handsome leading man like Cary Grant being so often flustered by women. The genre's ties to farce, as well as its initial need to coexist with the film industry's self-imposed censorship (the Motion Picture Production Code of 1934) could be examined along Freudian comedy as sexual taboo lines. But the purpose here is to analyze the comedy theory most broadly applicable to the screwball genre: superiority.

The superiority theory stretches back to the writings of Aristotle and his definition of comedy as the "imitation of baser men," often drawn from subjects of "deformity." Such a description hardly makes comedy seem like a positive pastime. What often is neglected is that Aristotle's goal was to remove the slur which . . . [Plato] had placed on comedy by considering it fit only for slaves and strangers.

Accordingly, Aristotle transferred the ignominy from the comedians to the subject-matter of comedy itself.[1]

And though Aristotle removed the slur, the majority of theorists following him in the superiority approach continue to produce often unpleasant-sounding definitions, the most famous probably being Thomas Hobbes's observation that laughter was "the apprehension of some deformed thing in another, by comparison whereof they [the viewers] suddenly applaud themselves."[2]

Because of this harsh-toned, seemingly one-dimensional approach, the superiority theory has sometimes alienated people. Max Eastman downplays this theory in his chapter "Derision" from his provocative *The Sense of Humor*.[3],

The root of this unpleasantness is lodged in the conservative nature of the theory, in its non-romantic view of humans outside civilization. To quote another superiority theorist, Henri Bergson:

Laughter is, above all, a corrective. Being intended to humiliate, it must make a painful impression on the person against whom it is directed. By laughter, society avenges itself for the liberties taken with it . . . [Laughter] . . . must have a *social* signification.[4]

These superiority references underline the conservative nature of this approach to comedy theory. Before examining screwball comedy more closely in terms of Bergson's superiority model, which seems custom-made for the genre, it is imperative to survey the inherently conservative nature of the genre itself, focusing on three key barometers: the concept of implosion, genre space and conflict, and the comic tendencies of pivotal directors.

Andrew Bergman has observed, "If early thirties comedy was explosive, screwball comedy was implosive: it worked to pull things together."[5] The focal point of Bergman's use of the term "implosion" is applied to the joining of economically diverse classes largely within the Capra films he sees as the heart of the genre. But while the post-*It Happened One Night* (1934) Capra films do not work as screwball comedy models (see Chapter 3) because of the politics which dominate them, the term "implosion" can still be relevant to the genre's inherently two-part conservative base.

First, while the comedy of the pre-MGM Marx Brothers and W. C. Fields is truly iconoclastic toward high society, screwball comedy merely pokes survivable—status quo—fun at the eccentricities of the rich. While satire can and does exist, the screwball comedy viewer generally is allowed to grow fond of these wealthy wackos, in a superior sort of way, while also enjoying the escapism of beautiful people in beautiful settings. Most screwball comedies minimize any socioeconomic differences of the leading duo and key on their initial conflicts concerning eccentric behavior. A marked exception to this, however, is *It Happened One Night*, which focuses on a coupling from different classes with the viewer's initial loyalties manipulated toward the blue-collar camp.

Second, despite the general superiority in the genre of the female over the male, with her apparently antisocial approach to the traditionally male-dominated courtship ritual, the game still has the most conservative of goals: the heroine's madcap maneuvers are often used to capture a male and break him—or save him—from any real antisocial rigidity. This is best summed up with the term *marriage*, or the promise of marriage, which ends the screwball comedy, reaffirming one of the most traditional institutions in Western society. But the apparent duality of the heroine helps explain the often contradictory views of screwball comedy from feminist critics. For example, Molly Haskell's *From Reverence to Rape: The Treatment of Women in the Movies* spends a great deal of time on the genre, sketching it as a generally positive, rebellious trend; Majorie Rosen's *Popcorn Venus: Women, Movies and the American Dream* all but ignores it.[6]

As a teacher who frequently uses the genre in class, the author has found the same divided response with regard to the heroine. Students, especially feminists, have ambivalent feelings toward the heroine. They generally tend to like her madcap means but have difficulty accepting the end: all this just for a man. The negativist position among feminist critics is probably articulated most baldly by Karyn Kay: "In modern screwball comedies the narrative inevitably unwinds to a reiteration of this man-above-woman world order."[7]

Yet, even if one ignores the nonpolitical nature of implosion in the genre, particularly the aforementioned age-old female capture of the male, political implosion in screwball comedy would more logically seem to have occurred *outside* the film, between a genre that amicably ridiculed the rich and a public that enjoyed seeing this done. Without turning this into an example of rhetorical analysis with audience response charts and accompanying financial statements, it is safe to say that the 1930s leftist was slightly appalled at Hollywood's general ability to steer clear of depression issues, whether in the screwball comedy mold or whatever other genre happened to be in the limelight. Documentary filmmaker and 1930s activist Leo Hurwitz makes much the same point in his fascinating "One Man's Voyages: Ideas and Films in the 1930's."[8]

After implosion, the second key factor underlining the conservative nature of screwball comedy is the genre's relationship to space and conflict. As noted in Chapter 1, screwball comedy is not part of the traditional "determinate space" genres in which action generally occurs at a specific time and place, as with the western, the gangster picture, and the war film.[9] The determinate space genre generally has its hero enter a specific physically contested space, achieve a definite resolution, then exit said space. Thus, in an archetypal western like John Ford's *My Darling Clementine* (1946), Wyatt Earp (Henry Fonda) and his brothers ride into a contested space called Tombstone, a town suffering under the presence of the evil Clantons (led by Walter Brennan). After a "battle" at the OK Corrall, in which the Clantons are killed and Tombstone's conflict is resolved, Wyatt Earp and one surviving brother move on.

In contrast, screwball comedy is a genre of indeterminate time and space, like the musical and the melodrama. It is not limited to one time or place and is defined more through the interaction of characters. Screwball comedy deals "not with threatened space, but with a 'civilized' society whose characters have no exit and must learn to adjust their own personal dispositions to accommodate that of their cultural milieu."[10] Thus, it is conservative in the sense that to coexist in a society is to know compromise. Moreover, unlike the sometimes vigilante violence which closes determinate time and space genres, screwball comedies occasionally even add courtroom scenes at or near the film's end. Though comic, they represent another attempt at civilized compromise. (And at no time is the genre's courtroom comedy so outrageous that it totally undercuts the system—something the Marx Brothers's courtroom scene is designed to do in *Duck Soup*, 1933).

Film theorist Stanley Cavell has difficulty accepting the collapsing brontosaurus conclusion of *Bringing Up Baby,* where Cary Grant finally confesses his love for Katharine Hepburn—despite her causing the destruction of his epic academic project.[11] Cavell's hesitancy is not directed, however, at the scene's pivotal breaking of the last and most symbolic metaphor for Grant's rigidity (examined in Chapter 3) but rather at the seemingly unrealistic plot demand that Grant should still want to embrace Hepburn. Yet, besides saving him from a damnable rigidity, this union (of Grant and Hepburn) is the ultimate and closing compromise in a genre based in compromise. Such endings might seem uneasy, since they often bridge ninety previous minutes of largely comic differences, but marriage or the promise of marriage is a final humorous concession to the "conflicts which had opposed those principals throughout the narrative."[12]

Before the romantic conclusion of *You Belong to Me* (1941), which reteamed *The Lady Eve* (1941) stars Barbara Stanwyck and Henry Fonda, she observed: "What a pair . . . about as much chance for happiness as two ducks in the desert." It is a description which could be applied to any number of screwball couples, at least until the conclusion of each story. Moreover, Preston Sturges even opens *The Palm Beach Story* (1942) with a joke on the suspension of disbelief necessary in the screwball comedy conclusion. He begins with a madcap rush to a wedding ceremony and an equally rushed ceremony (to the strains of *The William Tell Overture*) with the superimposed title "and they lived happily ever after." However, a second superimposition soon queries: ". . . or do they?" Thus, the story proper now begins five years after that ceremony, and the viewer can now examine a screwball comedy couple having comic differences. Yet, as might be expected, Sturges ends this "exposé" of the screwball comedy ending with an even greater tongue-in-cheek conclusion. *Palm Beach Story* stars Claudette Colbert and Joel McCrea must naturally be reunited without hurting two equally winsome supporting players (Mary Astor and Rudy Vallee), who have fallen for them. Preston—deus ex machina—Sturges suddenly reveals that Colbert and McCrea each have an identical twin. Once again there is a closing marriage (only now with three couples). The camera pulls back and once more there is the "and they lived happily ever after" superimposition followed by the "or did they?" But this time there is the sound of breaking glass, as if the camera and/or cameraperson can no longer handle close scrutiny of a screwball comedy conclusion.

Cavell's hesitation might be logical, but screwball comedy is not. As Carole Lombard biographer Larry Swindell observes, the genre "permitted poetic license, and made the most of it."[13] Moreover, if one questions the close of *Bringing Up Baby*, one would need to question the close of most other screwball comedies, from Lombard and Powell in *My Man Godfrey* (1936), to Rosalind Russell and Don Ameche in *The Feminine Touch* (1941)—where another professor (Ameche) loves a woman (Russell) despite her destruction of his epic academic project (in this case a book on jealousy). In addition, Cavell is on record earlier in *Pursuits of Happiness* as defending suspension of disbelief in comedy. Writing on the heroine as director in *The Lady Eve*, he credits Northrop Frye for the observation "that the inclusion of some event particularly hard to believe is a common feature of Shakespeare's comedy [to which Cavell is comparing screwball comedy], as if placed there to exact the greatest effort from his dramatic powers and from his audience's imagination."[14]

It is dangerous, moreover, to attack most comedy conclusions (regardless of comic type). To do so contradicts the fundamental pattern of comedy itself, which moves toward the happy ending after overcoming some initial problems—just the opposite of the tragedy. The beginnings of comedy are tied to ancient fertility rituals and rites of spring, events commensurate with rebirth, with marriage, with a new world, and with the happy ending. As Frye so nicely articulates in his *Anatomy of Criticism* (1957), the comedy happy endings are not there to "impress us as true, but as desirable, and they are brought about by manipulation."[15] No matter how unlikely the maneuvering, it is inseparable from both comedy and the audience anticipation of comedy.

The third key spotlighting the conservative makeup of screwball comedy is the comic tendencies of some pivotal directors. This discussion will be limited to three men whose work covers the history (yesterday and today) of screwball comedy—Howard Hawks, Leo McCarey, and Blake Edwards—the best contemporary screwball comedy director.

If one had to identify a single, central director of the genre, Hawks would be the obvious choice. No other artist made quality screwball comedies as long or as well. Hawks's floundering comic males are the antithesis of his cool and capable adventure heroes. Moreover, as film critic Robin Wood observes in his landmark study *Howard Hawks* (1968), the director's comedies provide a special fascination through their "lure of irresponsibility."[16] In Hawks's world civilization and chaos battle each other toe to toe, be it the release of the symbolic semi-wild leopard in *Bringing Up Baby*, or Cary Grant's "release" by the youth serum in *Monkey Business* (1952). Yet, as Wood so correctly notes in a statement very reminiscent of Bergson on superiority (see note 4): "As elsewhere in Hawks's work (*Monkey Business* offering the extremist instance), our yearnings for total irresponsibility are evoked to be chastised."[17] Either way, and still generally applicable to the genre, a conservative comic humiliation is celebrated. (Moreover, in Hawks's *I Was a Male War Bride*, Cary Grant suffers even greater comic humiliation without succumbing to the "lure of irresponsibility.") Hawks said it all himself when he observed, first of *I Was a Male War Bride*, and then of his screwball comedies in general:

> Anything we could do to humiliate him [Grant], to put him down and let her [Ann Sheridan] sail blithely along, made it what I thought was funny. I think it's fun to have a woman dominant and let the man be funniest [most frustrated]. Katie [Hepburn] and Rosalind Russell and Ann Sheridan . . . did their share in being funny, but they . . . left the other [comedy of frustration] to Cary.[18]

In McCarey's world, civilization and chaos also battle each other toe to toe, but it is without the more dramatic examples of Hawks's at large leopard in *Bringing Up Baby* or Cary Grant literally going on the war path in *Monkey Business*. The roots of this for McCarey are in what he referred to as "the tit-for-tat" gags he introduced to Laurel & Hardy, what film historian John McCabe refers to as "reciprocal destruction."[19] For example, in the classic Laurel & Hardy *Big Business* (1929; McCarey provided the story and supervised the production), the antiheroic duo are selling Christmas trees door-to-door, until they run into their frequent nemesis James Finlayson. A conflict arises, and they methodically take turns destroying each other's property. The comic uniqueness is in what film comedy historian Gerald Mast describes as "the quiet deliberateness with which these child-adults go about their petty revenges. . . . They perform these vicious and childish actions with the greatest slowness, calm, and reason."[20]

When McCarey adapted his antiheroic pattern to the feature film and what became screwball comedy "reciprocal destruction" is toned down, but it is still very much present. Thus, hero and heroine take turns doing battle, such as the scene in *My Favorite Wife* in which Irene Dunne thinks she has successfully passed off a milquetoast type as her island companion to husband Cary Grant. But Grant knows differently, and he asks her to lunch at the Pacific Club, where Dunne's real and very virile former companion (Randolph Scott) is staying. At this point Grant begins to laugh, in anticipation of the comic humiliation he is about to render. And Dunne then joins in, enjoying what she still believes to have been a successful comic humiliation of Grant. Each one's laughter increases before the scene closes.

As with Laurel & Hardy, however, McCarey's screwball comedy male suffers both the most frequent humiliations and the ultimate story-closing one. (*My Favorite Wife* continues as the focus because the film's dichotomy of urban, antiheroic Grant and muscled man of nature Scott provide the closest corollary to the Hawksian civilization-chaos confrontation.) At film's close Dunne subjects Grant to a prolonged humiliation as he struggles with his antiheroic indecisiveness (see Chapter 3), just as occurred between the two in McCarey's *The Awful Truth*. Bosley Crowther's *New York Times* rave review of *My Favorite Wife* manages to capsulize nicely this McCarey tradition of the comically humiliating heroine:

> Do you remember *The Awful Truth*. . . . Do you remember . . .
> Miss Dunne's tantalizing contrariness? Then you know . . .
> what to expect in *My Favorite Wife*. . . . McCarey is, without
> compare, a master of the technique of the prolonged and
> amorous tease; and with an actress such as Miss Dunne through
> whom to apply it . . . —mere man is powerless before it. . . .
> Mr. Grant, a normally susceptible male, is thrown about, be-
> wildered and helpless, like an iron filing, when he comes within
> the magnetic field of Miss Dunne's allure.[21]

Contemporary director Blake Edwards, whose forays into screwball comedy include *10* (1978) and *Victor/Victoria* (1982), is the best active filmmaker in the genre. A strong disciple of McCarey, Edwards describes his theory of comedy as very much in the McCarey conservative superiority track:

> humor is based, if you will, on cruelty. There's a certain cruel
> quality about the poor guy in *10* who, once he'd set upon his
> guest, fell down hills and fell in the pool . . . you have to
> remember that in comedy you can do *terrible* things to other
> people! [McCarey's] Laurel & Hardy did terrible things to each
> other.[22]

Comic superiority is very apparent in screwball comedy.

These, then, have been the three key barometers of screwball comedy's inherently conservative base: implosion, the genre's relationship to time and conflict, and the comic tendencies of key directors. They prepare the way for a better understanding of the genre when analyzed according to Bergson's theory of superiority.

Bergson's approach is closely tied to the concept of "mechanical inelasticity": "Any arrangement of acts and events is comic which gives us, in a single combination, the illusion of life and the distinct impression of a mechanical arrangement."[23] Comedy theorist and novelist George Meredith, a contemporary of Bergson, applies much the same concept in his "malady of sameness," from the "Prelude" of *The Egoist*.[24] The Bergson model will be followed because it is the more detailed.

Mechanical inelasticity, which on occasion also has been tied to comic incongruity, was a reaction by Bergson "against the coarse logic, the 'machinery,' of the nineteenth century, against everything cut-and-dried."[25] It anticipates the *New Yorker* antihero school and its comic rebellion against the nineteenth-century rational, "logical" world of the cracker-barrel Yankee. Moreover, Bergson's metaphorical attack on the machine compliments nicely the real attack of *The New Yorker* group on the frustrations of the mechanical, a comic problem often carried over into screwball comedy.

Bergson's theory of superiority can best be applied to the screwball genre by examining the effects on character development of three of its components: (1) "absentmindedness," (2) "inversion" or "topsyturvydom"— where character roles are switched, and (3) supporting comedy character types as satellites of the lead performer.

First, the main thrust of comic rigidity comes about by way of absentmindedness, a state Bergson ranks as nearly "the fountain-head of the comic," where there is a "growing callousness to social life. Any individual is comic who automatically goes his own way without troubling himself about getting into touch with the rest of his fellow-beings."[26] Bergson notes that this rigidity is most apt to occur among career professionals, a narrowness which he labels as the "professional comic," and exemplifies with the teacher who has concern only for his own subject.[27]

This Bergsonian composite character articulates beautifully the state of most screwball comedy males. Bergson has all but said the absent-minded professor, a central figure in screwball comedy, is equally central to his theory of superiority. Moreover, even when Bergson refers to a nonteacher model of absent-minded rigidity, there are frequently eccentric professor roots. For example, he discusses the classic rigidity of Don Quixote, a figure also dealt with in the comedy superiority theory of Bergson contemporary George Meredith.[28] But just how does the windmill-attacking rigidity of Quixote connect with the absent-minded professor, beyond a mutual tunnel vision approach to the world? The answer lies in the evolution of Quixote's comic rigidity—a self-administered academic straitjacket normally associated with the absent-minded professor:

he [Quixote] made away many acres of arable land to buy him
books of that kind [on knighthood], and therefore he brought to
his house as many as ever he could get . . . the poor gentleman
grew distracted [with difficult passages], and was breaking his
brains day and night, to understand and unbowel their sense, an
endless labour. . . . In resolution, he plunged himself so deeply
in his reading of these books, as he spent many times in the
lecture of them whole days and nights; and in the end, through
his little sleep and much reading, he dried up his brains in such
sort as he lost wholly his judgement.[29]

The screwball comedy frequently focuses on some professionally rigid male,
often a professor or someone professorial in his actions, and on the
heroine's attempt to perform the "corrective" act of bringing him back to
social gregariousness.

As noted in Chapter 3, the heroine's ability to loosen up the stiff
professor is best demonstrated in the screwball films of Howard Hawks,
especially when showcasing Cary Grant. (Interestingly enough, *the* great
unrealized joint film project of screwball comedy's greatest director and
actor, Hawks and Grant, was the making of Don Quixote.[30]) But one need
not reiterate long lists of the genre's aforementioned stiff professors or even
related forms of male rigidity (bankers, butlers) to highlight this
phenomenon. By the time of what might be called Preston Sturges's
summing up of the genre, his films of the early 1940s, references to male
rigidity and stiffness were just as likely to show up in film dialogue.
Sturges's *The Palm Beach Story* provides two such examples.

In the first case, after innocently taking money from a wealthy eccentric,
Claudette Colbert tells jealous husband Joel McCrea: "You don't have to
get [morally] rigid about it. It was perfectly innocent, I assure you."

Later in the film Mary Astor compliments Colbert on romantically
loosening up Astor's overly rational brother (Rudy Vallee): "How did you
manage it? He's [normally] stiffer than a plank. This [romance] must have
done him a power of good."

Not surprisingly, the roles of both McCrea and Vallee have stereotyped
professorial qualities. McCrea is a scientist/inventor who is a poor
businessman; Vallee is a round-shouldered, bespectacled individual with a
constantly absent-minded expression and a little notebook in which he
neatly records his purchases (though, as he tells Colbert, he never adds them
up).

To compound this case of genre summation, McCrea and Vallee also
represent two screwball comedy variations on the comically rigid professor
type. Vallee, though not so perfect an example as Grant in *Bringing Up
Baby,* has the overly rational, overly detached academic mind which has
allowed other goals and/or values to get in the way of romance. This

characteristic is most economically presented in *Ball of Fire* (1941) by way of a name. The only one of eight professors in that film who has had a heterosexual relationship, though now a widower, is the one named *Oddly* (Richard Haydn)! This innocent and/or asexual male is most common to the genre, and the ongoing personification of Bergson's absent-minded professor.

The rigidity of McCrea is initially divorced from screwball comedy in an entirely different manner. This less frequently showcased development links professor types with old (conservative) ideas about sexuality—probably because tradition has them studying old things. Thus, in *I Met Him in Paris* (1937) the nickname of "professor" is interchanged with that of "grandmother" to describe the snoopy character activities of Melvyn Douglas to Claudette Colbert and Robert Young. "Professor" Douglas (the story actually casts him as a playwright, an equally vacuous profession for middle America) will eventually loosen up and win the heart of the girl.

An interesting variation of this second type occurs in *Vivacious Lady* (1938), in which Jimmy Stewart is actually cast as a professor. His is a very rational world, modeled after the tradition-bound nature of his father, professor *and* president of the college, Charles Coburn. But when this serious young man is sent to sin city New York to retrieve a colleague mesmerized by a nightclub singer (Ginger Rogers), he also melts and marries Rogers immediately. This is just the beginning, however. Once the newlyweds return to the small-town college fiefdom of his father, Stewart suffers some rigidity regression—he is afraid to cross his father with this impulsive wedding. It is up to Rogers eventually to thaw out both professors, with the able assistance of Stewart's perennial screen mother Beulah Bondi—who has also been revitalized by Rogers's appearance.

In *The Doctor Takes a Wife* (1940) Ray Milland accepts a college promotion (from instructor to professor) under a false pretense based entirely upon a conservative morality: his dean feels that academics studying psychotic disorders are more stable if married. Though the history of the genre, not to mention the chapter entitled *The Doctor Takes a Wife*, suggests otherwise, Milland is too timid to rock a successful promotion when he is mistakenly thought to be married to feminist author Loretta Young. Moreover, neither Young nor Milland want the accompanying scandal the truth would generate. As in *Vivacious Lady*, Milland also has a tradition-bound professor for a father (Edmund Gwenn).

As for the traditional absent-minded professor type, Bergson has anticipated the added humor to be found in certain performers repeating and embellishing on a given absentmindedness—"Still more laughable will be the absentmindedness [rigidity] we have seen springing up and growing before our very eyes, with whose origin we are acquainted and whose life-history we can reconstruct.[31]

This statement further helps explain why a performer like Grant can have such a strong continuing impact on a genre, especially in the carryover comic successes of his professor roles from *Bringing Up Baby* to *Monkey Business* (see Chapter 5). Regardless of the manner in which screwball rigidity is approached, however, there can be no denying its presence in the genre. The opening of *Nothing Sacred* even seems to make a black comedy joke about this characteristic. When reporter Fredric March's "exclusive" proves to be the "hoax of the century," his newspaper demotes him figuratively and literally—to the basement obituary department. Like Grant's *Bringing Up Baby* paleontologist, March's life's work has now become the dead—the ultimate *stiff*ness. Again the heroine must come to the rescue, though in *Nothing Sacred* her mere story is enough to get March a reprieve.

A second element of Bergson's theory of comedy superiority to be applied to character development in screwball comedy has to do with "inversion" or "topsyturvydom," where "certain characters in a certain situation" pull a switch:

> Thus, we laugh at the prisoner at the bar lecturing the magistrate; at a child presuming to teach its parents; in a word, at everything that comes under the heading of "topsyturvydom."[32]

"Topsyturvydom" seems an especially appropriate term for a genre born in the depression. And Bergson's example of "a child presuming to teach its parents" is doubly appropriate for the antihero male of the genre. This is because, as demonstrated in Chapter 3, the male is closely associated with childhood and is ruled by the motherly female. Topsyturvydom for the male, then, means he likes to think he is in charge of his life, especially in his interactions with the opposite sex. Such is not the case, however.

Screwball comedy turns the American courtship system on its ear: the female leads the charge while the male holds back in the manner of the stereotyped weaker sex. Even the rare appearance of a strong male does not change this situation. In *My Man Godfrey*, William Powell as a butler seems more than capable, but once he serves Carole Lombard breakfast that first morning, she more correctly predicts *their* future: "You're my responsibility now. See you in church." If there are still doubtful observers here, it is not long before Powell tells his best friend he has that "foolish feeling [love] again." And the film closes with a Lombard/Powell marriage.

The more typical genre situation finds the male in a predicament like Cary Grant's at the close of *My Favorite Wife* (1940). He nervously and laboriously ponders which wife to choose, like a child with limited funds in a candy shop, thinking he still has some say in the decision. However, the viewer knows that wife number one, Irene Dunne, has won long ago, much as she did at the close of *The Awful Truth* (1937). In fact, it has been the author's experience, after using *My Favorite Wife* in several film comedy seminars, that students are somewhat bothered by Dunne's power plays at the close, suggesting she is unnecessarily baiting or toying with Grant. Certainly there can be no question it is comedy of superiority.

In *Bringing Up Baby* Katharine Hepburn uses any number of tricks to win over the already-spoken-for Cary Grant. They alternate between actions that allow Grant to *think* he is playing the logical masculine role and actions that more correctly display the gender reversal that has also taken place. In the former case, Hepburn plays upon the stereotype of male as decisive protector when she fakes being attacked by a leopard while on the phone to Grant; he drops everything to come to her rescue. In the latter instance, once she has kidnapped him using the threat of physical violence (turning a leopard loose on him), she uses one of the hoariest examples of male lechery: she takes *his* clothes. Grant completes the sex reversal when he must don women's clothing.

In *The Lady Eve* Barbara Stanwyck has an equally impressive array of tricks that allow her to woo and win Henry Fonda not once but twice, and he does not even suspect she is the same girl. Both times Stanwyck plays the gracious screwball heroine by allowing Fonda to think he is the romantic instigator. When Stanwyck and Fonda are reteamed later the same year (1941) for *You Belong to Me*, the focus is on their marriage (as opposed to the courtship of *The Lady Eve*), but once again there is "topsyturvydom." Fonda is the live-at-home millionaire; Stanwyck's medical practice frequently keeps her out of the home. Thus, every morning finds Fonda waving off his working wife. He is both more awkward and more childlike in *You Belong to Me* than in *The Lady Eve*, despite the antiheroic gifts he brought to the latter film. Stanwyck sometimes assists his frustrations in the earlier film, such as tripping him on the ocean liner, but Fonda authors all his boners in *You Belong to Me*. These range from a comic skiing accident while trying to show off for Stanwyck to pulling on his pants backwards in a fit of anger.

Fonda's association with the Nervous Nell screwball male role was so strong that for a while he was given the left-handed compliment of being the model for a key figure (Major Major) in *the* post–World War II comic antihero novel, *Catch 22*. The Fonda connection with the character of Major Major is noted throughout the work by author Joseph Heller, as if in tribute to a film genre that grew from the original American comic antihero movement.[33]

As was the case when the screwball male had to pay for the sins of his stiffness, "topsyturvydom" also brings comic humiliation to the male. This is necessary for a comedy theory based on superiority:

> laughter cannot be absolutely just. . . . Its function is to intimidate [and change for the social good] by humiliating. Now, it would not suceed . . . had not nature implanted . . . even in the best of men, a spark of spitefulness or, at all events, of mischief.[34]

This is a softening of the superiority theory, as opposed to Hobbes's observation at the opening of the chapter. The genre further pads things by following its ritual of male humiliation with the healing salve of a forthcoming marriage to the eccentric, though always beautiful, screwball heroine. It is hardly banishment to a life of poverty, which is what many in the depression audience would return to once the theater lights went up.

But what about the topsyturvy positioning of the screwball heroine, as well as what some might call the rigid nature of her eccentricity? Why is there not a certain degree of superiority shown toward her?

There are three key items in the genre that differentiate female activity from that of the male. First, the heroine often assumes her eccentricity, as the title *Theodora Goes Wild* (1936) so nicely footnotes, merely to win over the male. This is a trademark of *Theodora* star Irene Dunne, especially in *The Awful Truth* and *My Favorite Wife,* but several other screwball heroines followed the same "assumed" eccentricity, including Stanwyck in *The Lady Eve* and Colbert in *Midnight.* And even those heroines who merely seem pleasantly potted from the beginning of a film (Lombard in any number of roles) often display clues of a screwball masterplan. For example, in *My Man Godfrey,* when Lombard's sister tells her she should throw herself at Godfrey, the girl you thought was operating without either oar in the water calculatingly observes: "You can't rush a man like Godfrey."

By being in this command position, the heroine removes herself from a key premise of the comedy theory of superiority, that "there be some aspect of his person of which he is unaware [and thus mechanical]."[35] This same principle is honored among standup comics, whose golden rule is never to laugh at their own material.

Second, there has always been a sexual double standard as to how society responds to the reversal of stereotype gender activity. A girl with certain masculine overtones is perfectly acceptable; the notion of a tomboy is actually celebrated in our society. But any male attempts to reciprocate such a gender crossover are still strongly verboten in American culture, Boy George notwithstanding.

This allows the screwball heroine to be more aggressive in her male hunt without leaving the accepted normal range of female activity. At the same time she often is able to break down the male's rigidity, an antisocial state not allowing for his interaction with society, by driving him to some further cultural taboo, such as wearing women's clothing.

The third and final key difference between male and female activity in the genre deals with another double standard in the age-old battle of the sexes. Job markets, both yesterday and today, have no doubt created handicaps for women due simply to their gender, but courting "market" societal standards, especially in the 1930s, tended to favor them. It is as if the saying "all's fair in love and war" were written especially for them. And since all this female eccentricity is pointed toward marriage, there is nothing antisocial about it. Marriage is one of the key foundations of society.

This duality of the heroine—the apparent iconoclastic victory over the male that really reconfirms the societal status quo—helps explain the often divided comments directed at screwball comedy by feminist critics discussed earlier in this chapter.

A third and final element of Bergson's theory of comedy superiority as applied to character development in screwball comedy deals with the concept of the supporting comedy character satellite:

> a remarkable instinct . . . impels the comic poet, once he has elaborated his central character, to cause other characters, displaying the same general traits, to revolve as satellites around him.[36]

Bergson, and many other theorists, believe that while tragedy is based upon the individual, comedy is drawn from whole classes or groups of people, until a composite type is drawn. Bergson's concept of the satellite comedy type merely expands upon this:

> If the comic poet's object is to offer us types, that is to say, characters capable of self-repetition, how can he set about it better than by showing us, in each instance, several different copies of the same model.[37]

Consequently, not only are the leading screwball males antiheroic, but the key supporting characters are often the same, though they sometimes have a fatherly interest in the well-being of the genre's heroine, especially in the area of matrimony. But as would be expected of a fatherly yet antiheroic type, few people within the story pay any attention to him, especially the daughterly one. Thus it seems apropos to christen the character after that popular depression phrase "the forgotten man," (though unlike the scavenger-hunt search for a "forgotten man" in *My Man Godfrey*, financial woes are not among his problems; being a male is). Robert Benchley would seem to have legitimized the phrase's use in this manner by his 1941 short film subject about a father lost among his daughter's wedding preparations: *A Forgotten Man*.

Among screwball comedies, *the* forgotten man scene that always comes to mind first is that of Eugene Pallette's attempt at breakfasting in *The Lady Eve*. He has been quite forgotten pending the arrival of his future daughter-in-law, who is masquerading as royalty. Director Sturges handsomely mounts this short but pivotal scene by placing the wealthy Pallette at a very elaborate breakfast table with beautiful, covered silver serving dishes before him. Like Pavlov's "assistants," Pallette is near salivating as he surveys what appears to be one of the seven wonders of the breakfast world. Then he starts lifting the lids of one dish after another. Nothing. No one has given a thought to his breakfast with all the important female preparation going on. Like his film son, Henry Fonda, he does not count for much. Sturges then tops the surprise of the empty dishes by having Pallette pick up a silver serving dish lid in each hand and clash them together repeatedly like cymbals as the scene slowly dissolves to this "music" of frustration.

Pallette, with his roly-poly body and frog's voice, would not seem a most logical entry for the category of forgotten men. But as with Cary Grant's hold on the role of screwball comedy leading man, Pallette turns up often in the satellite father category, including performances in *The Ghost Goes West* and *My Man Godfrey* (both 1936).

As is to be expected of a genre loaded with absent-minded academicians, there are also a number of satellite professors in these productions, best exemplified by Professor Gary Cooper's Seven Dwarfs-styled associates in *Ball of Fire*. Though older, they are hardly wiser, and they represent a perfect satellite reflection of the antiheroic Cooper. At the same time, they are comically touching in their attempts to play the fatherly role jointly to both Grant and heroine Stanwyck. However, as would be expected of anti-heroic clones, they depend on a mother-like housekeeper to care for them.

In *Bringing Up Baby*, several possible academic satellites exist, but the best example would be Major Horace Applegate (Charles Ruggles, brother of screwball comedy director Wesley Ruggles), a dinner guest at the home of heroine Katharine Hepburn's aunt. Robin Wood's description of Applegate as an "effeminate and ineffectual big-game hunter, is interesting as a crazy-mirror reflection of the [Hawks adventure genre] men of action."[38] This applies equally well to the professor that Grant is playing, especially with Hepburn constantly taking him on hunting parties to find the escaped leopard.

There is also a certain metaphorical sense of the academic in Major Horace Applegate. He holds a title, bears a famous literary name, and tends to "lecture" on just about any subject that comes to mind, including animal calls. And as with the *Ball of Fire* professors, there is a certain fatherly presence to his being in the home of Hepburn's aunt.

As Wood infers in the last reference, if there seems to be an added incentive on the part of Howard Hawks to humiliate figures such as Applegate or Grant's professor, it is because they purposely represent what might be called the characters of the director's adventure genres (the western, film noir, the gangster film) gone topsyturvy. As observed earlier, the title *Nothing Sacred* describes the screwball philosophy quite nicely, and for directors like Hawks, who seemingly use the genre for a satire of their straight drama, a comedy theory based in superiority through humiliation is the only logical choice, whether dealing with leading performers or supporting satellites.

The assignment of fatherly duties to the satellite figure also addresses another genre misconception from the Capra-equals-screwball comedy equation (see Chapter 3). In *It Happened One Night* Claudette Colbert's father (Walter Connolly) actually knows what is best for her and eventually even masterminds her escape with Clark Gable. But this is an atypical father-daughter relationship in a screwball comedy (though as with the more representational antiheroic examples previously cited, Gable and Connolly do have much in common).

Consequently, on those occasions when a satellite fatherly figure exists, he is much more likely to be in the antiheroic mold of the frustrated central male, especially when portrayed by Eugene Pallette or Edward Everett Horton. In fact, he can be comically self-centered about his daughter's love life; witness Horton's desire to see a Claudette Colbert-Gary Cooper union in *Bluebeard's Eighth Wife* for purely economic reasons (Horton is an aristocrat without money), or, more recently, Liza Minnelli's delightfully greedy father (Barney Martin, a man without even a title) in *Arthur,* who cries when Minnelli will not accept a sizable monetary gift from wealthy Dudley Moore when they initially break up.

Instead of chronicling additional examples, however, a more insightful manner in which to close this section on the supporting character would be to examine briefly an elevation of what should have been a satellite's role to near co-star status, which can occur if the story's central male is more capable than the norm. Ralph Bellamy receives the boost in *His Girl Friday.* He is the beautifully mechanical insurance salesman still living with mother whom Rosalind Russell plans as replacement for ex-husband and newspaper editor Grant, more capable yet equally mechanical in his actions (no behavior is without a newspaper connection).

Bellamy's success in the role is aided by the fact that he often played the best friend who loses the girl, most noticeably his Oscar-nominated performance in *The Awful Truth*, which *His Girl Friday* role often resembles. Bergson sees such role identification as increasing the humor potential, because Bellamy has "become a [comedy] category . . . himself, ready for others to succumb to."[39]

Bellamy is the antiheroic balance to Grant that screwball comedy demands. But should not the added status of Bellamy's role generate its own comedy satellite figure? Yes, and just such a figure exists—Billy Gilbert's Silas F. Pinkus, the state courier trying to deliver a reprieve to the mayor throughout the film. Gilbert's character is so nicely antiheroic that one article on the film even notes the threatening nature of his off-screen wife, whom the viewer never sees.[40] The nature of the role is also assisted by Gilbert's long association with the comedy studio of Hal Roach, where he appeared in a number of short subjects, including those of Laurel & Hardy, thus helping to pioneer the move to antiheroic comedy. The honest, simple-minded, umbrella-carrying Gilbert represents a perfect comedy enlargement of the honest, simple-minded, umbrella-carrying Bellamy. Even their henpecked status is similar in that Bellamy's dominate female, his mother, is largely a threatening off-screen phenomenon. Gilbert offers a convincing glimpse of what Bellamy's character should resemble in twenty years.

Film critic Robin Wood feels the Grant-Bellamy "choice offered Hildy [Russell] is much too narrow to be acceptable."[41] Yet, it is comically defensible in a manner which reaffirms the purpose of this chapter—examining the screwball genre according to the theory of superiority. With the romantic deck firmly in Grant's favor, the viewer is not distracted from comedy by the need for a difficult decision. For example, while *Too Many Husbands* is a funny film, the humor is undermined by the equality of male choices left to Jean Arthur (Melvyn Douglas versus Fred MacMurray), and the nearly choiceless conclusion, which ends with all three dancing together. In contrast, most screwball comedies "telegraph" the hero's, or heroine's, choice long before the conclusion—generally because there is such a marked difference between the competition, such as Claudette Colbert choosing between Clark Gable and Jameson Thomas in *It Happened One Night*, Carole Lombard's decision between Grady Sutton and William Powell in *My Man Godfrey*, Dunne choosing between another Grant-Bellamy lineup in *The Awful Truth*, Grant's choice between Dunne and Gail Patrick in *My Favorite Wife*, Colbert comparing Joel McCrea to Rudy Vallee in *Palm Beach Story*, and more recently, Ryan O'Neal faced with Barbra Streisand or Madeline Kahn in *What's Up, Doc?* and Dudley Moore faced with Liza Minnelli and Jill Eikenberry in *Arthur*. In fact, historians Thomas Sobchack and Vivian C. Sobchack even define this suitor discrepancy as a basic component of the genre, though they inexplicably focus only on males: "the gallery of male suitors who surround the female . . . are potently inappropriate mates . . . made to seem asexual or ridiculously vain."[42]

Screwball comedy's ties with superiority make all the more understandable its inherently conservative nature—a genre in which truly "nothing is sacred." Yet, Molly Haskell says it much more poetically, and with even a glimmer of hope:

> The characters dance the screwball dance on a precipice as steep
> as the Cliffs of Dover in King Lear; their fall is but a pratfall,
> but from the moment of humiliation—their metaphorical
> nudity—they work their way back to salvation.[43]

NOTES

1. James K. Feibleman, *In Praise of Comedy: A Study in its Theory and Practice* (1938; rpt. New York: Horizon Press, 1970), p. 79.

2. Thomas Hobbes, *Leviathan*, ed. Michael Oakeshott (1651; rpt. New York: The Macmillan Company, 1970), p. 52.

3. Max Eastman, *The Sense of Humor* (New York: Charles Scribner's Sons, 1921), pp. 137-51.

4. Henri Bergson, "Laughter," in *Comedy*, ed. Wylie Sypher (Garden City, New York: Doubleday & Company, 1956), pp. 6t5, 187.

5. Andrew Bergman, *We're in the Money: Depression America and Its Films* (1971; rpt. New York: Harper & Row, 1972), p. 134.

6. Molly Haskell, *From Reverence to Rape: The Treatment of Women in the Movies* (Baltimore: Penguin Books, 1974), pp. 126, 130-35, 137-38; Marjorie Rosen, *Popcorn Venus: Women, Movies and the American Dream* (New York: Avon Books, 1974).

7. Karyn Kay, *Part-Time Work of a Domestic Slave* review, *Film Quarterly*, Fall 1975, p. 56.

8. Leo Hurwitz, "One Man's Voyage: Ideas and Films in the 1930's," *Cinema Journal*, Fall 1975, p. 9. This paper was also presented at a Brandeis University symposium on documentary film in February 1972, and for the American Civilization/ American Cinema program at the University of Iowa, March 1975.

9. Thomas Schatz deals with determinate and indeterminate space throughout his "Hollywood Film Genre As Ritual: A Theoretical and Methodological Inquiry" (Ph.D. dissertation, University of Iowa, 1976), which served as the foundation for his recent *Hollywood Genres: Formulas, Filmmaking, and the Studio System* (New York: Random House, 1981).

10. Ibid., p. 145.

11. Stanley Cavell, *Pursuits of Happiness: The Hollywood Comedy of Remarriage* (Cambridge, Massachusetts: Harvard University Press, 1981), p. 121.

12. Schatz, "Hollywood Film Genre As Ritual: A Theoretical and Methodological Inquiry," p. 260.

13. Larry Swindell, *Screwball: The Life of Carole Lombard* (New York: William Morrow and Company, 1975), p. 190.

14. Cavell, *Pursuits of Happiness: The Hollywood Comedy of Remarriage*, p. 66.

15. Northrop Frye, *Anatomy of Criticism: Four Essays* (1957; rpt. Princeton, New Jersey: Princeton University Press, 1973), p. 170.

16. Robin Wood, Chapter 3, "The Lure of Irresponsibility," in *Howard Hawks* (1968; rpt. London: British Film Institute, 1981), pp. 58-88.

17. Ibid., p. 64.

18. Joseph McBride, *Hawks on Hawks* (Los Angeles: University of California Press, 1982), p. 70.

19. John McCabe, *The Comedy World of Stan Laurel* (Garden City, New York: Doubleday and Company, 1974), p. 64.

20. Gerald Mast, *The Comic Mind: Comedy and the Movies* (Indianapolis: Bobbs-Merrill Company, 1973), p. 191.

21. Bosley Crowther, *My Favorite Wife* review, *New York Times*, May 31, 1940, p. 15.

22. Harlan Kennedy, "Blake Edwards: Life After 10," *American Film*, July-August 1981, p. 28.

23. Bergson, "Laughter," p. 105.

24. George Meredith, "Prelude," in *The Egoist* (1879; rpt. Boston: Houghton Mifflin Company, 1958), p. 6.

25. Wylie Sypher, "Introduction," in *Comedy*, ed. Wylie Sypher (Garden City, New York: Doubleday and Company, 1956), p. ix.

26. Bergson, "Laughter," pp. 68, 147.

27. Ibid., pp. 174-75.

28. Ibid., pp. 69, 178-79; George Meredith, "An Essay on Comedy," in *Comedy*, ed. Wylie Sypher (Garden City, New York: Doubleday and Company, 1956), p. 44.

29. Miguel de Cervantes, *Don Quixote of the Mancha*, trans. Thomas Shelton (1605; rpt. New York: P. F. Collier & Son, 1969), pp. 18-19.

30. Joseph McBride and Michael Wilmington, " 'Do I Get to Play the Drunk This Time?': An Encounter with Howard Hawks," *Sight and Sound*, Spring 1971, p. 98.

31. Bergson, "Laughter," p. 68.

32. Ibid., p. 121.

33. Joseph Heller, *Catch-22* (1955; rpt. New York: Dell Publishing Company, 1968), pp. 22, 85, 87, 91, 92.

34. Bergson, "Laughter, " p. 188.

35. Ibid., p. 155.

36. Ibid., p. 166.

37. Ibid., p. 167.

38. Wood, *Howard Hawks* ,p. 69.

39. Bergson, "Laughter," p. 157.

40. Tom Powers, "His Girl Friday: Screwball Liberation," *Jump Cut: A Review of Contemporary Cinema* (April 1978), p. 26.

41 Wood, *Howard Hawks*, p. 77.

42. Thomas Sobchack and Vivian C. Sobchack, "Genre films," in *An Introduction to Film* (Boston: Little, Brown and Company, 1980), p. 208.

43. Haskell, *From Reverence to Rape: The Treatment of Women in the Movies*, pp. 137-38.

7.

A SCREWBALL COMEDY BIBLIOGRAPHICAL ESSAY

This bibliographical essay is an attempt to organize, in chronological order, those key reference materials which both directly address screwball comedy and are most helpful in studying the genre. However, in three cases works had special applicability to the genre despite not having referred to it specifically and exceptions were made for their inclusion: Manny Farber and W. S. Poster's "Preston Sturges: Success in the Movies" (1954), Robin Wood's "The Lure of Irresponsibility" (1968), and Wes D. Gehring's "Mc-Carey vs. Capra: A Guide to American Film Comedy of the '30's" (1978).

All works are divided by length. The first section is limited to book-length sources; the second is comprised of shorter works and includes articles, book chapters, and monographs. In addition, a brief account of screwball comedy archives is included.

There is always a temptation to note every source of related interest. But this can open such a floodgate of material that pivotal works are short-changed. Thus, this bibliographical essay attempts the most disciplined of configurations. The reader/researcher who must have other related sources is invited to study the scores of notes which close each of the proceeding chapters.

BOOKS

There are only two book-length studies of the genre: Ted Sennett's *Lunatics and Lovers* (1971) and Stanley Cavell's *Pursuits of Happiness: The Hollywood Comedy of Remarriage* (1981). Interestingly enough, the books take diametrically opposite approaches. Sennett looks through the small end of the telescope, briefly examining 230 films, while Cavell uses the telescope's large end, scrutinizing a mere seven works in seven chapters.

Sennett is a publishing executive who served as the general editor of the sixteen-book popular film art series, *Pyramid Illustrated History of the Movies*. He is also the author of *Warner Brothers Presents Great Hollywood Movies*, *Hollywood Musical*, *Your Show of Shows*, and the editor of *The Movie Buff's Book*. As both his credits and his approach to *Lunatics and Lovers* suggest, Sennett's forte is detail. Thus, the book's main strength is as a reference text, especially the appendix material and the filmography.

Appendix I is devoted to paragraph-length biographies of key screwball comedy players. Appendix II applies the same approach to genre directors, while Appendix III examines the writers. The appendix material is followed by a 230-entry filmography (arranged by year, 1932-44), with each film also receiving a one-sentence synopsis.

The main text of the book is divided into ten chapters, each representing a subgrouping of the genre. The self-explanatory titles of the chapters are: "The Cinderella Syndrome," "Wife, Husband, Friend, Secretary," "Poor Little Rich Girls (and Boys)," "Lamb Bites Wolf," "Bats in Their Belfry," "The Thin Man, Topper, and Friends," "Boss-Ladies and Other Liberated Types," and "Stage to Screen." The only exceptions to this subgenre categorizing are in the opening chapter overview, "A World of Lunatics and Lovers" (from which the book's title is taken), and a late chapter devoted to a genre director, "The Amazing Mr. Sturges."

Sennett's group of films and facts is truly amazing, but he does not take one beyond this. Instead of topping off this impressive and important body of information with some big-picture analysis of the genre, or what it might mean in relationship to American comedy, film art, and the individual and/or the society at large, one merely receives more information. This does not negate it as a reference work, but it could have been so much more, especially given Sennett's fine grasp of so many films. With such an impressive array of facts, so neatly arranged, the ending arrives just as things should be beginning.

Another problem is that Sennett establishes no criteria to determine just what screwball comedy is. Granted, this is no easy task. But some filter devise is necessary, or else all lines of demarcation become unclear. For example, he includes material which should be in a personality comedian genre, such as Harold Lloyd's *The Milky Wave* (1936), Bob Hope's *Ghost Breakers* (1940), Red Skelton's *Whistling in Brooklyn* (1944), and Joe E. Brown's *Alibi Ike* (1935). Consequently, while Sennett provides a wealth of material, his undefined approach to the genre seems a bit too broad.

In contrast, Stanley Cavell's *Pursuits of Happiness* examines a mere seven films: *The Lady Eve* (1941), *It Happened One Night* (1934), *Bringing Up Baby* (1938), *The Philadelphia Story* (1940), *His Girl Friday* (1940), *Adam's Rib* (1949), and *The Awful Truth* (1937).

Cavell is the Walter M. Cabot Professor of Aesthetics and the General Theory of Value at Harvard University. He is also the author of *Must We Mean What We Say?*, *The Senses of Walden*, *The Claim of Reason*, and *The World Viewed*. In *Pursuits of Happiness* Cavell more than makes up for the absence of analysis in *Lunatics and Lovers*. Indeed, his positions have already generated much attention in the volume at hand (see especially Chapters 3 and 6). While this author has sometimes disagreed with Cavell, his book is frequently insightful and always intellectually provocative. Some items, however, bear discussion.

First, Cavell's forty-two-page introduction, sometimes brilliant, sometimes meanderingly obtuse, can also be irritating. For example, he frequently takes an apologetic stance toward film study, as if he were writing in an earlier era when the medium's position in academic circles was on shaky ground: "I AM NOT INSENSIBLE, whatever defenses I may deploy, of an avenue of outrageousness in considering Hollywood films in the light, from time to time, of major works of thought."[1] Thus, his frequent flights of intellectual comparison, such as his juxtaposing Kant and Capra (while not without interest) sometimes seem an extension of that apologetic stance, as if mere film or film figures could be elevated by association. In fact, Cavell seems to inadvertently imply just that when he later observes, "If my citings of philosophical texts along the way hinder more than they help you, skip them."[2]

The introduction takes the interestingly provocative position of defining a new genre based upon the aforementioned seven films—"the comedy of remarriage," drawing much from Shakespearean romantic comedy. But Cavell can be at the same time annoyingly cavalier:

> I am for myself satisfied that this group of films is the principal
> group of Hollywood comedies after the advent of sound. . . .
> But I will not attempt to argue directly for that here, any more
> than I will attempt explicitly to convince anyone that film is an
> art.[3]

Cavell seems to confuse his outdated bugaboo about film as art with the basic intellectual courtesy of providing some background, however brief, on why this unique status. It is not a question of art, but, rather, why this art?

Also cavalier is the fact that while all seven films are obviously screwball comedies (with the possible exception of *Adam's Rib*), Cavell makes reference to the genre in neither the introduction nor the rest of the book. Even stimulating developments, like his attempt to define a new genre called "The Hollywood Comedy of Remarriage" has an obligation to its cinematic roots. For example, Thomas Schatz includes "The divorce-remarriage variation" as a subheading (one type of screwball comedy) in the chapter on the genre in his *Hollywood Genres: Formulas, Filmmaking, and the Studio*

System (1981).[4] Earlier, Brian Henderson's essay on the genre, "Romantic Comedy Today: Semi-Tough or Impossible?" (1978), used the same idea but a simpler wording, "old love/new love," as its basic division of the genre.[5] Thus, while Sennett's book became too entangled in an almost film-by-film tradition of the genre, Cavell's work suffers from tunnel vision. For example, in his examination of *The Lady Eve*, Cavell insightfully observes that Barbara Stanwyck is "Some kind of stand-in for the role of director."[6] Yet, as this author demonstrates in Chapter 3, this is hardly an isolated example in the unmentioned screwball genre. Consequently, screwball comedy and comedy of remarriage should be treated as one and the same.

Second, Cavell and this author interpret a number of basic screwball issues differently. Since these conflicting arguments were addressed in the main text, they need not be reiterated here. It would seem appropriate, however, to note the key questions themselves: Is it hero or heroine who undergoes change in the genre? Just how universally applicable to the genre are the events in *A Midsummer Night's Dream?* How realistic (if at all) should a screwball comedy conclusion be?

Third, despite such differences, Cavell and this author were in agreement on several pivotal issues: the exclusion of the Capra trilogy of *Mr. Deeds Goes to Town* (1936), *Mr. Smith Goes to Washington* (1939), and *Meet John Doe* (1941); the length of the initial screwball comedy movement (1934 to the early 1940s); the self-conscious nature of the genre (comically feeding upon itself); and the close ties between the screwball comedy player and his or her real-life identity.

Cavell's book is provocatively stimulating. Even when the reader disagrees, which occurred frequently with this author, one is challenged to reevaluate his basic concept of the genre. (The absence of this quality is what ultimately made Sennett's *Lunatics and Lovers* a disappointment.)

SHORTER WORKS

A good place to begin is Lewis Jacobs's brief discussion of the genre in his chapter on "Contemporary Film Content" in the watershed *The Rise of the American Film: A Critical History* (1939). As the chapter title indicates, Jacobs was writing during the period in question. Correctly defining what he calls "daffy" comedies (though he later calls the antics of the performers "screw-ball") as being a mixture of slapstick and sophistication, he notes such examples as *It Happened One Night* (1934), *Twentieth Century* (1934), *My Man Godfrey* (1936), *Theodora Goes Wild* (1936), *Topper* (1937), *The Awful Truth* (1937), *Nothing Sacred* (1937) and *Bringing Up Baby*. The only Capra film included was *It Happened One Night* (though *Mr. Smith Goes to Washington* had not yet been made).

As a sociological historian, Jacobs ties the birth of the genre to the depression—crazy activities in a "crazy world." The performers he mentions

(Carole Lombard, Katharine Hepburn, Cary Grant, Fred MacMurray, and Melvyn Douglas) are still recognized as stellar examples of the genre (see Chapter 5), though, as film critic Andrew Sarris notes, Jacobs can be rather misleading in reading a performer. He describes Grant as a strong rebel figure in *Holiday* (1938), who "tells the heroine and the rich and dignified where to go, and dashes off and on the scene with a complete disdain of conventionality."[7]

Jacobs also makes a fascinating but unfortunately rather vague connection between the eccentric screwball comedy performer and some period personality clowns, such as the Marx Brothers and W. C. Fields. Jacobs's point is that the comically offbeat characteristics of the screwball performer are present in the personality type—but in a greatly exaggerated state. As already noted in this book (see Chapter 4), there were direct ties between screwball comedy and personality clowns, such as Gregory La Cava's connection with Fields, or Leo McCarey's with Laurel & Hardy. But unfortunately, Jacobs does not expand on this statement, and it is sufficiently vague for readers to misconstrue. Thus, Sarris questions it in his article on screwball comedy.[8] Still, both because of its brevity and the time period in which it was written, Jacobs has done a credible job.

The important 1930s film critic Otis Ferguson's "While We Were Laughing" (1940) makes an excellent companion piece to Jacobs's work. While discussing a wide gamut of American film comedy, it pays particular attention to screwball comedy, especially to *It Happened One Night* (1934). It also focuses on pivotal 1934, and the two other key films to join *It Happened One Night: The Thin Man* and *Twentieth Century*. And as noted in Chapter 1, Ferguson both discusses the first appearance of the term screwball (as applied to a film) and insightfully recognizes the genre's ability to integrate what would normally be solo slapstick material by a comic personality into a comic narrative.

The Manny Farber-W. C. Poster essay "Preston Sturges: Success in the Movies" (1954) examines this director's short but memorable 1940s film career. While providing numerous insights to the world of Sturges, it is most valuable when it draws a parallel between his fast-paced, slapstick-like dialogue and the comparable *visual* antics of silent film comedy. As already noted in Chapter 4, this is an important analogy applicable to other screwball directors.

Sociological film historians Richard Griffith and Arthur Mayer devote a segment of their chapter "The New Deal" to screwball comedy in *The Movies* (1957), which examines American film history largely through stills and commentary. It sees the genre as an outgrowth of the depression, and notes the importance of *It Happened One Night* and *The Thin Man* (both 1934). Though the twelve accompanying stills are well-chosen, the commentary is disappointingly brief for a reference which is noted in other screwball comedy essays. (For example, Raymond Durgnat's "Lightly and Politely," 1970, expands upon it, and Andrew Sarris's "The Sex Comedy

Without Sex," 1978, uses it as a point of departure for his censorship-produced screwball comedy hypothesis.)

William Thomaier's "Early Sound Comedy" (1958) was devoted entirely to the evolution of screwball comedy. It is a brief but informative survey of the genre from 1934 to 1941, proceeding at a methodical year-by-year pace. Of special interest is his observation that Capra films pointed the viewer to a "better life," whereas screwball comedy focused on a "to hell with everything" foundation.[9] (See also Bernard Drew's less methodical overview, "High Comedy in the Thirties," 1976, which despite its title does not limit itself to that decade.)

Andrew Sarris's "The World of Howard Hawks" (1961) includes an excellent early examination of the dark side of the director's screwball comedy. Later included in editor Joseph McBride's anthology, *Focus on Howard Hawks* (1972), it is the best screwball-related essay in the text. In fact, the comedy segments were strong enough that they were later edited into the 100 percent screwball comedy Hawks essay entitled "Hawksian Comedy," which was anthologized in *Movie Comedy* (1977).

Robin Wood's *Howard Hawks* (1968) was a watershed work on a director who, at that time, had only received a minimal amount of serious attention. His chapter on "The Lure of Irresponsibility" is of particular interest to the study of screwball comedy. Though it does not address the genre directly, its examination of *Scarface* (1932), *Bringing Up Baby* (1938), *His Girl Friday* (1940), *Monkey Business* (1952), and *I Was a Male War Bride* (1949) posits several characteristics, most specifically the title-repeating "lure of irresponsibility," which are frequently applicable to screwball comedy. While this author does not always agree with the Wood position (such as the question of male choice given Rosalind Russell in *His Girl Friday*, examined in Chapter 6), it is a not-to-be-avoided essay. (See also Gerald Mast's "The Dialogue Tradition," 1973, in *The Comic Mind: Comedy and the Movies*. While never addressing screwball comedy directly, it does examine several genre films, and like Wood—it is most insightful on Hawks.)

In 1971 pluralist film critic Pauline Kael's controversial *The Citizen Kane Book* was published. The excitement was really the result of the lengthy essay which opens the work—"Raising Kane," which more than lives up to its pun of a title. The purpose of both the essay and the book was to prove that Herman J. Mankiewicz, not Orson Welles, created the script for *Citizen Kane* (1941; they have always been credited as co-authors). In addition, Kael's book also celebrates 1930s film comedy and the neglected screenwriter. Yet, just as she can overstate her main thesis, anti-auteurist Kael would seem to overreact to neglect of screenwriters by suddenly granting them the lion's share of the credit.

Andrew Bergman's "Frank Capra and the Screwball Comedy, 1931-1941," Chapter 10 from his book *We're In the Money: Depression America and Its Films* (1971), brings the reader back to a specific auteur. Capra *is* screwball comedy to Bergman. Since this essay has been frequently addressed in this volume, it should be sufficient to say this is normally the starting point for those who endorse the post–*It Happened One Night*, Capra-equals-screwball comedy formula. (Probably the most ambitious expansion of this Capra position comes from the aforementioned chapter on the genre in Thomas Schatz's *Hollywood Genres*.)

Donald W. McCaffrey's "Sophisticated and Almost Satirical," Chapter 7 from his *The Golden Age of Sound Comedy: Comic Films and Comedians of the Thirties* (1973), is a genre overview which takes *Easy Living* (1937) as its model, including to a lesser extent *Nothing Sacred* (1937). The key screwball years for McCaffrey are 1934-38, and the early-1940s revival by Preston Sturges. The essay is refreshing because McCaffrey is unconventional. Although his focus films are *Easy Living* and *Nothing Sacred*, he provides commentary on such other genre works as *The Ghost Goes West* (1936), *Topper* (1937), *Vivacious Lady* (1938), and *Mad Miss Manton* (1938). Such breadth is unusual in most essays on this genre.

Molly Haskell's chapter "The Thirties," from her *From Reverence to Rape: The Treatment of Women in the Movies* (1974), examines a myriad of women's issues from the decade, including a brief but insightful look at screwball comedy. She anticipates the thesis of Andrew Sarris's later link between the Censorship Code and screwball comedy, and has an answer in waiting for feminists who attack the genre (see following entry). And like the poetical Haskell quote which closed the previous chapter, she is forever a master at concentrating much into a few words. (See also Ray Hagen's affectionate look at the 1930s and screwball comedy: "The Day of the Runaway Heiress," 1966).

The summer 1976 *Film Quarterly* contained Leland A. Poague's "A Short Defense of Screwball Comedy," which was a response to a fall 1975 Karyn Kay feminist review of *Part-Time Work of a Domestic Slave*. Kay had, in a lengthy aside, linked twentieth-century screwball comedy with the "Noah" plays of the medieval ages, in which Mr. and Mrs. Noah battle as to whether she is going to board the ark. In either case, Kay saw the male as clearly dominate. Poague's interpretations diametrically opposed this. Immediately following Poague's article, a Kay rebuttal appeared. Among other things, she incorporated *The Taming of the Shrew* into her defense. Ironically, Haskell had already written the best of defenses two years earlier when she observed screwball comedies "celebrate difficult and anarchic love rather than security and the suburban dream . . . favoring movement over status, and speech and argument over silent compliance."[10]

Jim Leach's "The Screwball Comedy," from the Barry K. Grant-edited anthology *Film Genre: Theory and Criticism* (1977) is one of the most insightful essays ever done on the genre. Leach begins by addressing the danger of defining a genre like comedy both too narrowly (fit only for pedantics), or too broadly ("a genre which encompasses the visions of Jerry Lewis *and* Ernst Lubitsch is already in trouble."[11]).

He goes on to discuss screwball comedy's relationship to slapstick, sexuality, and even film noir. Several screwball comedy directors are discussed, but Hawks, appropriately, receives the most sustained attention, with even a reference to Robin Wood's important "The Lure of Irresponsibility" (examined earlier in this chapter). And Capra's post-*It Happened One Night* work is seen as populist, not screwball, based in part on the observation that the emphasis is not sexual (the genre's all-important couple) but rather social. Finally, Leach briefly examines some modern (1970s) screwball comedies and closes with a plea for both flexibility in viewing variations of the genre as well as an awareness of the multitude of comedy genres which exist.

Auteur critic Andrew Sarris's "The Sex Comedy Without Sex," from the March 1978 *American Film*, should also have the subtitle "With Review." Because, while Sarris's underlying argument is that the genre was a result of censorship code implementation—thus the title "The Sex Comedy Without Sex"—the article's main strength is in its examination of the sociological positions taken by film historian Lewis Jacobs in his *The Rise of the American Film*. To a lesser extent Sarris also interprets the sociological positions of Andrew Bergman, Richard Griffith, and Arthur Mayer.

Sarris finds Jacobs too broad in his late-1930s views of screwball comedy (though as noted earlier, even with this broadness Jacobs's only Capra film is *It Happened One Night*). Moreover, by examining pivotal Jacobs examples of the genre, Sarris makes a strong case for screwball comedy being "only fitfully concerned with the economic problems of the era."[12] Certainly, reading screwball comedy as escapist fare during the depression must count for something, but even if Sarris has overreacted in preparation for presenting his own hypothesis, he is frequently effective on the attack. For example, he reminds the reader that *Holiday* (another Jacobs model) was originally a 1920s play.

Sarris is not so convincing, however, in his shorter examinations of other screwball historians/theorists (also found to be faulty), such as Bergman's approach to the genre as being conservative. Moreover, once Sarris finally fleshes out his own code-influenced screwball genre premise, after having negated all the other theorists, his hypothesis (though plausible as a contributing factor) hardly seems able to carry the whole weight of a genre. But his closing discussion of the genre's few constants is good, and brings him full circle to the screwball universals for which he was searching at the article's beginning. (See Molly Haskell's "The Thirties," for an earlier but much briefer discussion of the Code and screwball comedy, and E. Rubinstein's later "The End of Screwball Comedy: *The Lady Eve* and *The Palm Beach Story,* which takes a Preston Sturges focus.) Brian Henderson's "Romantic Comedy Today: Semi-tough or Impossible?," from the summer 1978 *Film Quarterly*, opens with a lament that there has never been one umbrella of a comedy theory which could cover all that is comic. Moving to the opposite extreme, it then surveys the controversy which surrounds defining even one type of comedy—the screwball variety—which he includes in a larger romantic comedy category (with comedy of manners and marriage).

The rest of Henderson's essay is largely composed of fluctuations between an analysis of the 1977 romantic comedy *Semi-Tough* (which is also punned in the title of the article) and discussion of romantic comedies from the 1930s. These examples are generally screwball in nature, such as *Bringing Up Baby* and *Holiday*. The inclusion of material on Noel Coward's *Design for Living* and Ben Hecht's film adaptation (1933) for Ernst Lubitsch should remind the reader that Henderson is still addressing a larger *romantic* comedy category, with *Design for Living* fitting the aforementioned grouping: comedy of manners.

The article provides some interesting observations on screwball comedy, such as the "old love/new love" division, which, as mentioned earlier, anticipates Cavell's book-length study. But while that romantic comedy umbrella reminds the viewer of the comedy family in which screwball comedy is included, it can also be a liability. It disregards certain unique characteristics of screwball comedy, such as the frequency of its unconventional approach to (parody of) romanticism, especially with the aggressive, zany female and the retiring male.

In 1978 this author wrote "McCarey vs. Capra: A Guide to American Film Comedy of the '30s." While not speaking directly to screwball comedy, the antihero-crackerbarrel dichotomy is pivotal to an American humor-oriented understanding of the genre, as well as the reason why Capra's post–*It Happened One Night* inclusion is a mistake. A slightly larger version of this essay later appeared as Chapter 5 in the author's *Leo McCarey and the Comic Anti-Hero in American Film* (1980). While completely divorced from screwball comedy, the author's "The Electric Horseman: A 'Capra' Film for the 1980s" (*Journal of Popular Film and Television*, Winter 1983) presents a more contemporary look at the populist, non-screwball world in which Capra is best associated.

Thomas Sobchack and Vivian C. Sobchack address screwball comedy as a subdivision of romantic comedy in the "Genre Films" chapter of their *An Introduction to Film* (1980). Though much briefer than is Henderson in his essay, they avoid the romantic comedy ambiguity which flaws that article, directly addressing the formula change necessary for screwball comedy. The Sobchacks nicely update the genre's ties to ancient Greece's New Comedy. They recognize screwball comedy is more likely to vest additional wisdom in one member of the couple as opposed to an outside adviser in the pure New Comedy tradition. They further note, using examples such as *Bringing Up Baby* and *The Lady Eve* (1941), that it is the female who generally dominates.

The Sobchacks close their analysis by providing some basic screwball conventions—the most pointed examples being the mismatch of suitor choices facing the female, as well as her generally dominate position.

"Screwball Comedy: Defining a Film Genre" (1983) is a monograph-length examination of the movement by this author. It focuses on the genre's interrelationship with the evolution of the comic antihero in American humor, and is the foundation for the book at hand. As the monograph subtitle states, "Defining a Film Genre," it is also an attempt to affix a body criteria to what has too often been a shapeless genre (an ongoing goal in this book-length study). The meat of the monograph appears in expanded form as Chapter 3 in this volume. For another shorter variation on this material see the author's "Screwball Comedy: An Overview" (*Journal of Popular Film and Television*, Winter 1985).

SCREWBALL COMEDY ARCHIVES

Unfortunately, there is no single library with a center for screwball comedy research. The student of the genre is largely dependent upon searching out materials based upon specific film titles and persons involved in their production. The writing of this volume was greatly assisted by the diversified holdings of five libraries: the Library of Congress (Washington, D.C.), the Billy Rose Theatre Collection (New York Public Library at Lincoln Center), the Academy of Motion Picture Arts and Sciences Library (Los Angeles), the American Film Institute Library (Los Angeles), and the University of Iowa main library (Iowa City).

In particular, this involved the motion picture clipping files at both the Billy Rose and Academy libraries, the oral histories (especially Leo McCarey's) at the American Film Institute, and the general periodical holdings at the Library of Congress and the University of Iowa.

It is hoped that this work may be a starting point for further study of screwball comedy and its ongoing impact on popular culture, and that it will represent one more proof of comedy's equality with the "more serious arts."

NOTES

1. Stanley Cavell, *Pursuits of Happiness: The Hollywood Comedy of Remarriage* (Cambridge, Massachusetts: Harvard University Press, 1981), p. 8.
2. Ibid., p. 16.
3. Ibid., p. 11.
4. Thomas Schatz, "The Screwball Comedy," in *Hollywood Genres: Formulas, Filmmaking, and the Studio System* (New York: Random House, 1981), p. 162.
5. Brian Henderson, "Romantic Comedy Today: Semi-Tough or Impossible?" *Film Quarterly*, Summer 1978, p. 17.
6. Cavell, *Pursuits of Happiness*, p. 66.
7. Lewis Jacobs, Chapter 25, "Contemporary Film Content," in *The Rise of the American Film: A Critical History* (1939; rpt. New York: Teachers College Press, 1971), p. 536; Andrew Sarris, "The Sex Comedy Without Sex," *American Film*, March 1978, p. 10.
8. Sarris, "The Sex Comedy Without Sex," pp. 9-10.

9. William Thomaier, "Early Sound Comedy Was Influenced by the Instability of the '30s and Was Therefore Screwball," *Films in Review*, May 1958, p. 257.

10. Molly Haskell, "The Thirties," in *From Reverence to Rape: The Treatment of Women in the Movies* (Baltimore: Penguin Books, 1974), p. 126.

11. Jim Leach, "The Screwball Comedy," in *Film Genre: Theory and Criticism*, ed. Barry K. Grant (Metuchen, New Jersey: The Scarecrow Press, 1977), p. 75.

12. Andrew Sarris, "The Sex Comedy Without Sex," *American Film*, March 1978, p. 10.

8.

BIBLIOGRAPHICAL CHECKLIST OF KEY SCREWBALL COMEDY SOURCES

BOOKS ON SCREWBALL COMEDY

Cavell, Stanley. *Pursuits of Happiness: The Hollywood Comedy of Remarriage.* Cambridge, Massachusetts: Harvard University Press, 1981.

Sennett, Ted. *Lunatics and Lovers.* New Rochelle, New York: Arlington House, 1971.

SHORTER WORKS ON SCREWBALL COMEDY: ARTICLES, BOOK CHAPTERS, AND MONOGRAPHS

Bergman, Andrew. Chapter 10, "Frank Capra and the Screwball Comedy, 1931-1941." In *We're In the Money: Depression America and Its Films.* 1971; rpt. New York: Harper & Row, 1972.

Drew, Bernard. "High Comedy in the Thirties" (1976). In *Movie Comedy.* Edited by Stuart Byron and Elisabeth Weis. New York: Penguin Books, 1977.

Durgnat, Raymond. Chapter 19, "Lightly and Politely." In *The Crazy Mirror: Hollywood Comedy and the American Image.* 1970; rpt. New York: Delta, 1972.

Farber, Manny, and W. S. Poster. "Preston Sturges: Success in the Movies" (1954). In *Negative Space.* New York: Frederick Praeger, 1972.

Ferguson, Otis. "While We Were Laughing" (1940). In *The Film Criticism of Otis Ferguson.* Edited by Robert Wilson. Philadelphia: Temple University Press, 1971.

Gehring, Wes D. "McCarey vs. Capra: A Guide to American Film Comedy of the '30s," *The Journal of Popular Film and Television* 7, no. 1 (1978): 67-84. (For a contemporary look at the populist, non-screwball world in which Capra is best associated, see the author's "The Electric Horseman: A 'Capra' Film for the 1980s," *Journal of Popular Film and Television*, Winter 1983, pp. 10-18.)

_____. "Screwball Comedy: Defining a Film Genre." Muncie, Indiana: Ball State University Press Monograph Series, 1983.

_____. "Screwball Comedy: An Overview," *The Journal of Popular Film and Television*, Winter 1985.

Griffith, Richard, and Arthur Mayer. "The New Deal." In *The Movies*. New York: Simon and Schuster, 1957. (The latest update, 1981, added a third author, Eileen Bowser.)

Hagen, Ray. "The Day of the Runaway Heiress," *Film and Filming*, April 1966, pp. 40-43.

Haskell, Molly. "The Thirties." In *From Reverence to Rape: The Treatment of Women in the Movies*. Baltimore: Penguin Books, Inc., 1974.

Henderson, Brian. "Romantic Comedy Today: Semi-Tough or Impossible?" *Film Quarterly*, Summer 1978, pp. 11-23.

Jacobs, Lewis. Chapter 25, "Contemporary Film Content." In *The Rise of the American Film: A Critical History*. 1939; rpt. New York: Teachers College Press, 1971.

Kael, Pauline. "Raising Kane." In *The Citizen Kane Book*. Boston: Little, Brown and Company, 1971.

Kay, Karyn. "Controversy and Correspondence: Karyn Kay Replies," *Film Quarterly*, Summer 1976, pp. 63-64.

_____. "Part-Time Work of a Domestic Slave," *Film Quarterly*, Fall 1975, pp. 52-57.

Leach, Jim. "The Screwball Comedy." In *Film Genre: Theory and Criticism*. Edited by Barry K. Grant. Metuchen, New Jersey: The Scarecrow Press, Inc., 1977.

McCaffrey, Donald W. Chapter 7, "Sophisticated and Almost Satirical." In *The Golden Age of Sound Comedy: Comic Films and Comedians of the Thirties*. New York: A. S. Barnes and Company, 1973.

Mast, Gerald. Chapter 16. "The Dialogue Tradition." In *The Comic Mind: Comedy and the Movies*. 2d ed. Chicago: The University of Chicago Press, 1979.

Poague, Leland A. "Controversy and Correspondence: A Short Defense of Screwball Comedy," *Film Quarterly*, Summer 1976, pp. 62-63.

E. Rubinstein, "The End of Screwball Comedy: *The Lady Eve* and *The Palm Beach Story*," *Post Script*, Spring/Summer 1982, pp. 33-47.

Sarris, Andrew. "The Sex Comedy Without Sex," *American Film*, March 1978, pp. 8-15.

Sarris, Andrew. "The World of Howard Hawks" (1961). In *Focus on Howard Hawks*. Edited by Joseph McBride. Englewood Cliffs, New Jersey: Prentice-Hall, Inc., 1972. See also Andrew Sarris. "Hawksian Comedy." In *Movie Comedy*. Edited by Stuart Byron and Elisabeth Weis. New York: Penguin Books, 1977.

Schatz, Thomas. Chapter 6, "The Screwball Comedy." In *Hollywood Genres: Formulas, Filmmaking, and the Studio System*. New York: Random House, 1981. (The Capra position.)

Sobchack, Thomas, and Vivian C. Sobchack. "Genre Films." In *An Introduction to Film*. Boston: Little, Brown and Company, 1980.

Thomaier, William. "Early Sound Comedy Was Influenced by the Instability of the '30s and Was Therefore Screwball," *Films in Review*, May 1958, pp. 254-62.

Wood, Robin. Chapter 3, "The Lure of Irresponsibility." In *Howard Hawks*. 1968; rpt. London: British Film Institute, 1981.

APPENDIX: FILMOGRAPHY

This filmography of selected screwball comedies keys on the heyday of the genre (1934-44), which is also the focus of this volume. It does include, however, a section on notable post-1944 screwball comedies.

Because the majority of these films were done during the golden age of the American studio system (1930-45), a time when crossing craft lines was tantamount to heresy (a director was supposed to direct, a write to write . . .), the writing of pivotal screwball directors like Howard Hawks, Leo McCarey, and Gregory La Cava is invariably absent from the following credits. (See Chapter 4 on the director for an expanded look at the writing side of these men, as well as how another focus screwball director, Preston Sturges, helps break this tradition.)

Films are listed in the order of their *New York Times* review date.

SCREWBALL COMEDY, 1934–1944

1934   *It Happened One Night* (105 minutes).
       Columbia. Producer: Harry Cohn. Director: Frank Capra. Screenplay: Robert Riskin, from the Samuel Hopkins Adams story "Night Bus." Cinematography: Joseph Walker. Cast: Clark Gable (Peter Warne), Claudette Colbert (Ellie Andrews), Walter Connolly (Alexander Andrews), Roscoe Karns (Oscar Shapeley), Jameson Thomas (King Westley), Ward Bond and Eddy Chandler (bus drivers), Alan Hale (Danker), Arthur Hoyt (Zeke), Blanche Frederici (Zeke's wife), Charles C. Wilson (Joe Gordon), Wallis Clark (Lovington), Harry C. Bradley (Henderson), Harry Holman (auto camp manager), Maidel Turner (manager's wife), Irving Bacon (station attendant), Charles D. Brown and Hal Price (reporters).

1934   *Twentieth Century* (91 minutes).
Columbia. Producer/Director: Howard Hawks. Screenplay: Ben Hecht, Charles MacArthur, from their play, based on the Charles Bruce Milholland play *Napoleon on Broadway*. Cinematography: Joseph August. Cast: John Barrymore (Oscar Jaffe), Carole Lombard (Mildred Plotka/Lily Garland), Walter Connolly (Oliver Webb), Roscoe Karns (Owen O'Malley), Charles Levison (Max Jacobs), Etienne Girardot (Matthew J. Clark), Dale Fuller (Sadie), Ralph Forbes (George Smith), Billie Seward (Anita), Clifford Thompson (Lockwood), James P. Burtis (conductor), Gigi Parrish (Myrtle Schultz), Edgar Kennedy (Mr. McGonigle), Ed Gargan (sheriff), Snowflake (porter), Herman Bing (first beard), Lee Kohlmer (second beard), Pat Flaherty (Flannigan).

1934   *The Thin Man* (91 minutes).
Metro-Goldwyn-Mayer. Producer: Hunt Stromberg. Director: W. S. Van Dyke II. Screenplay: Albert Hackett, Frances Goodrich, from the Dashiell Hammett novel. Cinematography: James Wong. Cast: William Powell (Nick Charles), Myrna Loy (Nora Charles), Maureen O'Sullivan (Dorothy), Nat Pendleton (Lieutenant John Guild), Minna Gombell (Mimi Wynant), Porter Hall (McCauley), Henry Wadsworth (Tommy), William Henry (Gilbert Wynant), Harold Huber (Nunheim), Cesar Romero (Chris Jorgenson), Natalie Moorhead (Julia Wolf), Edward Brophy (Joe Morelli), Clay Clement (Quinn), Thomas Jackson (reporter), Walter Long (Stutsy Burke), Ben Roach (Foster), Ben Taggart (police captain). (Five additional *Thin Man* "films" followed between 1936 and 1947.)

1935   *The Gilded Lily* (85 minutes).
Paramount. Producer: Albert Lewis. Director: Wesley Ruggles. Screenplay: Claude Binyon, from a Melvinne Baker, Jack Kirkland story. Cinematography: Victor Milner. Cast: Claudette Colbert (Lillian David), Fred MacMurray (Peter Dawes), Ray Milland (Charles Gray/Granville), C. Aubrey Smith (Lloyd Granville). Luis Alberni (Nate), Edward Craven (Eddie), Donald Meek (Hankerson), Charles Irwin (Oscar), Ferdinand Munier (Otto Bushe), Grace Bradley (Daisy), Charles Wilson (city editor), Jerry Mandy (waiter), Warren Hymer (taxi driver), Tom Dugan (tramp), Forrester Harvey (Hugo), Mary Gordon (Hugo's wife), Leonid Kinsky (vocal teacher).

1935   *Ruggles of Red Gap* (91 minutes).
Paramount. Producer: Arthur Hornblow, Jr. Director: Leo McCarey. Screenplay: Walter Deleon, Harlan Thompson, adaptation by Humphrey Pearson of the Harry Leon Wilson novel. Cinematography: Alfred Gilks. Cast: Charles Laughton (Marmaduke Ruggles), Mary Boland (Effie Floud), Charlie Ruggles (Egbert Floud), Zazu Pitts (Mrs. Judson), Roland Young (Earl of Burnstead), Leila Hyams (Nell Kenna), Maude Eburne (Ma Pettingill), Lucien Littlefield (Charles Belknap-Jackson), James Burk (Jeff Tuttle), Dell Henderson (Sam), Leota Lorraine (Mrs. Belknap-Jackson),

Clarence Wilson (Jake Henshaw), Brenda Fowler (Judy Ballard), Augusta Anderson (Mrs. Wallaby), Sarah Edwards (Mrs. Myron Carey), Rafael Storm (clothing salesman), George Burton (Hank), Victor Potel (cowboy), Frank Rice (Buck), William J. Welsh (Eddie), Harry Bernard (cowboy), Alice Ardell (Lisette), Rolfe Seden (barber).

1935 *The Whole Town's Talking* (95 minutes).
Columbia. Producer: Lester Cowan. Director: John Ford. Screenplay: Jo Swerling, from the W. R. Burnett novel. Film Dialogue: Robert Riskin. Cinematography: Joseph H. August. Cast: Edward G. Robinson (Arthur Ferguson Jones /"Killer" Mannion), Jean Arthur (Miss "Bill" Clark), Wallace Ford (Mr. Healy), Arthur Byron (Mr. Spencer), Arthur Hohl (Det. Sgt. Michael Boyle), Donald Meek (Mr. Hoyt), Paul Harvey (J. G. Carpenter), Edward Brophy ("Slugs" Martin), J. Farrell McDonald (Warden), Etienne Girardot (Mr. Seaver), James Donlan (Howe), John Wray (henchman), Effie Ellsler (Aunt Agatha), Robert Emmett O'Connor (police lieutenant), Joseph Sawyer (extra), Francis Ford (extra), Robert Parrish (extra).

1935 *She Married Her Boss* (90 minutes).
Columbia. Producer: Everett Riskin. Director: Gregory La Cava. Screenplay: Sidney Buchman, from a Thyra Samter Winslow story. Cinematography: Leon Shamroy. Cast: Claudette Colbert (Julia Scott), Melvyn Douglas (Richard Barclay), Michael Bartlett (Leonard Rogers), Raymond Walburn (Franklyn), Jean Dixon (Martha Pryor), Katherine Alexander (Gertrude Barclay), Edith Fellows (Annabel Barclay), Clara Kimball Young (Parsons), Grace Hayle (Agnes), Charles Arnt (manager, department store), Schuyler Shaw (chauffeur), Selmer Jackson (Andrews), John Hyams (Hoyt), Robert E. Homans (detective), Lillian Rich (telephone operator), Arthur S. Byron (store watchman), David O'Brien (man), Buddy Roosevelt (chauffeur), Ruth Cherrington (old maid saleswoman), Lillian Moore (department head).

1935 *Hands Across the Table* (80 minutes).
Paramount. Producer: E. Lloyd Sheldon. Director: Mitchell Leisen. Screenplay: Norman Krasna, Vincent Lawrence, Herbert Fields, from the Vin Delmar story "Bracelets." Cinematography: Ted Tetzlaff. Cast: Carole Lombard (Regi Allen), Fred MacMurray (Theodore Drew III), Ralph Bellamy (Allen Macklyn), Astrid Allwyn (Vivian Snowden), Ruth Donnelly (Laura), Marie Prevost (Nona), Joseph Tozer (Peter), William Demarest (Natty), Edward Gargan (Pinky Kelly), Ferdinand Munier (Miles), Harold Minjir (Valentine), Marcelle Corday (French maid).

1936 *The Ghost Goes West* (95 minutes).
London Films. Producer: Alexander Korda. Director: René Clair. Screenplay: Robert E. Sherwood, René Clair, from the Eric Keown story "Sir Tristram Goes West." Cinematography: Harold Rosson. Special Effects:

Ned Mann. Cast: Robert Donat (Murdoch Glourie/Donald Glourie), Jean Parker (Peggy Martin), Eugene Pallette (Joe Martin), Elsa Lanchester (Lady Shepperton).

1936   *The Ex-Mrs. Bradford* (80 minutes).
RKO-Radio. Producer: Edward Kaufman. Director: Steven Roberts. Screenplay: Anthony Veiller, from a James Edward Grant story. Cinematography: J. Roy Hunt. Cast: William Powell (Dr. Bradford), Jean Arthur (Paula Bradford), James Gleason (Inspector Corrigan), Eric Blore (Stokes), Robert Armstrong (Nick Martel), Lila Lee (Miss Prentiss), Grant Mitchell (Mr. Summers), Erin O'Brien-Moore (Mrs. Summers), Ralph Morgan (Mr. Hutchins), Frank M. Thomas (Mike North), Frankie Darro (Salisbury), Frank Reicher (Henry Strand), Charles Richman (Turf Club President), John Sheehan (Murphy), Paul Fix (Lou Pender).

1936   *My Man Godfrey* (93 minutes).
Universal. Producer/Director: Gregory La Cava. Screenplay: Morrie Ryskind, Eric Hatch, from the Eric Hatch novel. Cinematography: Ted Tetzlaff. Cast: William Powell (Godfrey Parke), Carole Lombard (Irene Bullock), Alice Brady (Angelica Bullock), Gail Patrick (Cornelia Bullock), Jean Dixon (Molly), Eugene Pallette (Alexander Bullock), Allan Mowbray (Tommy Gray), Mischa Auer (Carlo), Robert Light (Faithful George), Pat Flaherty (Mike), Franklin Pangborn (master of ceremonies), Grady Sutton (Van Rumple), Ed Gargan (detective), James Flavin (second detective), Robert Perry (doorman).

1936   *Theodora Goes Wild* (94 minutes).
Columbia. Producer: Everett Riskin. Director: Richard Boleslawski. Screenplay: Sidney Buchman, from a Mary McCarthy story. Cinematography: Joseph Walker. Cast: Irene Dunne (Theodora Lynn), Melvyn Douglas (Michael Grant), Thomas Mitchell (Jed Waterbury), Thurston Hall (Arthur Stevenson), Rosalind Keith (Adelaide Perry), Spring Byington (Rebecca Perry), Elisabeth Risdon (Aunt Mary), Margaret McWade (Aunt Elsie), Nana Bryant (Ethel Stevenson), Henry Kolker (Jonathan Grant), Leona Maricle (Agnes Grant), Robert Greig (Uncle John), Fredrick Burton (Governor Wyatt).

1936   *The Libeled Lady* (98 minutes).
Metro-Goldwyn-Mayer. Producer: Lawrence Weingarten. Director: Jack Conway. Screenplay: Maurine Watkins, Howard Emmett Rogers, George Oppenheimer, from a story by Wallace Sullivan. Cinematography: Norbert Brodine. Cast: William Powell (Bill Chandler), Myrna Loy (Connie Allenbury), Jean Harlow (Gladys Benton), Spencer Tracy (Warren Haggerty), Walter Connolly (James B. Allenbury), Charles Grapwin (Hollis Bane), Cora Witherspoon (Mrs. Burns-Norvell), E. E. Clive (Evans), Charles Trowbridge (Graham), Spencer Charters (magistrate), Greta Meyer (Connie's maid), Richard Tucker (Barker), Hattie McDaniel (maid),

Howard Hickman (cable editor), Harry C. Bradley (justice of the peace), Bodil Rosing (justice of the peace's wife).

1937   *I Met Him in Paris* (86 minutes).
Paramount. Producer/Director: Wesley Ruggles. Screenplay: Claude Binyon, from a Helen Meinardi story. Cinematography: Leon Tover. Special Effects: Farciot Edouart. Cast: Claudette Colbert (Kay Denham), Melvyn Douglas (George Potter), Robert Young (Gene Anders), Mona Barrie (Helen Anders), George Davis (cutter driver), Alexander Cross (John Hailey), Lee Bowman (Berk Sutter), Fritz Feld (Swiss hotel clerk), Rudolph Amant (romantic waiter), George Sorel (hotel clerk), Louis LaBey (bartender), Egon Brecher (Emile, upper tower man), Hans Joby (lower tower man), Jacques Venaire (Frenchman—flirt), Eugene Borden (head waiter), Captain Fernando Garcia (elevator operator), Albert Pollet (conductor), Francesco Maran and Yola D'Avil (French couple in apartment), Alexander Schoenberg (porter), Joe Thoben (assistant bartender), Gennaro Curci (double talk waiter), Jean De Briac (steward).

1937   *Easy Living* (88 minutes).
Paramount. Producer: Arthur Hornblow, Jr. Director: Mitchell Leisen. Screenplay: Preston Sturges. Cinematography: Ted Tetzlaff. Special Effects Photography: Farciot Edouart. Cast: Jean Arthur (Mary Smith), Edward Arnold (J. B. Ball), Ray Milland (John Ball, Jr.), Luis Alberni (Mr. Louis Louis), Mary Nash (Mrs. Ball), Franklin Pangborn (Van Buren), Barlowe Borland (Mr. Gurney), William Demarest (Wallace Whistling), Andrew Tombes (E. F. Hulgar), Esther Dale (Lillian), Harlan Briggs (office manager), William B. Davidson (Mr. Hyde), Nora Cecil (Mrs. Swerf), Robert Greig (butler), Vernon Dent (1st partner), Edwin Stanley (2nd partner), Richard Barbee (3rd partner), Arthur Hoyt (jeweler), Gertrude Astor (saleswoman).

1937   *Topper* (89 minutes).
Distributing Company: Metro-Goldwyn-Mayer. Producing Company/Producer: Hal Roach. Director: Norman Z. McLeod. Screenplay: Jack Jerne, Eric Hatch, Eddie Moran, from the Thorne Smith novel *The Jovial Ghosts*. Cinematography: Norbert Brodine. Photographic Effects: Roy Seawright. Cast: Constance Bennett (Marion Kerby), Cary Grant (George Kerby), Roland Young (Cosmo Topper), Billie Burke (Mrs. Topper), Alan Mowbray (Wilkins), Eugene Pallette (Casey), Arthur Lake (elevator boy), Hedda Hopper (Mrs. Stuyvesant), Virginia Sale (Miss Johnson), Theodore Von Eltz (hotel manager), J. Farrell McDonald (policeman), Elaine Shepart (secretary), "Three Hits and a Miss" (themselves).

1937   *The Awful Truth* (89 minutes).
Columbia. Producer/Director: Leo McCarey. Screenplay: Vina Delmar, adaptation by Dwight Taylor of the Arthur Richman play. Cinematography: Joseph Walker. Cast: Irene Dunne (Lucy Warriner), Cary Grant

(Jerry Warriner), Ralph Bellamy (Daniel Leeson), Alexander D'Arcy (Armand Duvalle), Cecil Cunningham (Aunt Patsy), Marguerite Churchill (Barbara Vance), Esther Dale (Mrs. Leeson), Joyce Compton (Toots Binswanger/Dixie Belle Lee), Robert Allen (Frank Randall), Robert Warwick (Mr. Vance), Mary Forbes (Mrs. Vance), Claud Allister (Lord Fabian), Zita Moulton (Lady Fabian).

1937   *Nothing Sacred* (75 minutes).
Distributing Company: United Artists. Producing Company: Selznick-International. Producer: David O. Selznick. Director: William Wellman. Screenplay: Ben Hecht, from a story by William Street. Cinematography: W. Howard Greene. Photographic Effects: Jack Cosgrove. Cast: Carole Lombard (Hazel Flagg), Fredric March (Wally Cook), Charles Winninger (Dr. Donner), Walter Connolly (Stone), Sig Berman (Dr. Eggelhoffer), Frank Fay (master of ceremonies), Raymond Scott and his quintet (orchestra), Maxie Rosenbloom (Max), Alex Schoenberg (Dr. Kerchinwisser), Monty Wooley (Dr. Vunch), Alex Novinsky (Dr. Marachuffsky), Margaret Hamilton (drug store lady), Troy Brown (Ernest Walker), Hattie McDaniel (Mrs. Walker), Katherine Shelton (Dr. Donner's nurse), Olin Howland (baggage man), Ben Morgan (wrestler), Hans Steinke (wrestler), George Chandler (photographer), Claire Du Brey (Miss Rafferty), Nora Cecil (schoolteacher).

1937   *True Confession* (84 minutes).
Paramount. Producer: Albert Lewin. Director: Wesley Ruggles. Screenplay: Claude Binyon, from the Louis Verneuil, Georges Berr play *Mon Crime*. Cinematography: Ted Tetzlaff. Cast: Carole Lombard (Helen Bartlett), Fred MacMurray (Kenneth Bartlett), John Barrymore (Charley), Una Merkel (Daisy McClure), Porter Hall (prosecutor), Edgar Kennedy (Darsey), Lynne Overman (bartender), Fritz Field (Krayler's butler), Richard Carle (judge), John T. Murray (Otto Krayler), Tommy Dugan (typewriter man), Garry Owen (Tony Krauch), Toby Wing (Suzanne Baggart), Hattie McDaniel (Ella), Bernard Suss (pedestrian).

1938   *Bringing Up Baby* (102 minutes).
RKO Radio. Producer/Director: Howard Hawks. Screenplay: Dudley Nichols, Hager Wilde, from a Hager Wilde story. Cinematography: Russell Metty. Special Effects: Vernon L. Walker. Cast: Katharine Hepburn (Susan), Cary Grant (David Huxley), Charles Ruggles (Major Horace Applegate), Walter Catlett (Slocum), Barry Fitzgerald (Mr. Gogarty), May Robinson (Aunt Elizabeth), Fritz Feld (Dr. Lehmann), Leona Roberts (Mrs. Gogarty), George Irving (Mr. Peabody), Tala Birrell (Mrs. Lehmann), Virginia Walker (Alice Swallow), John Kelly (Elmer).

1938   *Bluebeard's Eighth Wife* (80 minutes).
Paramount. Producer/Director: Ernst Lubitsch. Screenplay: Charles Brackett, Billy Wilder, adaptation by Charlton Andrews of the Alfred Savior play. Cinematography: Leo Tover. Special Effects: Farciot

Edouart. Cast: Claudette Colbert (Nicole de Loiselle), Gary Cooper (Michael Brandon), Edward Everett Horton (Marquis de Loiselle), David Niven (Albert de Regnier), Elizabeth Patterson (Aunt Hedwige), Herman Bing (Monsieur Pepinard), Warren Hymer (Kid Mulligan), Franklin Pangborn (assistant hotel manager), Armand Cortes (assistant hotel manager), Rolf Sedan (floor-walker), Lawrence Grant (Professor Urganzeff), Lionel Pape (Potin), Tyler Brooke (clerk), Tom Ricketts (Uncle André), Barlow Borland (Uncle Fernandel), Charles Halton (extra), Sacha Guitry (extra).

1938   *Joy of Living* (90 minutes).
RKO-Radio. Felix Young Production. Director: Tay Garnett. Screenplay: Gene Towne, Graham Baker, Allan Scott, from a story by Dorothy Fields and Herbert Fields, Cinematography: Joseph Walker. Special Effects: Vernon Walker. Cast: Irene Dunne (Maggie), Douglas Fairbanks, Jr. (Dan), Alice Brady (Minerva), Guy Kibbee (Dennis), Jean Dixon (Harrison), Eric Blore (Potter), Lucille Ball (Salina), Warren Hymer (Mike), Billy Gilbert (cafe owner), Frank Milan (Bert Pine), Dorothy Steiner (Dotsy Pine), Estelle Steiner (Betsy Pine), Phyllis Kennedy (Marie), Franklin Pangborn (orchestra leader), James Burke (Mac), John Qualen (Oswego), Spencer Charters (magistrate).

1938   *Vivacious Lady* (90 minutes).
RKO-Radio. Producer: Pandro S. Berman. Director: George Stevens. Screenplay: P. J. Wolfson, Ernest Pagano, from a I.A.R. Wylie story. Cinematography: Robert DeGrasse. Cast: Ginger Rogers (Francey), James Stewart (Peter), James Ellison (Keith), Beulah Bondi (Mrs. Morgan), Charles Coburn (Mr. Morgan), Frances Mercer (Helen), Phyllis Kennedy (Jenny), Franklin Pangborn (apartment manager), Grady Sutton (Culpepper), Jack Carson (waiter captain), Alec Craig (Joseph), Willie Best (porter).

1938   *Holiday* (94 minutes).
Columbia. Producer: Everett Riskin. Director: George Cukor. Screenplay: Donald Ogden Stewart, Sidney Buchman, from the Philip Barry play. Cinematography: Franz Planer. Cast: Katharine Hepburn (Linda Seton), Cary Grant (Johnny Case), Doris Nolan (Julia Seton), Lew Ayres (Ned Seton), Edward Everett Horton (Professor Nick Potter), Henry Kolker (Edward Seton), Binnie Barnes (Laura Cram), Jean Dixon (Susan Potter), Henry Daniell (Seton Cram), Charles Trowbridge (banker), George Pauncefort (Thayer), Mitchell Harris (Jennings), Neil Fitzgerald (Edgar), Marion Ballou (Grandmother), Howard Hickman (man in church), Hilda Plowright (woman in church).

1938   *Four's a Crowd* (91 minutes).
Warner Brothers. Executive Producer: Hal B. Wallis. Director: Michael Curtiz. Screenplay: Casey Robinson, Sig Herzig, from a Wallace Sullivan story. Cinematography: Ernest Haller. Cast: Errol Flynn (Robert Kensington Lansford), Olivia de Havilland (Lorri Dillingwell), Rosalind Russell

(Jean Christy), Patric Knowles (Patterson Buckley), Walter Connolly (John P. Dillingwell), Hugh Herbert (Silas Jenkins), Melville Cooper (Bingham), Franklin Pangborn (Preston), Herman Bing (Herman, the barber), Margaret Hamilton (Amy), Joseph Crehan (Pierce the butler), Joe Cunningham (Young), Dennie Moore (Buckley's secretary), Gloria Blondell and Carole Landis (Lansford's secretaries), Renie Riano (Mrs. Jenkins), Charles Trowbridge (Dr. Ives), Spencer Charters (Charlie).

1938   *You Can't Take It With You* (127 minutes).
Columbia. Producer/Director: Frank Capra. Screenplay: Robert Riskin, from the George S. Kaufmann, Moss Hart play. Cinematography: Joseph Walker. Cast: Jean Arthur (Alice Sycamore), Lionel Barrymore (Grandpa Vanderhof), James Stewart (Tony Kirby), Edward Arnold (Anthony Kirby, Sr.), Spring Byington (Penny Sycamore), Mischa Auer (Kolenkhov), Ann Miller (Essie Carmichael), Dub Taylor (Ed Carmichael), Samuel S. Hinds (Paul Sycamore), Donald Meek (Poppins), H. B. Warner (Ramsey), Halliwell Hobbes (Mr. DePinna), Mary Forbes (Mrs. Anthony Kirby), Eddie Anderson (Donald), Lillian Yarbo (Rheba), Harry Davenport (judge).

1938   *Mad Miss Manton* (80 minutes).
RKO-Radio. Producer: Pandro S. Berman. Director: Leigh Jason. Screenplay: Philip G. Epstein, from a Wilson Collison story. Cinematography: Nicholas Musuraca. Cast: Barbara Stanwyck (Melsa Manton), Henry Fonda (Peter Ames), Sam Levene (Lt. Mike Brent), Frances Mercer (Helen Frayne), Stanley Ridges (Eddie Norris), Whitney Bourne (Pat James), Vicki Lester (Kit Beverly), Ann Evers (Lee Wilson), Catherine O'Quinn (Dora Fenton), Linda Terry (Myra Frost), Eleanor Hansen (Jane), Hattie McDaniel (Hilda), James Burke (Sgt. Sullivan), Paul Guilfoyle (Bat Regan), Penny Singleton (Frances Clark), Leona Maricle (Sheila Lane), Kay Sutton (Gloria Hamilton), Miles Mander (Fred Thomas), John Qualen (subway watchman), Grady Sutton (district attorney's secretary).

1938   *Topper Takes a Trip* (80 minutes).
Distributing Company: United Artists. Producing Company: Hal Roach. Producer: Milton H. Bren. Director: Norman Z. McLeod. Screenplay: Eddie Moran, Jack Jevne, Corey Ford, from the Thorne Smith novel. Cinematography: Norbert Brodine and Roy Seawright. Cast: Constance Bennett (Marion Kerby), Roland Young (Cosmo Topper), Billie Burke (Mrs. Topper), Alan Mowbray (Wilkins), Verree Teasdale (Mrs. Parkhurst), Franklin Pangborn (Louis), Alexander D'Arcy (Baron de Rossi), "Skippy" ("Mr. Atlas"), Paul Hurst (bartender), Eddy Conrad (jailer), Spencer Charters (judge), Irving Pichel (prosecutor), Paul Everton (defender), Duke York (Gorgan), Amand Kaliz (clerk).

1939   *Midnight* (92 minutes).
Paramount. Producer: Arthur Hornblow, Jr. Screenplay: Charles Brackett, Billy Wilder, from a Edwin Justus Mayer, Franz Schulz original screen

story. Cinematography: Charles Lang, Jr. Cast: Claudette Colbert (Eve Peabody), Don Ameche (Tibor Czerny), John Barrymore (Georges Flammarion), Francis Lederer (Jacques Picot), Mary Astor (Helen Flammarion), Elaine Barrie (Simone), Hedda Hopper (Stephanie), Rex O'Malley (Marcel), Monty Wooley (judge), Armand Kaliz (Lebon), Lionel Pape (Edouart), Ferdinand Munier (Major Domo), Gennaro Curci (Major Domo).

1939 *Good Girls Go to Paris* (75 minutes).
Columbia. William Perlberg Production. Director: Alexander Hall. Screenplay: Gladys Lehman, Ken Englund, from a Leonore Coffee, William Joyce Cowan story. Cinematography: Henry Freulich. Cast: Melvyn Douglas (Ronald Brooke), Joan Blondell (Jenny Swanson), Walter Connolly (Olaf Brand), Alan Curtis (Tom Brand), Joan Perry (Sylvia Brand), Isabel Jeans (Caroline Brand), Stanley Brown (Ted Dayton), Alexander D'Arcy (Paul Kingston), Henry Hunter (Dennis), Clarence Kolb (Dayton, Sr.), Howard Hickman (Jeffers).

1940 *His Girl Friday* (92 minutes).
Columbia. Producer/Director: Howard Hawks. Screenplay: Charles Lederer, from the Ben Hecht, Charles MacArthur play *The Front Page.* Cinematography: Joseph Walker. Cast: Cary Grant (Walter Burns), Rosalind Russell (Hildy Johnson), Ralph Bellamy (Bruce Baldwin), Gene Lockhart (Sheriff Hartwell), Porter Hall (Murphy), Ernest Truex (Bensiger), Cliff Edwards (Endicott), Clarence Kolb (mayor), Roscoe Karns (McCue), Frank Jenks (Wilson), Regis Toomey (Sanders), Abner Biberman (Diamond Louie), Frank Orth (Duffy), John Qualen (Earl Williams), Helen Mack (Mollie Malloy), Alma Kruger (Mrs. Baldwin), Billy Gilbert (Silas F. Pinkus), Pat West (Warden Cooley), Edwin Maxwell (Dr. Egelhoffer).

1940 *Too Many Husbands* (80 minutes).
Columbia. Producer/Director: Wesley Ruggles. Screenplay: Claude Binyon, from the W. Somerset Maugham play. Cinematography: Joseph Walker. Cast: Jean Arthur (Vicky Lowndes), Fred MacMurray (Bill Cardew), Melvyn Douglas (Henry Lowndes), Harry Davenport (George), Dorothy Peterson (Gertrude Houlihan), Melville Cooper (Peter), Edgar Buchanan (McDermott), Tom Dugan (Sullivan).

1940 *My Favorite Wife* (88 minutes).
RKO Radio. Producer: Leo McCarey. Director: Garson Kanin. Screenplay: Bella Spewack, Samuel Spewack, from a Bella Spewack, Samuel Spewack, Leo McCarey story. Cinematography: Rudolph Mate. Cast: Irene Dunne (Ellen), Cary Grant (Nick), Randolph Scott (Burkett), Gail Patrick (Bianca), Ann Schoemaker (Ma), Scotty Beckett (Tim), Mary Lou Harrington (Chinch), Donald MacBride (hotel clerk), Hugh O'Connell (Johnson), Granville Bates (judge), Pedro de Cordoba (Dr. Kohlmar), Brandon Tynan (Dr. Manning), Leon Belasco (Henri), Harold Gerard (assistant clerk), Murray Alper (bartender), Earl Hodgins (clerk of court).

1940   *Doctor Takes a Wife* (83 minutes).
Columbia. Producer: William Perlberg. Director: Alexander Hall. Screenplay: George Seaton, Ken Englund, from an Aleen Leslie story. Cinematography: Sid Hickox. Cast: Loretta Young (June Cameron), Ray Milland (Dr. Timothy Sterling), Reginald Gardiner (John Pierce), Gail Patrick (Marilyn Thomas), Edmund Gwenn (Dr. Lionel Sterling), Frank Sully (Slapcovitch), George Metaxa (Jean Rovere), Gordon Jones (O'Brien), Charles Halton (Dr. Streeter), Joseph Eggenton (Dr. Nielson), Paul McAllister (Dean Lawton), Chester Clute (Johnson), Hal K. Dawson (Charlie), Edward Van Sloan (Burkhardt).

1940   *Turnabout* (81 minutes).
Distributing Company: United Artists. Producing Company: Hal Roach. Producer/Director: Hal Roach. Screenplay: Mickell Novak, Berne Giler, John McClain, from the Thorne Smith novel; additional dialogue, Rian James. Cinematography: Norbert Brodine. Special Effects: Roy Seawright. Cast: Adolphe Menjou (Phil Manning), Carole Landis (Sally Willows), John Hubbard (Tim Willows), William Gargan (Joel Clare), Verree Teasdale (Laura Bannister), Mary Astor (Marion Manning), Donald Meek (Henry), Joyce Compton (Irene Clare), Inez Courtney (Miss Edwards), Franklin Pangborn (Mr. Pingboom), Marjorie Main (Nora), Berton Churchill (Julian Marlowe), Margaret Roach (Dixie Gale), Ray Turner (Mose), Norman Budd (Jimmy), Polly Ann Young (Miss Twill), Eleanor Riley (Lorraine), Murray Alper (Masseur), Micki Morita (Ito), Yolande Mollot (Marie), George Renavent (Mr. Ram).

1940   *The Philadelphia Story* (112 minutes).
Metro-Goldwyn-Mayer. Producer: Joseph L. Mankiewicz. Director: George Cukor. Screenplay: Donald Ogden Stewart, from the Philip Barry play. Cinematography: Joseph Ruttenberg. Cast: Cary Grant (C. K. Dexter Haven), Katharine Hepburn (Tracy Lord), James Stewart (Macauley Connor), Ruth Hussey (Elizabeth Imbrie), John Howard (George Kittredge), Roland Young (Uncle Willie), John Halliday (Seth Lord), Mary Nash (Margaret Lord), Virginia Weidler (Dinah Lord), Henry Daniell (Sidney Kidd), Lionel Pape (Edward), Rex Evans (Thomas), Russ Clark (John), Hilda Plowright (librarian).

1941   *Mr. and Mrs. Smith* (90 minutes).
RKO-Radio. Executive Producer: Harry E. Edington. Director: Alfred Hitchcock. Screenplay: Norman Krasna, from his story. Cinematography: Harry Stradling. Special Effects: Vernon L. Walker. Cast: Carole Lombard (Ann Smith), Robert Montgomery (David Smith), Gene Raymond (Jeff Custer), Jack Carson (Chuck Benson), Philip Merivale (Mr. Custer), Lucile Watson (Mrs. Custer), William Tracy (Sammy), Charles Halton (Mr. Deever), Esther Dale (Mrs. Krauscheimer), Emma Dunn (Martha), William Edmunds (proprietor of Lucy's), Betty Compson (Gertie), Patricia Farr (Gloria), Adele Pearce (Lily).

1941   *The Lady Eve* (97 minutes).
Paramount. Producer: Paul Jones. Director/Screenplay: Preston Sturges, from the Monckton Hoffe story "Two Bad Hats." Cinematography: Victor Milner. Cast: Barbara Stanwyck (Jean/Eve), Henry Fonda (Charles Pike), Charles Coburn ("Colonel" Harrington), Eugene Pallette (Mr. Pike), William Demarest (Muggsy/Ambrose Murgatroyd), Eric Blore (Sir Alfred McGlennan/Keith), Melville Cooper (Gerald), Martha O'Driscoll (Martha), Janet Beecher (Mrs. Pike), Robert Greig (Burrows), Dora Clement (Gertrude), Luis Alberni (Pike's chef), Frank Moran (bartender), Evelyn Beresford and Arthur Stuart Hall (guests at party), Harry Rosenthal (piano tuner), Julius Tannen (lawyer), Arthur Hoyt (lawyer at telephone), Jimmy Conlin, Al Bridge, and Vic Potel (stewards).

1941   *Topper Returns* (95 minutes).
Distributing Company: United Artists. Producing Company: Hal Roach. Producer: Hal Roach. Director: Roy Del Ruth. Screenplay: Jonathan Latimer, Gordon Douglas, based on fictional characters conceived by Thorne Smith. Cinematography: Norbert Brodine. Special Effects: Roy Seabright. Cast: Joan Blondell (Gail Richards), Roland Young (Cosmo Topper), Carole Landis (Ann Carrington), Billie Burke (Mrs. Topper), Dennis O'Keefe (Bob), Patsy Kelly (maid), H.B. Warner (Mr. Carington), Eddie "Rochester" Anderson (chauffeur), George Zucco (Dr. Jeris), Donald MacBride (Sgt. Roberts), Rafaela Ottiano (Lillian), Trevor Bardette (Rama).

1941   *The Devil and Miss Jones* (92 minutes).
RKO-Radio. Producer: Frank Ross. Director: Sam Wood. Screenplay: Norman Krasna. Cinematography: Harry Stradling. Special Effects: Vernon L. Walker. Cast: Jean Arthur (Mary Jones), Charles Coburn (John P. Merrick), Robert Cummings (Joe O'Brien), Edmund Gwenn (Hooper), Spring Byington (Elizabeth Ellis), S. Z. Sakall (George), William Demarest (first detective), Walter Kingsford (Allison), Montagu Love (Harrison), Richard Carle (Oliver), Charles Waldron (Needles), Edwin Maxwell (Withers), Edward McNamara (police sergeant), Robert Emmett Keane (Tom Higgins), Florence Bates (customer).

1941   *The Bride Came C.O.D.* (92 minutes). Warner Brothers. Executive Producer: Hal B. Wallis. Director: William Keighley. Screenplay: Julius J. Epstein, Philip G. Epstein, from the Kenneth Earl, M. M. Musselman story. Cinematography: Ernest Haller. Cast: James Cagney (Steve Collins), Bette Davis (Joan Winfield), Stuart Erwin (Tommy Keenan), Jack Carson (Allen Brice), George Tobias (Peewee), Eugene Pallette (Lucius K. Winfield), Harry Davenport (Pop Tolliver), William Frawley (Sheriff McGee), Edward Brophy (Hinkle), Harry Holman (Judge Sobler), Chick Chandler, Keith Douglas (later Douglas Kennedy), and Herbert Anderson (reporters), DeWolfe-William Hopper (Keenan's pilot).

1941   *Here Comes Mr. Jordan* (93 minutes).
Columbia. Producer: Everett Riskin. Director: Alexander Hall. Screenplay: Sidney Buchman, Seton I. Miller, from the Harry Segall play *Heaven Can Wait*. Cinematography: Joseph Walker. Cast: Robert Montgomery (Joe Pendleton), Evelyn Keys (Bette Logan), Claude Rains (Mr. Jordan), Rita Johnson (Julia Farnsworth), Edward Everett Horton (Messenger 7013), James Gleason (Max Corkle), John Emery (Tony Abbott), Donald MacBride (Inspector Williams), Don Costello (Lefty), Halliwell Hobbes (Sisk), Benny Rugin (Bugs).

1941   *Unfinished Business* (94 minutes).
Universal. Producer/Director: Gregory La Cava. Screenplay: Eugene Thackery. Cinematography: Joseph Valentine. Cast: Irene Dunne (Nancy Andrews), Robert Montgomery (Tommy Duncan), Preston Foster (Steve Duncan), Eugene Pallette (Elmer), Dick Foran (Frank), Esther Dale (Aunt Mathilda), Walter Catlett (Billy Ross), Richard Davies (Richard), Katharyn Adams (Katy), Samuel S. Hinds (Uncle), June Clyde (Clarisse), Phyllis Barry (Sheila).

1941   *You Belong To Me* (94 minutes).
Columbia. Producer/Director: Wesley Ruggles. Screenplay: Claude Binyon, from a Dalton Trumbo story. Cinematography: Joseph Walker. Cast: Barbara Stanwyck (Helen Hunt), Henry Fonda (Peter Kirk), Edgar Buchanan (Billings), Roger Clark (Vandemer), Ruth Donnelly (Emma), Melville Cooper (Moody), Ralph Peters (Joseph), Maude Eburne (Ella), Renie Riano (Minnie), Ellen Lowe (Eva), Mary Treen (Doris), Gordon Jones (Robert Andrews), Fritz Feld (desk clerk), Paul Harvey (Barrows), Harold Waldridge (Smithers), Lloyd Bridges and Stanley Brown (ski patrol), Jack Norton (Kuckel), Larry Parks (Blemish), Grady Sutton (clerk), Georgia Caine (necktie woman).

1941   *The Feminine Touch* (97 minutes).
Metro-Goldwyn-Mayer. Producer: Joseph L. Mankiewicz. Director: W. S. Van Dyke II. Screenplay: George Oppenheimer, Edmund L. Hartmann, Ogden Nash. Cinematography: Ray June. Special Effects: Warren Newcombe. Cast: Rosalind Russell (Julie Hathaway), Don Ameche (John Hathaway), Kay Francis (Nellie Woods), Van Heflin (Elliott Morgan), Donald Meek (Captain Makepeace Liveright), Gordon Jones (Rubber-Legs Ryan), Henry Daniell (Shelley Mason), Sidney Blackmer (Freddie Bond), Grant Mitchell (Dean Hutchinson), David Clyde (Brighton).

1941   *Two-Faced Woman* (94 minutes).
Metro-Goldwyn-Mayer. Producer: Gottfried Reinhardt. Director: George Cukor. Screenplay: S. N. Behrman, Salka Viertel, George Oppenheimer, from the Ludwig Fulda play. Cinematography: Joseph Ruttenberg. Cast: Greta Garbo (Karin), Melvyn Douglas (Larry Blake), Constance Bennett (Griselda Vaughn), Roland Young (O. O. Miller), Robert Sterling (Dick

Williams), Ruth Gordon (Miss Ellis), Frances Carson (Miss Dunbar), Bob Alton (dancer).

1941   *Ball of Fire* (111 minutes).
Distributing Company: United Artists. Production Company: Goldwyn Productions. Producer: Samuel Goldwyn. Director: Howard Hawks. Screenplay: Billy Wilder, Charles Brackett, from the Billy Wilder, Thomas Monroe story "From A-Z." Cinematography: Gregg Toland. Cast: Gary Cooper (Professor Bertram Potts), Barbara Stanwyck (Sugarpuss O'Shea), Oscar Homolka (Professor Gurkakoff), Henry Travers (Professor Jerome), S. Z. Sakall (Professor Magenbruch), Tully Marshall (Professor Robinson), Leonid Kinskey (Professor Quintana), Richard Haydn (Professor Oddly), Aubrey Mather (Professor Peagram), Allen Jenkins (garbage man), Dana Andrews (Joe Lilac), Dan Duryea (Duke Pastrami), Ralph Peters (Asthma Anderson), Kathleen Howard (Miss Bragg), Mary Field (Miss Totten), Charles Lane (Larsen), Charles Arnt (McNeary), Elisha Cook (waiter), Gene Krupa and His Orchestra (themselves).

1942   *Take a Letter, Darling* (93 minutes).
Paramount. Associate Producer: Fred Kohlmar. Director: Mitchell Leisen. Screenplay: Claude Binyon, from a George Beck story. Cinematography: John Mescal. Cast: Rosalind Russell (A. M. MacGregor), Fred MacMurray (Ton Varney), Macdonald Carey (Jonathan Caldwell), Constance Moore (Ethel Caldwell), Robert Benchley (G. B. Atwater), Charles Arnt (Bud Newton), Cecil Kellaway (Uncle George), Kathleen Howard (Aunt Minnie), Margaret Seddon (Aunt Judy), Dooley Wilson (Moses), George H. Reed (Sam), Margaret Hayes (Sally), Sonny Boy Williams (Mickey Dowling).

1942   *Lady in a Jam* (81 minutes).
Universal. Producer/Director: Gregory La Cava. Screenplay: Eugene Thackery, Frank Cockrell, Otho Lovering. Cinematography: Hal Mohr. Cast: Irene Dunne (Jane Palmer), Patric Knowles (Dr. Enright), Ralph Bellamy (Stanley), Eugene Pallette (Mr. Billingsley), Samuel S. Hinds (Dr. Brewster), Queenie Vassar (Cactus Kate), Jane Garland (Strawberry), Edward McWade (Ground-Hog), Robert Homans (Faro Bill).

1942   *The Major and the Minor* (100 minutes).
Paramount. Producer: Arthur Hornblow, Jr. Director: Willy Wilder. Screenplay: Charles Brackett, Billy Wilder, suggested by the Edward Childs Carpenter play *Connie Goes Home* and the Fannie Kilbourne story "Sunny Goes Home." Cinematography: Leo Tover. Cast: Ginger Rogers (Susan Applegate), Ray Milland (Major Kirby), Rita Johnson (Pamela Hill), Robert Benchley (Mr. Osborne), Diana Lynn (Lucy Hill), Edward Fielding (Colonel Hill), Frankie Thomas (Cadet Osborne), Raymond Roe (Cadet Wigton), Charles Smith (Cadet Korner), Larry Nunn (Cadet Babcock), Billy Dawson (Cadet Miller), Lela Rogers (Mrs. Applegate).

1942   *Once Upon a Honeymoon* (115 minutes).
RKO-Radio. Producer/Director: Leo McCarey. Screenplay: Sheridan Gibney, from a Leo McCarey story. Cinematography: George Barnes. Cast: Ginger Rogers (Katie O'Hara), Cary Grant (Pat O'Toole), Walter Slezak (Baron Von Luber), Albert Dekker (Gaston Leblanc), Albert Basserman (Marshal Borelski), Ferike Boros (Elsa), Harry Shannon (Ed Cumberland), Natasha Lytess (Anna Beckstein), Hans Conreid (tailor), Lionel Royce (German officer), Alex Melesh (waiter), Walter Stahl and Russell Gaige (guests of Baron), Dina Smivnova (traveler—Warsaw).

1942   *I Married a Witch* (76 minutes).
Distribution: United Artists. Production: Paramount. Producer: Preston Sturges. Director: René Clair. Screenplay: Robert Pirosh, Marc Connelly, from the Thorne Smith novel *The Passionate Witch*—completed by Norman Matson. Cinematography: Ted Tetzlaff. Special Effects: Gordon Jennings. Cast: Fredric March (Wallace Wooley), Veronica Lake (Jennifer), Robert Benchley (Dr. Dudley White), Susan Hayward (Estelle Masterson), Cecil Kellaway (Daniel), Elizabeth Patterson (Margaret), Robert Warwick (J. B. Masterson), Eily Malyon (Tabitha), Robert Greig (town crier), Helen St. Rayner (vocalist), Aldrich Bowker (justice of the peace), Emma Dunn (wife), Viola Moore (Martha), Mary Field (Nancy), Nora Cecil (Harriet), Emory Parnell (Allen), Charles Moore (Rufus), Al Bridge (prison guard), Arthur Stuart Hall (guest), Chester Conklin (bartender), Reed Hadley (young man).

1942   *The Palm Beach Story* (88 minutes).
Paramount. Associate Producer: Paul Jones. Director: Preston Sturges. Screenplay: Preston Sturges. Cinematography: Victor Milner. Cast: Claudette Colbert (Gerry Jeffers), Joel McCrea (Tom Jeffers), Mary Astor (Princess), Rudy Vallee (John D. Hackensacker III), Sig Arno (Toto), Robert Warwick (Mr. Hinch), Arthur Stuart Hull (Mr. Osmond), Torben Meyer (Dr. Kluck), Jimmy Conlin (Mr. Asweld), Vic Potel (Mr. McKeewie), Robert Dudley (Wienie King), Franklin Pangborn (manager), Arthur Hoyt (Pullman conductor), Al Bridge (conductor), Snowflake (bartender), Charles Moore (porter), Frank Moran (brakeman), Harry Rosenthal (orchestra leader), Esther Howard (Wienie King wife), William Demarest, Jack Norton, Robert Greig, Roscoe Ates, Dewey Robinson, Chester Conklin, and Sheldon Jett (members of the Ale & Quail Club).

1943   *The More the Merrier* (101 minutes).
Columbia. Producer/Director: George Stevens. Screenplay: Richard Flournoy, Lewis R. Foster, Robert Russell, Frank Ross, from a Robert Russell and Frank Ross story. Cast: Jean Arthur (Connie Milligan), Joel McCrea (Joe Carter), Charles Coburn (Benjamin Dingle), Richard Gaines (Charles J. Pendergast), Bruce Bennett (Evans), Frank Sully (Pike), Clyde Fillmore (Senator Noonan), Stanley Clements (Morton Rodakiewicz), Don Douglas (Harding).

1944   *The Miracle of Morgan Creek* (99 minutes).
Paramount. Producer/Director/Screenplay: Preston Sturges. Cinematography: John F. Seitz. Cast: Eddie Bracken (Norval Jones), Betty Hutton (Trudy Kockenlocker), Diana Lynn (Emmy Kockenlocker), William Demarest (Constable Kockenlocker), Porter Hall (justice of the peace), Emory Parnell (Mr. Tuerck), Al Bridge (Mr. Johnson), Julius Tannen (Mr. Rafferty), Vic Potel (Newspaper editor), Brian Donlevy (Governor McGinty), Akim Tamiroff (The Boss), Almira Sessions (justice of the peace's wife), Esther Howard (Sally), J. Farrell MacDonald (sheriff), Frank Moran (first M.P.), Connie Tompkins (Cecilia), Georgia Caine (Mrs. Johnson), Torben Meyer (doctor), George Melford (U.S. Marshal), Jimmy Conlin (the mayor), Harry Rosenthal (Mr. Schwartz), Chester Conklin (Pete), Byron Foulger (McGinty's secretary), Arthur Hoyt (McGinty's secretary), Robert Dudley (man).

1944   *Arsenic and Old Lace* (118 minutes).
Warner Brothers. Producer/Director: Frank Capra. Screenplay: Julius J. Epstein, Philip G. Epstein, from the Joseph Kesselring play. Cinematography: Sol Polito. Special Effects: Byron Haskin, Robert Burks. Cast: Cary Grant (Mortimer Brewster), Raymond Massey (Jonathan Brewster), Priscilla Lane (Elaine Harper), Josephine Hull (Abby Brewster), Jean Adair (Martha Brewster), Jack Carson (O'Hara), Edward Everett Horton (Mr. Witherspoon), Peter Lorre (Dr. Einstein), James Gleason (Lt. Rooney), John Alexander (Teddy "Roosevelt" Brewster), Grant Mitchell (Reverend Harper), Edward McNamara (Brophy), Gary Owen (taxi driver), John Ridgely (Saunders), Vaughn Glaser (Judge Cullman), Chester Clute (Doctor Gilchrist), Charles Lane (reporter), Edward McWade (Gibbs), Leo White (man in phone booth), Spencer Charters (marriage license clerk), Hank Mann (photographer), Lee Phelps (umpire).

NOTABLE POST-1944 SCREWBALL COMEDIES

1949   *I Was a Male War Bride* (105 minutes).
Twentieth Century-Fox. Producer: Sol C. Siegel. Director: Howard Hawks. Screenplay: Charles Lederer, Leonard Spigelgass, Hagar Wilde, from the Henri Rochard novel. Cinematography: Norbert Brodine, O. H. Borrodaile. Special Effects: Fred Sersen. Cast: Cary Grant (Captain Henri Rochard), Ann Sheridan (Lt. Catherine Gates), William Neff (Captain Jack Rumsey), Eugene Gericke (Tony Jewitt), Marion Marshall (WAC Kitty), Randy Stuart (WAC Mae), Ruben Wendorf (innkeeper's assistant), Lester Sharpe (waiter), Ken Tobey (seaman), Robert Stevenson (lieutenant), Alfred Linder (bartender), David McMahon (chaplain), Joe Haworth (shore patrol), John Whitney (Trumble), William Pullen and William Self (sergeants), John Zilly (shore patrol).

1952   *Monkey Business* (97 minutes).
Twentieth Century-Fox. Producer: Sol C. Siegel. Director: Howard Hawks. Screenplay: Ben Hecht, I. A. Diamond, Charles Lederer, from a Harry

Segall story. Cinematography: Milton Krasner. Cast: Cary Grant (Professor Barnaby Fulton), Ginger Rogers (Edwina Fulton), Charles Coburn (Oliver Oxly), Marilyn Monroe (Lois Laurel), Hugh Marlowe (Hank Entwhistle), Henri Letondal (Dr. Siegfried Kitzel), Robert Cornthwaite (Dr. Zoldeck), Larry Keating (O. J. Gulverly), Douglas Spencer (Dr. Bruner), Esther Dale (Mrs. Rhinelander), George Winslow (deep-voiced little Indian boy), Emmett Lynn (Jimmy), Kathleen Freeman (Mrs. Brannigan), Harry Carey, Jr., and Jerry Sheldon (detectives), Howard Hawks (off-screen voice in opening scene).

1953   *The Moon Is Blue* (99 minutes).
United Artists. Producers: Otto Preminger, F. Hugh Herbert. Director: Otto Preminger. Screenplay: F. Hugh Herbert, from his play. Cinematography: Ernest Laszlo. Cast: Maggie McNamara (Patty O'Neill), William Holden (Don Gresham), David Niven (David Slater), Dawn Addams (Cynthia Slater), Gregory Ratoff (taxi driver), Fortunio Bonanova (television announcer), Hardy Kruger and Johanna Metz (couple in final scene).

1964   *Man's Favorite Sport?* (127 minutes).
Distributing Company: Universal. Producing Company: Gibralter-Laurel. Producer/Director: Howard Hawks. Screenplay: John Fenton Murray, Steve McNeil, from the Pat Frank story "The Girl Who Almost Got Away." Cinematography: Russell Harlan. Cast: Rock Hudson (Roger Willoughby), Paula Prentiss (Abigail Page), Maria Perschy (Isolde "Easy" Mueller), John McGiver (William Cadwalader), Charlene Holt (Tex Connors), Roscoe Karns (Major Phipps), James Westerfield (policeman), Norman Alden (John Screaming Eagle), Forrest Lewis (Skaggs), Regis Toomey (Bagley), Tyler McVey (Bush), Kathie Brown (Marcia).

1972   *What's Up, Doc?* (94 minutes).
Distributing Company: Warner Brothers. Producing Company: Saticoy Production (Peter Bogdanovich). Producer/Director: Peter Bogdanovich. Screenplay: Buck Henry, Robert Benton, David Newman, from a Peter Bogdanovich story. Cinematography: Laszlo Kovacs. Cast: Barbra Streisand (Judy Maxwell), Ryan O'Neal (Professor Howard Bannister), Kenneth Mars (Hugh Simon), Madeline Kahn (Eunice Burns), Austin Pendleton (Frederick Larrabee), Sorrell Booke (Harry), Stefan Gierasch (Fritz), Mabel Albertson (Mrs. Van Hoskins), Michael Murphy (Mr. Smith), Liam Dunn (Judge Maxwell), Graham Jarvis (bailiff), John Hillerman (Mr. Kaltenborn), Phil Roth (Mr. Jones), George Morfogen (Rudy), Randy Quaid (Professor Hosquith), M. Emmet Walsh (arresting officer), Eleanor Zee (banquet receptionist), Kevin O'Neal (delivery boy).

1979   *10* (122 minutes).
Distributing Company: Warner Brothers. Producing Company: A Geoffrey Production for Orion Pictures. Producers: Blake Edwards, Tony Adams. Director/Screenplay: Blake Edwards. Cinematography: Frank

Stanley. Cast: Dudley Moore (George Webber), Julie Andrews (Samantha Taylor), Bo Derek (Jennifer Miles), Robert Webber (Hugh), Dee Wallace (Mary Lewis), Sam Jones (David Hanley), Brian Dennehy (Don, the bartender), Max Showalter (reverend), Rad Daly (Josh), Nedra Volz (Mrs. Kissel), James Noble (Dr. Fred Miles), John Hawker (Covington), Deborah Rush (dental assistant), Don Calfa (neighbor), Walter George Alton (Larry), Annette Martin (redhead), John Hancock (Dr. Croce), Larry Goldman (Bernie Kauffman, TV director).

1979   *Starting Over* (106 minutes).
Distributing Company: Paramount. Producing Company: James L. Brooks Production. Producers: James L. Brooks, Alan J. Pakula. Director/Screenplay: Alan J. Pakula, from the Dan Wakefield novel. Cinematography: Sven Nykvist. Cast: Burt Reynolds (Phil Potter), Jill Clayburgh (Marilyn Holmberg), Candice Bergen (Jessica Potter), Charles Durning (Mickey Potter), Frances Sternhagen (Marva Potter), Austin Pendleton (Paul), Mary Kay Place (Marie), MacIntyre Dixon (Dan Ryan), Jay Sanders (Larry), Richard Whiting (Everett), Alfie Wise and Wallace Shawn (workshop members), Sturgis Warner (John Morganson).

1980   *Seems Like Old Times* (102 minutes).
Columbia. Producer: Ray Stark. Director: Jay Sandrich. Screenplay: Neil Simon. Cinematography: David M. Walsh. Cast: Goldie Hawn (Glenda), Chevy Chase (Nick), Charles Grodin (Ira), Robert Guillaume (Fred), Harold Gould (judge), George Grizzard (Governor), Yvonne Wilder (Aurora), T. K. Carter (Chester), Judd Omen (Dex), Marc Alaimo (Bee Gee).

1981   *Arthur* (96 minutes).
Distributing Company: Warner Brothers. Producing Company: Orion Pictures. Producer: Robert Greenhut. Director/Screenplay: Steve Gordon. Cinematography: Fred Schuler. Cast: Dudley Moore (Arthur Bach), Liza Minnelli (Linda Marolla), John Gielgud (Hobson), Geraldine Fitzgerald (Martha Bach), Jill Eikenberry (Susan Johnson), Stephen Elliott (Burt Johnson), Ted Ross (Bitterman), Barney Martin (Ralph Morolla), Thomas Barbour (Stanford Bach), Anne DeSalvo (Gloria), Marjorie Barnes (hooker), Dillion Evans (Oak Room maître d'), Maurice Copeland (Uncle Peter), Justina Johnson (Aunt Pearl).

1982   *Victor/Victoria* (133 minutes).
Distributing Company: Metro-Goldwyn-Mayer-United Artists. Producing Company: An M-G-M film, by Peerford Ltd., in association with Artists Management A.G. Producers: Blake Edwards, Tony Adams. Director/Screenplay: Blake Edwards, based on the 1933 Ufa-film *Viktor und Viktoria* —conceived by Hans Hoemburg, written and directed by Reinhold Schuenzel. Cinematography: Dick Bush. Cast: Julie Andrews (Victor/Victoria), James Garner (King), Robert Preston (Toddy), Lesley Ann Warren (Norma), Alex Karras (Squash), John Rhys-Daves (Cassell), Graham Stark (waiter), Peter Arne (Labisse), Sherloque Tanney (Bovin).

1984   *All of Me* (93 minutes).
Distributing Company: Universal. Producing Company: A King's Road Presentation. Producer: Stephen Friedman. Director: Carl Reiner. Screenplay: Phil Alden Robinson, adapted by Henro Olek from the Ed Davis novel *Me Two*. Cinematography: Richard Kleine. Cast: Steve Martin (Robert Cobb), Lily Tomlin (Edwina Cutwater), Victoria Tennant (Terry Hoskins), Madolyn Smith (Peggy Schulyer), Richard Libertini (Prahka Lasa), Dana Elcar (Burton Schulyer), Jason Bernard (Tyrone Wattell), Selma Diamond (Margo).

INDEX

Italicized page numbers indicate illustrations.

About the Author

WES D. GEHRING is Associate Professor of Film, Ball State University (Muncie, Indiana). He is the author of *Charlie Chaplin: A Bio-Bibliography, W. C. Fields: A Bio-Bibliography* (Greenwood Press, 1983, 1984), *Leo McCarey and the Comic Anti-Hero in American Film* and monographs on screwball comedy and Charlie Chaplin. His articles have appeared in numerous periodicals.

Recent Titles in
Contributions to the Study of Popular Culture

Tarzan and Tradition: Classical Myth in Popular Literature
Erling B. Holtsmark

Common Culture and the Great Tradition: The Case for Renewal
Marshall W. Fishwick

Concise Histories of American Popular Culture
M. Thomas Inge, editor

Ban Johnson: Czar of Baseball
Eugene C. Murdock

Putting Dell on the Map: A History of the Dell Paperbacks
William H. Lyles

Behold the Mighty Wurlitzer: The History of the Theatre Pipe Organ
John W. Landon

Mighty Casey: All-American
Eugene C. Murdock

The Baker Street Reader: Cornerstone Writings about Sherlock Holmes
Philip A. Shreffler, editor

Dark Cinema: American *Film Noir* in Cultural Perspective
Jon Tuska

Seven Pillars of Popular Culture
Marshall W. Fishwick

The American West in Film: Critical Approaches to the Western
Jon Tuska

Sport in America: New Historical Perspectives
Donald Spivey, editor